• *Volume 9* •

A REVIEW
of the
GREEK INSCRIPTIONS
and PAPYRI
Published in 1986-87

**NEW DOCUMENTS ILLUSTRATING
EARLY CHRISTIANITY**

• *Volume 9* •

A REVIEW

of the

GREEK INSCRIPTIONS
and PAPYRI

Published in 1986-87

edited by

S.R. Llewelyn

in collaboration with

M. Harding, J.R. Harrison, T.W. Hillard, E.A. Judge,
R.A Kearsley, J.M. Lieu, A.M. Nobbs & J.W. Pryor

In honour of Paul Barnett

ANCIENT HISTORY DOCUMENTARY RESEARCH CENTRE
MACQUARIE UNIVERSITY, N.S.W. AUSTRALIA

WILLIAM B. EERDMANS PUBLISHING COMPANY
GRAND RAPIDS, MICHIGAN / CAMBRIDGE, U.K.

— 2002 —

© 2002 Macquarie University

Published 2002 by Wm. B. Eerdmans Publishing Co.
255 Jefferson Ave. S.E., Grand Rapids, Michigan 49503 /
P.O. Box 163, Cambridge CB3 9PU U.K.
in association with
The Ancient History Documentary Research Centre,
Macquarie University, NSW 2109, Australia

Printed in the United States of America

08 07 06 05 04 03 02   7 6 5 4 3 2 1

ISBN 0-8028-4519-3 (pbk. : alk. paper)

The Ancient History Documentary Research Centre
(Director: Professor S. N. C. Lieu and Associate Professor A. M. Nobbs)
within the Division of Humanities at Macquarie University fosters research and professional
development in association with other organizations interested in the documentation of the ancient world.

Committee for *New Documents Illustrating Early Christianity*
P. W. Barnett (Chairman), P. Geidans, E. A. Judge, A. McComb, A. M. Nobbs, R. B. Tress

TABLE OF CONTENTS

TABLE OF CONTENTS

PREFACE

Volume 9 of *New Documents Illustrating Early Christianity*, in honour of Dr Paul Barnett, acknowledges with gratitude his profound contribution to the series as Chair of its Committee from its inception in 1980. He had returned to Sydney as Master of Robert Menzies College at Macquarie, while the University invited him to take responsibility in the School of History, Philosophy and Politics for teaching the undergraduate unit 'The New Testament in its Times', as well as for postgraduate units and research supervision in the field.

In 2002, with (obligatory) retirement from his primary vocation, he continues as a Senior Research Fellow in an honorary capacity within what is now the Department of Ancient History. His ongoing contribution to the *New Documents* project lies not only in the chairing of its Committee. He represents to us the interests of those it is designed to serve, that is all those involved in the study of the New Testament, especially those working at a professional level.

Associate Professor Alanna Nobbs
Director
Ancient History Documentary Research Centre

PAUL BARNETT AND NEW TESTAMENT HISTORY

Ancient History at Macquarie was conceived as a comprehensive approach to the sources of Western culture. The University had already decided not to introduce Classics as such, and there seems to have been no expectation of either Archaeology or Divinity (both of which turned out to be of compelling interest to some students). The leading idea was to span the provinces of the older disciplines through wide-ranging modern schools of study. Within the School of Historical, Philosophical and Political Studies (as it was still called in 1969) it then fell to the newly introduced Ancient History to catch up not only the history of Israel but also that of the New Testament. But a History unit cannot be about a book, objected Philosophy. Contemporary theologians may well have thought that 'New Testament history' risked missing its main point anyway.[1]

The regular undergraduate unit at Macquarie side-stepped the problem by calling itself 'The New Testament in its Times'. Six lecturers in turn have tackled it: R.J. Banks, R.J. Maddox, P.W. Barnett, Max Wilcox, J.M Lieu and now C.B. Forbes. Each has made specialised contributions to historical research on the New Testament. In the case of Paul Barnett, who has been with us longest, there has also developed a sustained drive to explore what it means to call the New Testament 'history'.

The seeds of this go back to his first encounter with Ancient History as a University discipline. Paul Barnett had completed his theological training with a London BD in 1963, and was appointed to a lectureship at Moore Theological College. The principal advised him to take up Ancient History and Greek, a combination which led in the end to the University of Sydney's Honours MA program in History, one of the country's most distinguished nurseries of historical research (dating from the pre-PhD age). In 1968 he took as a prerequisite the seminar on G.R. Elton's 'Tudor revolution in government' from the BA Honours program in History. He had been surprised earlier to discover that the Ancient History sequence simply skirted round the New Testament. You had to wait for Constantine to learn what that had been about. The MA Honours thesis did not quite get to the point either. Supervised by R.A. Bauman (the historian of Roman law), it was on *Disturbances in Judaea (4 BC — AD 73)* (Diss. Sydney 1974). This was followed by a PhD thesis on *The Jewish Eschatological Prophets AD 40 — 70 in their Theological and Political Setting* (Diss. London 1978), and several articles in New Testament journals. The London supervisor was T.F. Glasson, who had been exploring Greek influence on Jewish apocalyptic ideas.

Paul Barnett came to Macquarie in 1980 as Master of Robert Menzies College. His arrival coincided with a shift of emphasis in the University from teaching (and the training of teachers) to research. Ancient History now committed itself to field work in Israel, to Egyptology and to the project *New Documents Illustrating Early Christianity*. One of our researchers (B.W. Winter, a theologian by training) had challenged us to undertake the revision of Moulton and Milligan's *Vocabulary of the Greek Testament Illustrated from the Papyri and other non-literary Sources*. We brought C.J. Hemer from Cambridge to assess the need for and plausibility of that. To pave the way he advised us to publish the *New Documents* series. Both it and the Moulton and Milligan project

---

[1] On the recent shift away from historical criticism of the New Testament to literary ('reader-response') criticism see J. Barr, *History and Ideology in the Old Testament: Biblical Studies at the End of a Millennium* (Oxford 2000) 9-14, 16-24. On four types of historical criticism see 40-43, and 45 on the unhistorical character of much Pauline study; on four types of ideology, see 102-04.

proper were placed under the chairmanship of Paul Barnett, to ensure that the philologists kept the focus on the New Testament. He had learned word-hunting in R.K. Sinclair's 1966 unit at Sydney on Greek slavery and freedom.

In 1983, at Robert Menzies College, Paul Barnett commenced a School of Christian Studies, for the benefit typically of graduates in other disciplines. In the same year he commenced what was to become a series of six books on New Testament history. The first five were written for the general reader, neither theologian nor historian by profession. *Is the New Testament History?* (Sydney 1983) ends its opening chapter with the author's confession of faith in his discipline: 'Let the evidence speak for itself and lead where it will' (p. 15).

One catches the strenuous doctrine of G.R. Elton, whose work, *The Practice of History* (Sydney 1967), provoked a whole generation of Cambridge modern historians. The objective truth of past actions can be reconstructed through empirical study of the documents left by people, who had chosen to act as they did. Cast aside were social theory, abstract causes and ideology, the image in the eye of the beholder. Concurrently the opposite campaign was carrying all before it in Cambridge amongst the ancient historians.[2] But the New Testament field was led by the gentle Professor C.F.D. Moule. In *The Phenomenon of the New Testament* (London 1967) he stood in effect somewhat to the modern side: 'All I am trying to do is to present certain undoubted phenomena of the New Testament writings and to ask how the reader proposes to account for them' (p. 3). Barnett, in his later works, looks back consciously to these models from earlier days, Elton and Moule.

Reviewing *Is the New Testament History?* in *The Classical World* 83 (1989) 119-20, A.M. Devine considered it 'a good introduction to the historical context of the New Testament' (which it did not profess to be!), but dismisses its main point as historically unimportant: 'What gives Christianity its importance from the historical standpoint is not the historicity of its eponymous founder but the formulation and propagation of its doctrine by generations of theologians'. This neatly illustrates Paul Barnett's complaint

---

[2] Moses Finley arrived in Cambridge from America in 1955. 'He had a strong antipathy for Rankean scientific historicism and the notion that value-free facts and truth could be distilled from the sources ... a historian must generate his own data ... by using the conclusions of modern anthropology', C.R. Whittaker, *Proceedings of the British Academy* 94 (1997) 467-68. By coincidence, this posthumous appraisal follows immediately on that of Elton, by Patrick Collinson.

There are other incidental parallels. Both came from intellectual families of German-Jewish background. Both went to England as refugees (Elton from Hitler, Finley from McCarthy). Both anglicised their names during the war (formerly Ehrenberg and Finkelstein). Their manifestos were both launched in the mid-fifties: 'It is enough if a man knows what he is about — and Thomas Cromwell, at least, knew that', *The Tudor Revolution in Government* (Cambridge 1953) 426; 'A human society without myth has never been known, and indeed it is doubtful whether such a society is possible', *The World of Odysseus* (New York 1954, 2nd edn 1977) 25. The sixties and seventies saw their ascendancy in Cambridge. Both were knighted.

But in either case we do them an injustice by polarising their positions. Finley's mythic world was still rich in the detailed exegesis of the Homeric text, while Elton's personalised revolution led him into a complex systematic analysis of the evidence. See the two extensive obituaries in *PBA* 94 (1997), noted above, and (for Elton in particular) A. Munslow, *The Routledge Companion to Historical Studies* (London 2000). G. Roberts, 'Geoffrey Elton and the philosophy of history', *The Historian* 57 (1998) 29-31, brings out our obligation to respect the human individuality of those we study — this applies especially to contemporary post-modernists claiming the freedom to impose their own intelligibility on the past.

against the professional ancient historians — they by-pass the primary historical phenomena documented within the New Testament itself, pursuing instead its consequences in later times.

Such an attitude has in effect been entrenched by the New Testament specialists. Although the intricate disciplines of the field were methodologically historical, the convention was to use the term 'history' for the study of its cultural and social setting. F.V. Filson, *A New Testament History* (London 1965) did this explicitly: its theme is 'the emerging church' and whatever is needed to give the context or background to that. See my critique in *Reformed Theological Review* 25.2 (1966) 65-67. F.F. Bruce, *New Testament History* (London 1969), reviewed by me in *Journal of Religious History* 7.2 (1972) 163-65, 'surveys the events recorded in New Testament writings from a historical point of view' (according to the publisher). The meaning of this is not explained, but in practice it meant focussing not on the main points of the New Testament at all, but on the points of intersection with the general history of the times.

Paul Barnett's first book was praised (on its back cover) by F.F. Bruce along much the same lines, and the most recent one, *Jesus and the Rise of Early Christianity* (Downers Grove 1999), is said on its dust-jacket to be 'a worthy sequel to F.F. Bruce's effort to write a history of the New Testament period' (Ben Witherington III), and to supply 'a fresh benchmark' to F.F. Bruce's 'standard' work (Robert W. Yarborough). In the publisher's news-sheet, *Academic Alert*, p. 5, Barnett himself rates F.F. Bruce as 'one of the two great historians of the New Testament period', the other being Martin Hengel. All this glides over the fact that what Barnett means by 'New Testament history' is something fundamentally different from the 'history of the New Testament period' as treated by F.F. Bruce. Barnett notes the fact discreetly: 'such distractions have not always been avoided' (p. 17 and n. 8). What then is the distinctive thing Paul Barnett has done for our subject?

The central question in *Is the New Testament History?* had been 'How confident may we be that Matthew, Mark, Luke and John have told us the truth about Jesus and not given us some idealised, romantic version?' (p. 49). A preliminary concern of the book was 'fixing the time-frame' (p. 33). The second book, *Bethlehem to Patmos: The New Testament Story* (Sydney 1989), attempts to reconstruct 'the story-line of the New Testament', recognising that it is 'incomplete' in the sense of having 'information gaps', but not attempting to 'plug them up with guesses' (p. 10). Some political and social context was to be provided, as well as a challenge to the assumption that New Testament writers were 'not concerned with history'. In the 'Foreword' Michael Green invites us to watch 'an honest man sifting the truth'.

In *The Two Faces of Jesus* (Sydney 1990) Paul Barnett draws attention to the recent dramatic shift in the 'Quest for the Historical Jesus'. Bultmann in 1934 had said 'We can now know almost nothing concerning the life and personality of Jesus'. But E.P. Sanders in 1985 could say 'We can know pretty well what Jesus was out to accomplish'. It makes sense 'in the world of first-century Judaism'. For Barnett, however, that 'public face' falls short of the full reality because it excludes the 'filial face' as seen by the intimate disciples. Our author offers an analysis of this profile, working not from the credal formulae, but from the historical evidence.

In *The Truth about Jesus* (Sydney 1994) Paul Barnett pursues the way in which the testimony of the disciples was structured and transmitted through the four personal strands of the tradition, and its successive stages across the first generation or two. He uses the differences to identify 'core facts', and notes how 'gratuitous' (or incidental) testimony reinforces them.

Jesus and the Logic of History (Leicester 1997) confronts the multiplication of 'Jesuses' characteristic of our 'deconstructionist' postmodern era. An opening chapter on 'Jesus and the practice of history' appeals to the principles of Elton and Moule against the application of social science models, insofar as the latter make only selective use of the available evidence. The reflective and biographic focus of the gospels, and their later compilation, may be checked through the more diverse and gratuitous evidence for Jesus preserved in the earlier letters.

These five shorter books offer successive probes into the evidence that must be used for an historical appraisal of the New Testament events. The major work that followed, *Jesus and the Rise of Early Christianity* (Downers Grove 1999) is far from being a re-run. Only *Jesus and the Logic of History* is (occasionally) referred to, along with half a dozen of Barnett's more technical articles. The distracting sub-title, *A History of New Testament Times*, was, I am told, requested by the publisher. The work reaches further and far more deeply into the historical complex of the New Testament than is implied by that.

Paul Barnett discloses in the Preface that the experience of writing this book was for him revelatory. 'I am now at last beginning to grasp the message and meaning of the New Testament' (p. 11). This can hardly refer to his technique. He is still willing only to go as far as the evidence will take him. But he seeks now to get inside it, to uncover the dynamic nexus between the mission of Jesus and the later preaching of his disciples. Jesus' conception of his place in the history of Israel is the 'engine' that 'drives the story' (p. 10).

The opening chapter on 'The New Testament as History', with its excursus on 'History and Myth', explains the force of this conclusion. At various points throughout the historical analysis its probabilities are put to the test: for example in excursus 8B 'The criterion of dissimilarity' and 8C, 'Did Jesus make claims to deity?'. The writings of the New Testament are manifestly conceived and shaped under the impulse of the message they convey. Yet they are built up not out of mythological thinking but from the narrative of remembered experience.

Massive though Paul Barnett's contribution has been in this kind of study, there has been coupled with it the concurrent task of interpreting and commenting on the texts book by book. He is the author of four shorter commentaries, on Second Corinthians (1988), the Revelation (1988), Mark's Gospel (1991) and First Corinthians (2000), but in this field also there is a monumental work, his contribution on Second Corinthians for the New International Commentary on the New Testament (Grand Rapids and Cambridge 1997). Together these two sequences of studies constitute a masterly demonstration of how one may come to terms with the New Testament as a phenomenon of history.

E.A. Judge

PAUL BARNETT — MAJOR BIBLIOGRAPHY

BOOKS

The Quest for Power (Sydney 1972) (with P.F. Jensen)

Is the New Testament History? (Sydney 1983)

Is the New Testament Reliable? (Downer's Grove 1986)

The Message of 2 Corinthians: Power in Weakness (Leicester 1988)

The Message of Second Corinthians (Leicester 1988)

Bethlehem to Patmos (Sydney 1988); U.S. title *Behind the Scenes of the New Testament* (Downer's Grove, 1990)

Apocalypse Now and Then: Reading Revelation Today (Sydney 1989)

The Two Faces of Jesus (Sydney 1990)

The Servant King: Reading Mark Today (Sydney 1991)

The Truth about Jesus (Sydney 1994)

Resurrection: Truth and Reality (Sydney 1994) (with D. Peterson and P. Jensen)

Commentary on Paul's Second Epistle to the Corinthians, New International Commentary on the New Testament (Grand Rapids 1997)

Jesus and the Logic of History (Grand Rapids 1997)

Jesus and the Rise of Early Christianity (Downer's Grove 1999)

The New Millennium: Christians and Hope (Sydney 1999) (with P.F. Jensen, B. Newman and M. Raiter)

1st Corinthians: Holiness and Hope of a Rescued People (Fearn 2000)

ARTICLES

'Paul's Preaching Reconsidered', *Interchange* 2.2 (1969) 104-109

'Church and Denomination', *Interchange* 12 (1972) 237-245

'Baptism in the Holy Spirit', *Interchange* 13 (1973) 11-18

'*Apographe* and *Apographesthai*', *Expository Times* 85 (1974) 377-380

'Under Tiberius all was Quiet', *New Testament Studies* 21 (1974/5) 564-571

'Who were the "BIASTAI"?', *Reformed Theological Review* 35 (1977) 65-70

'The Jewish Sign-Prophets, AD 60-70: Their Intentions and Origin', *New Testament Studies* 27 (1981) 679-697

'Opposition in Corinth', *Journal for the Study of the New Testament* 22 (1984) 3-17

'The Feeding of the Multitude, Mark 6 / John 6', *Gospel Perspectives* vol. 6, D. Wenham & C. Blomberg (eds), (Sheffield 1987) 273-293

'Agrippa the Elder and Early Christianity', in D.G. Peterson & P.T. O'Brien (eds), *God Who is Rich in Mercy: Essays Presented to D.B. Knox* (Homebush West/Grand Rapids 1986) 123-37

'Polemical Parallelism: Some Further Reflections on the Apocalypse', *Journal for the Study of the New Testament* 35 (1989) 111-120

'Wives and Women's Ministry', *Evangelical Quarterly* 61.3 (1989) 225-238

'Women in the Church: With Special Reference to 1 Tim 2', in *The Bible and Women's Ministry* (Sydney 1990) 49-64

'Revelation in its Roman Setting', *Reformed Theological Review* 50.2 (1991) 59-68

'Mark: Story and History', in D.G. Peterson & J. Pryor (eds), *In the Fullness of Time* (Sydney 1992) 29-44

'The Importance of Paul for the Historical Jesus', *Crux* 29.1 (1993) 29-32

'The Apostle Paul, the Bishop of Newark and the Resurrection of Jesus', *Crux* 30.3 (1994) 2-11

'Doing Theology for the Corinthians', in D. Lewis & A. McGrath (eds), *Doing Theology for the People of God* (Leicester, IVP 1996) 123-136

'Jesus and the Logic of History', *Crux* (March 1997) 2-10

'Jesus and the Logic of History', *Reformed Theological Review* 57.1 (April 1998) 22-35

'Christian Community and the Gospel', in T. Bradshaw (ed.), *Grace and Truth in the Secular Age* (Grand Rapids 1998) 128-139

'Why Paul Wrote Second Corinthians', in T.W. Hillard et. al. (eds), *Ancient History in a Modern University*, vol. 2 (Grand Rapids 1998) 138-152

'Galatians and Earliest Christianity', *Reformed Theological Review* 59.3 (2000) 112-129

'Jewish Mission in the Era of the NT and the Apostle Paul', forthcoming

Dictionary of Paul and His Letters, G.F. Hawthorne, R.P. Martin & D.G. Reid (IVP 1993): articles on 'Apostle', 'Opponents of Paul', 'Revolutionary Movements', 'Tentmaking'.

Dictionary of the Later New Testament and its Developments, R.P. Martin & P.H. Davids (IVP 1997), articles on 'Apostasy' and 'Salvation'.

                                                            C.B. Forbes

INTRODUCTION

The ninth volume in the *New Documents Illustrating Early Christianity* series has adopted a somewhat different format from that of the preceding volumes with the documentary evidence no longer grouped exclusively under subject headings. The two subject headings of Judaica and Ecclesiastica are retained for their inherent relevance to the aim of the series; however, the remaining documents are grouped according to their type, namely, inscriptions and papyri. Within each group the documents are arranged chronologically.

As always, the intended reader of *New Docs* is the researcher, teacher or student in biblical studies and other related fields. The series is offered as a tool to broaden the context of scholarship in these areas. In order to assist the reading of the Greek text, the translation has attempted to reflect, as far as practicable, the formal structure of the document. This means that the translation is line-by-line, with doubtful and restored readings marked by *sigla* in the English translation. Naturally, one cannot translate the Greek document into flowing English if at the same time one pays strict regard to formal structures. Thus something of a compromise has resulted. For example, the indication of doubtful and restored readings can only be approximate. Again not all documents can be rigidly translated line-by-line. Words and expressions may need to appear on different lines in the Greek and English texts for syntactic reasons. Where this occurs to a significant degree the reader will be alerted to the fact by the translation's continued indentation. Resumption of line-by-line translation is indicated by the cessation of indentation. It is hoped that all these devices will help the non-Greek reader to use the documents in a more critical fashion, knowing what the text actually says and what the editor has restored to it.

Most quotations from other ancient texts or secondary sources are also translated to assist the English reader. Exceptions exist. For example, where the reader's access to an adequate translation can be assumed or when the quotation is paraphrased in the preceding sentence, translation may be omitted. If I have used the translation of another author, this is acknowledged in the text. My own translations, however, are those not otherwise acknowledged.

In view of a past review criticism it needs to be pointed out to the reader that the Greek of the documentary texts is not that which one has come to expect from the published literary texts of antiquity. This is particularly the case with orthography. Spelling was not standardised and persons typically wrote as they heard the word pronounced. The correct spelling will generally be indicated below the document in its critical apparatus.

New Docs 9 covers documents which were first published or significantly re-edited in the years 1986-87. The selected documents in this volume represent only part of a large number of documents of potential interest from the culled material. Of these the more significant have been chosen to be representative of the review years.

Abbreviations

Abbreviations follow standard conventions, except where altered for clarity.

Journals - as in *L'Année philologique*.

Papyrological works - as in S.R. Pickering, *Papyrus Editions held in Australian Libraries* (North Ryde 1984); ibid., *Papyrus Editions: Supplement* (North Ryde 1985).

Epigraphical works according to generally used conventions (see LSJ), preceded where necessary by *I*. (e.g. *I. Ephesus*).

Ancient authors, biblical and patristic works - generally as in LSJ, BAGD, and Lampe (see below).

Textual sigla used are as follows:

αβ	—	letters not completely legible
. . . .	—	4 letters missing
...	—	indeterminate number of letters missing
[αβ]	—	letters lost from document and restored by editor
[±8 letters]	—	about 8 letters lost
‹αβ›	—	letters omitted by scribe and added by editor
«αβ»	—	editorial correction of wrong letters in the text
(αβ)	—	editor has resolved an abbreviation in the text
{αβ}	—	letters wrongly added by scribe and cancelled by editor
⟦αβ⟧	—	a (still legible) erasure made by scribe
`αβ´	—	letters written above line
ᾱ	—	letter stands for a numerical equivalent
v., vv., vac.	—	one, two, several letter spaces left blank (*vacat*) on document
m.1, m.2	—	first hand (*manus*), second hand

Acknowledgements

The efforts of a number of people need to be acknowledged in this introduction. Professor E.A. Judge and Dr J.W. Pryor joined me on the editorial committee for this volume. Judge read and made a selection of documents from the relevant volumes and journals published in 1986 and 1987. He also contributed four entries and undertook proof-reading of the manuscript. Pryor liaised with contributors to the volume as well as undertaking the writing of two entries. Other contributors to the volume are Dr J.R. Harrison (5 entries), Dr M. Harding (1 entry), Dr T.W. Hillard (2 entries), Dr R.A. Kearsley (2 entries), Associate Professor A.M. Nobbs (1 entry) and Professor J.M. Lieu (1 entry). The appraisal of Paul Barnett's contribution to the study of New Testament History was prepared by E.A. Judge, while C.B. Forbes compiled the Bibliography of his MAJOR works. I am also deeply indebted to E.A. Lewis whose careful typing of the Greek documents and assistance in the typesetting of the volume have been much appreciated. I would like to express my thanks to P. Geidans of the Ancient History Documentary Research Centre, who has helped in various ways in the production of this volume. Finally, I wish to acknowledge the contribution of the New Documents Administrative Committee (P.W. Barnett, E.A. Judge, A. McComb, A.M. Nobbs and R.B. Tress) and more particularly its chairman over the past twenty-two years, Dr Paul Barnett, to whom this volume is gratefully dedicated.

S.R. Llewelyn

INSCRIPTIONS

§1   A Share in all the Sacrifices

Mylasa   Rectangular stone   IIᵃ
(originally part of a wall)

Ed. — W. Blümel, *Die Inschriften von Mylasa*, I (Bonn 1987) no. 119, 45-46 (= I. Mylasa I 119).

μεγαλομερῶς καὶ εὐ[   ]
[κ]αὶ εὐεντ[εύ]τως· ὅπως οὖν κα[ὶ
ἡ φυλὴ τοὺς ἀ]-
γαθοὺς τῶν ἀνδρῶν [κ]α̣ὶ ἀξίου[ς
ἐπισημα]-
[σ]ίας καὶ τιμ[ῆ]ς ἀποδεχο[μ]ένη
κα[ὶ τιμῶσα]
5   φαίνητα[ι] ἕνεκεν τοῦ π[ο]λλοὺς
[τὸν πρὸς ἀ]-
[ρ]ετὴ[ν] ζηλοῦν βίον· ἀγαθῆι
τύ[χηι· ἐπηνῆσθαι]
[Δ]ιονύσιον καὶ στεφανῶσα[ι
αὐτ]ὸν χρυσ[ῶι στε]-
φάνωι· στῆσαι δὲ αὐτοῦ [εἰκόνα
χ]αλ[κῆν ἐ]-
πὶ βήματος λευκοῦ λίθου [ἐν] ᾧ
ἂν αὐτὸς [βού]-
10   [λ]ηται τόπῳ· δίδοσσθ[αι] δὲ
[αὐ]τῷ ἕως [ζωῆς]
[κ]αὶ μερίδα ἐκ τῶν θυσιῶν
πασῶν τῶν ὑπὸ
[τ]ῆς φυλῆς συντελουμέν[ων·
ἐπιγρ]αφὴν [δὲ]
[γ]ενέσθαι ἐπὶ τοῦ βήματο[ς
τήνδε·] ἡ φυλὴ
ἡ Κονοδωρκονδέων Διο[νύσιο]ν
'Ιατροκ[λεί]-
15   [ο]υς τοῦ Διονυσίου [   ]
[τ]ῶν νέων ἐτίμησεν χρυσ[ῶι
στεφάνωι καὶ]
[εἰκόνι χ]αλκῇ καὶ με[ρί]δι ἕως
ζ[ωῆς ἐκ]
[τῶν θυσι]ῶν τῶν ὑπ' αὐτῆς
συ[ντελουμένων πα]-

magnificently and [   ]
and affably; and therefore in order that
[the tribe] may
manifestly approve and [honour] the
virtuous
among men and (those) worthy of notice
and of honour
so that many may imitate (their) manner of
life
[in regard to] merit, with good
fortune: (it was decided to) [praise]
[D]ionysius and crown
him with a gold
crown; and to erect a bronze [statue]
of him
on a rostrum of white stone [in] whatever
place he
wishes; and also to give
to him for [life]
a share from all the sacrifices
contributed by
the tribe; and to put up [this]
inscription
on the rostrum:
the Konodorkondeis tribe
honoured Dionysius,
(son) of Iatrok[l-
]e]s, (son) of Dionysius, [   ]
of the young men, with a gold
[crown and]
with a bronze [statue] and with a share for
life [from
all the] sacrifices contributed by
(the tribe) itself

	[σῶν ἀρετ]ῆς ἕνεκεν καὶ	on account of (his) merit and
	καλοκ[ἀγαθίας τῆς]	nobleness
20	[εἰς τὴν φυλὴν καὶ εἰς τὴν]	[to the tribe and to his]
	πα[τρίδα]	native land.

The manifesto clause of our decree (*ll.*2-13) throws light on the re-definition of honour in early Christianity. Dionysius' honours are listed for the emulation of posterity. He is voted a gold crown, the erection of a bronze image, a share of the public sacrifices and the production of an inscription. By contrast, the early Christians either rejected these honours or formulated them differently.

First, the New Testament postponed the allocation of crowns until the *eschaton* (1 Cor. 9.25; Phil. 4.1; 1 Thess. 2.19; 2 Tim. 2.5; 4.8; Jam. 1.12; 1 Peter 5.4; Rev. 2.10; 3.11). There was little interest in the wide variety of hellenistic crown-types (Regling, *art. cit.*, 1592-1594.). In this respect, Paul dismissed one well-known coronal honour as 'fading' (φθαρτός: 1 Cor. 9.25). Moreover, the New Testament viewed the crowning ritual as a corporate experience. While the *demos* of a hellenistic city state did occasionally crown another city state (I. Assos 8; Demosthenes, *De cor.* 92-93), usually the ritual was reserved for members of the civic elite or local dignitaries like Dionysius. Only the decrees of the local associations — which aped the honorific conventions of the hellenistic city-states — extended their titles, awards and privileges down the social ladder.

Moreover, in crowning the *ekklesia* at the *eschaton*, God inverts social hierarchy and status (Matt. 19.28-30; Luke 14.7-11). The New Testament portrait of Christ — the unrequited benefactor requited by God — underscores this reversal. Christ, made lower than the angels and reduced to slave status (Heb. 2.9a; Phil. 2.7-8), suffered dishonour (1 Cor. 1.23; 2 Cor. 13.4a; Gal. 3.13b). But crowned by God's intervention, he became the focal point of all honour (Heb. 2.9b; Phil. 2.9-11). In the heavenly court, God remains the object of adoration and honour: so the twenty-four elders discard their crowns in front of God (Rev. 4.9-11). Thus, in democratising the crowning ritual and redirecting honour towards God and Christ, the New Testament writers were engaging in a critique of the Graeco-Roman honour system.

Second, the monotheism of early Christianity (1 Cor. 8.5-6; Rom. 1.23; cf. Ex. 20.4) ensured that images erected in honour of men were regarded with distrust by believers (cf. Rev. 13.14-15; 14.9-11; 16.2; 19.20; 20.4). In Paul's view, the only legitimate εἰκών was Christ into whose likeness we are changed (Rom. 8.29; 1 Cor. 15.49; 2 Cor. 3.18; Col. 1.15).

Third, the monotheistic and non-cultic nature of early Christianity made a share in the public sacrifices illegitimate for the believer (1 Cor. 10.18-22). Nonetheless, Paul appeals to the practice of the Levitical priesthood sharing in the temple sacrifices in order to legitimate his right to apostolic support (1 Cor. 9.13-14; cf. Lev. 6.16, 26; Dt. 18.1). Interestingly, the phrase μερὶς ἐκ τῶν θυσιῶν (*l.*11) is very rare in the inscriptions (L. Robert, *Le sanctuaire de Sinuri près de Mylasa. I. Les inscriptions* [Paris 1945] nos 16, 18, 20, 21, 22). In honorific contexts, the New Testament use of μερίς — and its cognate μέρος — is stripped of its association with the Gentile sacrificial cults. As we have seen, the Jewish background is paramount. Believers are made fit for a share in the inheritance of the saints in the kingdom of light (μερίς: Col. 1.12; cf. Dan. 12.13; Wis. 5.5). They have a share in the first resurrection (μέρος: Rev. 20.6; cf. Dan. 12.2) and in the tree of life (μέρος: Rev. 22.19; cf. Gen. 2.9). Again, the emphasis is corporate and non-elitist.

Last, the New Testament displays a surprising disregard for the erection of honorific inscriptions. ἐπιγραφή is seldom used. Where the word occurs, the context involves either the ironic reversal of honour (Mk. 15.26; Lk. 23.38) or the primacy of God's honour (Mk. 12.16; Lk..20.24; Acts 17.23 [cf. vv.24ff]; Rev. 21.12 [cf. vv.11, 22ff).

Bibliography

See H. **Balz**, μερίς and G. **Nebe**, μέρος, μερίζω in H. Balz and G. Schneider (eds), *EDNT* vol. 2 (Grand Rapids 1991) 408-10. K. **Baus**, *Der Kranz in Antike und Christentum* (Bonn 1940). On Graeco-Roman crowns, see W.F. **Boyd**, 'Crown', in J. Hastings (ed.), *Dictionary of the Apostolic Church* (Edinburgh 1915) 269. O. **Broneer**, 'The Isthmian victory crown', *AJA* 66/3 (1962) 259-63. J.B. **Campbell**, 'Crowns and Wreaths', *OCD* (Oxford 1996) 411. F.W. **Danker**, *Benefactor: Epigraphic Study of a Graeco-Roman and New Testament Semantic Field* (St Louis 1982) 467-71. L. **Deubner**, 'Die Bedeutung des Kranzes im klassischen Altertum', *ARW* 30 (1933) 70-104. W. **Grundmann**, στέφανος, στεφανόω, in G. Kittel and G. Friedrich (eds), *TDNT* vol. 7 (Grand Rapids 1971) 615-636. C.J. **Hemer**, στέφανος, in C. Brown (ed.), *DNTT* vol.1 (Exeter 1975) 405-406. G.H.R. **Horsley** , 'Funerary Practice in Hellenistic and Roman Rhodes', *New Docs* 2 (1982) §14 50. A. **Papathomas**, 'Das agonistiche Motiv 1 Kor 9.24ff. im Spiegel zeitgenössicher dokumentarischer Quellen', *NTS* 43/2 (1997) 223-41. On μερίς and cognates, K. **Regling**, 'Kranz', *RE* 11/2, cols.1588-1607. J. **Schneider**, μέρος in G. Kittel and G. Friedrich (eds), *TDNT* vol. 4 (Grand Rapids 1967) 594-98. G.M. **Stevenson**, 'Conceptual background to the golden crown imagery in the Apocalypse of John (4.4, 10; 14.14)', *JBL* 114/2 (1995) 257-72.

J.R. Harrison

§2 Saviour of the People

Cilicia   Marble statue-base   II^a

Ed. — G. Dagron and D. Feissel, *Inscriptions de Cilicie* (Paris 1987) no. 69, 113-14 (= I. KilikiaDF 69).

Ὁ δῆμος ὁ Μαλλωτῶν	The people of Mallos
Δημέαν Ἑρμοκράτου	(honour) Demeas, son of Hermocrates,
κοινὸν εὐεργέτην γεγενημένον	who has been a public benefactor
καὶ πεπολιτευμένον	and who has held public office
5 ἐπὶ σωτηρίαι τοῦ δήμου.	for the salvation of the people.

In antiquity there were many 'saviours' who brought σωτηρία ('safety'). Σωτήρ ('saviour', 'deliverer', 'preserver') was used as an epithet of protecting gods such as Jupiter. It was also an official title for sovereigns in the Hellenistic ruler cult and in the Roman imperial cultus. The word could equally refer to philosophers such as Epicurus (*Epicureus Herc.* 346.4b.7 Vogliano; *SIG*³ 834.20; Mott, 280-81), physicians (Foerster, 1006-1007), wealthy benefactors (Spicq, 352), priests and priestesses (Nock, 728), Roman generals (Foerster, 1008) and a host of other dignitaries. The twenty-four occurrences of σωτήρ in the New Testament are restricted to Christ (sixteen references) and God (eight references). Presumably the early Christians did not credit ordinary human beings with the honorific of σωτήρ (cf. Luke 22.25-26; Acts 4.12; 12.21-23).

This does not mean that the early Christians were indifferent to the terminological opportunities provided by the soteriological language of the inscriptions. The cosmological and eschatological status ascribed to Augustus is a case in point. The terminology of the Priene inscription, which honours Augustus as a Saviour-Benefactor (σωτήρ, σωτηρία: DocsAug §98 *ll* .36, 50; Danker, §33), throws light on Paul's portrait of the 'reign of grace' in Romans 5.12-21. Undoubtedly, the Adam-Christ typology in Rom. 5.12ff reflects traditional Jewish apocalyptic-eschatological motifs. But Paul's language of grace (χάρις), excess (ὑπερβάλλειν, ὑπερβολή) and abundance (περισσεύειν) — and each word (or its cognate) is present in the Priene inscription — alludes to the fact that Christ's grace surpassed the χάριτες of the Caesars (Harrison).

The Priene inscription provides extra examples of terminology reminiscent of Christ's work of beneficence (σωθησόμεθα: Rom. 5.9, 10). Like Augustus, Christ had brought peace (εἰρήνη, Rom. 5.1) and hope (ἐλπίς, Rom. 5.2, 4, 5). The arrival of Christ, as with Augustus, marked a culminating point in history (τὸ τελήοτατον τῶι βίωι, DocsAug §98 *ll*.33-34; cf. Rom. 5.6; Gal. 4.4), in that Christ was the τέλος of the Jewish law (Rom. 10.4). Christ — like Augustus — was the beginning of new life (ἀρχή τοῦ βίου καὶ τῆς ζωῆς, DocsAug §98 *l*.10; cf. Rom. 5.17, 18, 20; Col. 1.18). Whereas Augustus restored a world which was 'collapsing and falling into disarray' (DocsAug §98 *ll*.6-7), Christ would liberate the groaning creation at the *eschaton* (Rom. 8.18ff). Thus in describing Christ's work in Romans 5, Paul reflects elements of Augustus' soteriological propaganda. For a similar Augustan inscription at Halicarnassus, see DocsAug §98a. In *SEG* 36 (1986) 1207 the indigenous Myleis of Pisidia call Augustus their personal (*idios*) saviour. See also Philo, *Leg.*, 143-47.

The term σωτηρία ('safety', 'salvation', 'deliverance') — as found in our inscription — refers to Demeas' acts of deliverance, performed in his capacity as a benefactor and public official. Paul, by contrast, reserves σωτηρία for the saving acts of God (19 references). 1 Peter understands salvation to be eschatological (4 references: cf. Heb. 2.3, 10; 9.28). Elsewhere, the permanency of divine deliverance is underscored by the expression 'eternal salvation' (Heb. 5.9). Finally, the New Testament also speaks of God's salvation in contexts of liturgical praise (Luke 1.69, 71, 77; Rev. 7.10; 12.10; 19.1).

Bibliography

F.W. **Danker**, *Benefactor: Epigraphic Study of a Graeco-Roman and New Testament Field* (St. Louis 1982). W. **Deonna**, 'La légende d'Octave-Auguste: dieu, sauveur et maître du monde', *RHR* 83 (1921) 32-58; *RHR* 84 (1921) 77-107. W. **Foerster** and G. **Fohrer**, σώζω, σωτηρία, σωτήρ, σωτήριος, in G. Kittel and G. Friedrich (eds), *TDNT* vol. 7 (Grand Rapids 1971) 965-1024. D. **Georgi**, *Theocracy in Paul's Praxis and Theology* (Minneapolis 1991: Gmn orig. 1987). J.R. **Harrison**, *Paul's Language of Grace [χάρις] in its Graeco-Roman Context* [diss. Macquarie 1996], §6.1.2.4. S.C. **Mott**, *The Greek Benefactor and Deliverance from Moral Distress* [diss. Harvard 1971). A.D. **Nock**, '*Soter* and *euergetes*', in *id., Essays on Religion and the Ancient World* vol. 2 (Cambridge, Mass. 1972) 720-35. J. **Schneider** and C. **Brown**, 'Redemption', in C. Brown (ed.), *DNTT* vol. 3 (Exeter 1978) 177-223, esp. 205-21. C. **Spicq**, σώζω, σωτήρ, σωτηρία, σωτήριος, in *id., Theological Lexicon of the New Testament* vol. 3 (Peabody, Mass. 1994) 344-57.

J.R. Harrison

§3 Benefactor of the People

Smyrna   Statue base?   Hellenistic
                              (now lost)

Ed. — G. Petzl, *Die Inschriften von Smyrna*, II, 1 (Bonn 1987) no. 616, 111 (= I. Smyrna II 1.616).

Ὁ δῆμος	The people
Διονύσιον Διονυσίου	(honour) Dionysius, the son of Dionysius
ἄνδρα ἀγαθὸν ὄντα περὶ τὴν	who is a virtuous man with regard to the
πολιτείαν	body of citizens
καὶ εὐεργέτην τοῦ δήμου.	and a benefactor of the people.

The phrase ἀνὴρ ἀγαθός regularly appears in the inscriptions as an honorific for civic benefactors. Clarke (168-69) has drawn attention to Paul's use of ὁ ἀγαθός in Rom. 5.7b. In Clarke's view, Paul suggests the almost inconceivable idea that someone, in an act of reciprocity, might sacrifice himself for a civic benefactor (ὁ ἀγαθός) — but not for enemies (cf. ἀσεβεῖς, v.6; ἁμαρτωλοί, v.8).

Peterman (193-94) cites Pseudo-Demetrius (*Epistolary Types* 21) to demonstrate the reciprocal situation envisaged by Paul: 'For I know that what I am doing for you is less than I should, for even if I gave my life for you, I should still not be giving adequate thanks for the benefits I have received'. Valerius Maximus (*Noteworthy Doings and Sayings* 4.7.5) refers to L. Petronius who reciprocated the munificence of his benefactor, Caelius, in costly manner. Petronius took his own life and that of Caelius, thereby sparing his benefactor an ignominious death at the hands of his enemies. Our inscription, to some extent, helps us understand why such extreme acts of reciprocation were proposed in antiquity and even carried out.

The honorific, εὐεργέτης τοῦ δήμου, registers the gratitude of the *polis* towards its benefactor. It forms the background to Luke's portrayal of Christ as an exorcising and healing benefactor (Acts 10.38: εὐεργετῶν καὶ ἰώμενος πάντας τοὺς καταδυναστευομένους ὑπὸ τοῦ διαβόλου). However, in contrast to our inscription, the honour accorded Christ is redirected towards God. For εὐεργεσία: Acts 4.9, 1 Tim. 6.2; εὐεργέτης: Luke 22.25. On the New Testament avoidance of εὐ-compounds, see *New Docs* 2 (1982) 106.

Bibliography

A.D. **Clarke**, *Secular and Christian Leadership in Corinth: A Socio-Historical and Exegetical Study of 1 Corinthians 1-6* (Leiden-New York-Cologne 1993) 159-169. F.W. **Danker**, *Benefactor: Epigraphic Study of a Graeco-Roman and New Testament Semantic Field* (St Louis 1982). J. **Gerlach**, *ANHP ΑΓΑΘΟΣ* (München 1932) 7-14. G.W. **Peterman**, *Paul's Gift from Philippi: Conventions of Gift Exchange and Christian Giving* (Cambridge 1997).

J.R. Harrison

§4 Times of Necessity

Clarus   Tablet fastened to a column   Last third of II[a]

Ed. pr. — S. Şahin, *EA* 9 (1987) 62 no. 3; *SEG* 37 (1987) 957.

	ὁ δῆμος	The people (honour)
	Μένιππον Ἀπολ-	Menippus, (son) of Apol-
	λωνίδου τὸν θύ-	lonides (by adoption), according to nat-
	σει Εὐμήδους	ure (son) of Eumedes,
5	εὐεργέτην ὄντα	who is a benefactor
	καὶ περὶ τὴν πολι-	and in the interests of the body
	τείαν ἐκτενῆ καὶ	of citizens zealous and
	φιλάγαθον καὶ προσ-	devoted to (their) good and at
	τάντα τῆς πατρί-	the head of the father-
10	δος ἐν καιροῖς	land in times
	ἀναγκαίοις.	of necessity.

L. Robert has dated Menippus, a citizen of Colophon, to the last third of the second century BC. At the end of the reign of the Attalids, Menippus was again honoured by Clarus in a long decree. The honorifics of our decree are replicated there. See L. and J. Robert, *Claros* I: *Décrets hellénistiques* (Paris 1989) 63-104.

The phrase ἐν καιροῖς ἀναγκαίοις is rare in Greek documents and literature. The superlative form of ἀναγκαίοις is usually used in honorific inscriptions. ἐν καιροῖς ἀναγκαίοις draws our attention to Menippus' unswerving commitment to his community in times of crisis. As such, the phrase provides a backdrop against which New Testament portrayals of benefaction can be assessed. For Christ and the apostles as 'impoverished' benefactors, see 2 Cor. 6.10b; 8.9. For Paul as the 'endangered' and — paradoxically — 'cowardly' benefactor, see 2 Cor. 11.26-33. For discussion, see Danker (417-35); Harrison (§6.2; 7.4.2).

The phrase ἐν καιροῖς ἀναγκαίοις may also throw light on Paul's use of διὰ τὴν ἐνεστῶσαν ἀνάγκην (1 Cor. 7.26). Winter (*passim*) argues that Paul is referring there to the hardship of recent famines in the east during the forties and fifties (cf. Acts 11.28). The appointment of the wealthy benefactor — Tiberius Claudius Dinippus — as curator of Corinth's grain supply in *c.* AD 51-52 underscored the gravity of the situation. Traditionally, benefactors like Menippus played a similar role in critical times and rescued their *poleis* from disaster. For Paul, the 'pressing times' of famine at Corinth presaged the onset of the eschatological birth pangs (1 Cor. 7.29, ὁ καιρὸς συνεσταλμένος; cf. Mk 13.8) and exposed the transitory nature of the world and its relationships (1 Cor. 7.31).

For inscriptional examples of ἐν καιροῖς ἀναγκαιοτάτοις, see Michel 236, 998; Welles §63; I. Délos IV 1517 (154 BC); IG II(2) 971 (140-139 BC); I. Iasos 152; I. Keramos 6. For the papyri, see *UPZ* I 71 (152 BC). For Greek literature, Philo, *Jos.* 241; Dio Chrysostom, *Or.* 34.42. Note the variation on the theme in *SEG* 37 (1987) 1210 (*New Docs* 9 §9): [ἐν δει]νοτάτοις καὶ ἐπε[ί]γουσιν καιροῖς.

Bibliography

B.B. **Blue**, 'The house church at Corinth and the Lord's Supper: Famine, food supply, and the present distress', *Criswell Theological Review* 5/2 (1991) 221-39. F.W. **Danker**, *Benefactor: Epigraphic Study of a Graeco-Roman and New Testament Semantic Field* (St Louis 1982). P.D.A. **Garnsey**, *Famine and Food-Supply in the Graeco-Roman World* (Cambridge 1988), ch. xv. J.R. **Harrison**, *Paul's Language of Grace [χάρις] in its Graeco- Roman Context* (diss. Macquarie 1996). B.W. **Winter**, 'Secular and Christian responses to Corinthian famines', *Tyn Bul* 40 (1989) 86-106.

J.R. Harrison

§5 Faithful Words

Akcapinar   Marble base   I^a

Ed. pr. — E. Schwertheim, *Die Inschriften von Hadrianoi und Hadrianeia* (Bonn 1987) no. 24, 21-24; *SEG* 37 (1987) 1012.

Γαῦρος προφητῶν εἰλό-
μην πιστοὺς λόγους | καὶ ἐπέ-
γραψα νίκην Καίσαρος καὶ ἄ[θ]-
λους θεῶν, | ἐξ ὧν κατευχαῖς εἶ-
5 χον πάντα ἀπ' ἀρχῆς ἰς τέ-
λος | καὶ δῶρα ἀμισῶς ἀπο-
δίδων γαυρύνομαι· |
Γαῦρος 'Ασκληπιάδου Τορηανὸς
τὸν ἀνδρηάντα ἐκ τοῦ ἰδίου.

I, Gaurus, have obtained the prophets'
faithful words and inscribed
the victory of Caesar and the contests
of the gods, through whom by prayers
I grasped all things from start to
finish, and repaying ungrudgingly
the gifts I exult.
Gaurus, son of Asclepiades, from Torea
(set up) the statue at his own expense.

4 ἄ[λλ]ους ed.pr.   9 *l.* ἀνδριάντα

The inscription records the dedication of a statue. In view of the choice of term to describe it (ἀνδριας rather than ἄγαλμα) the editor (24) surmises that the statue was of a man rather than a deity. Line 3 contains reference to νίκη Καίσαρος. As neither term is perceived by the writer to require further clarification, it is assumed that the expression refers to the victory either of Julius Caesar at Pharsalus or Augustus at Actium. The phrase is used to refer to both victories.

The editor takes the inscription as evidence for the existence of an oracle at this site. As such it was one of the many oracles (μαντεῖα) to be found throughout the ancient world (Lucian, *De dea Syr.* 36). The assumption is reasonable given other dedications found at the site and made at the instigation of prophecy. In these, various persons are named as giving the prophecy: Apollonius (nos 6, 23), Zaeilas (12), Agothopous (19), Phosphorus (25, 32), Asclepiodorus (29, 34, 35) and Lyron (33); there are two dedications where the name is lost (26, 30). The editor also assumes that Gaurus inscribed the prophecies, i.e. πιστοὶ λόγοι. This follows from his restoration of ἄλλους in *ll.*3-4. Gaurus had thus inscribed other faithful words, not only about Augustus' victory but also about the gods. From this he concludes that Gaurus may have been a scribe in the office where oracles were recorded (χρησμογράφιον; I. Didyma 31 and 32). But again this assumption rests on the restoration of ἄλλους rather than ἄθλους in the text. It is this reconstruction that is doubtful. See article in *AE* 32 (2000) 147-49.

An interesting, but contrasting, example is provided by *SEG* 10 (1949) 410. The inscription is most probably an epitaph to the fallen Athenians, defeated at Coronea in 447 BC. The inscription attributes the defeat to the agency of a demigod because, as it seems from the last lines, the Athenians ignored or misunderstood a divine oracle.

τλέμονες Ηοἶον [ἀ]γῶνα μάχες
   τελέσαντες ἀέλπ[τος]
φσυχὰς δαιμονίος ὀλέσατ' ἐμ
   πολέμοι·
οὐ κατὰ δ[υσ]μενέ[ο]ν ἀνδρὸν
   σθένος, ἀλλά τις Ηυμᾶς
Ηεμιθέον, θείαν ε⟨ἴ⟩σοδον
   ἀντιάσας,
5 ἔβλαφσεν· πρόφρον ⌣⌣—⌣ δε
   δύσμαχον ἄγραν
ἐχθροῖς θερεύσας [— ⌣⌣
   Η]υμετέροι
σὺν κακῶι ἐχσετέλεσσε,
   βροτοῖσι δὲ πᾶσι τὸ λοιπὸν
φράζεσθαι λογίον πιστὸν
   ἔθεκε τέλος.

Stout-hearted men, what a contest of battle
   you have finished beyond all hope
and lost your souls by divine power in
   war!
not by hostile strength of men,
   but one
of the demigods, having made divine
   entry,
hurt you. Eager ... a prey
   unconquerable
to its enemies having hunted ...
   with your
ruin he fulfilled,
   and for all mortals in future
he has ordained to consider the sure fulfilment
   of oracles.

1 ἀέλπτως   2 δαιμονίως   8 λογίων

In the above inscription it is the end (τέλος) which is πιστόν and not the word or oracle of the gods. On a more general level it needs to be noted that the use of πιστοὶ λόγοι to describe an oracle of the gods is unusual. One would more reasonably have expected to find this described as ἱεροὶ λόγοι or θεῖοι λόγοι.[1] That these are not found prompts one to ask what actually is the purpose of this phrase. To assist in this, a sample of collocations has been taken and classified according to the variables of the noun's number (singular/plural) and the adjective's relation to the noun (predicative/attributive). Within each classification occurrences have been listed in accordance with the perceived subject matter of the λόγος or λόγοι, i.e. whether the subject matter is political, scientific, religious etc.

Predicative singular

In such usages the noun λόγος has a collective sense, as indeed it must. Though often translated by the English term 'word', λόγος does not mean a single word (ῥῆμα or ὄνομα) but refers to the formulation of thought in speech. It views the utterance or speech act as a whole. Thus the term must be variously translated as 'report', 'explanation', 'rumour' etc.

a. General

The λόγος that the nocturnal favours of a woman confuse the minds of men is not believable (Libanius, *Orat.* 28, 11). Just as Aristotle (see *EN* 1172a below) notes the adverse effect of a bad reputation on the credibility of one's words, Isocrates (*Antid.* 280) observes that a good reputation makes one's word more trustworthy. The trustworthiness of one's word can be compared with that of an oath. John Chrysostom, for example, observes that among friends one's word is more trustworthy than an oath (*De fug. simul. spec.* in *PG* 48, 1073). Interestingly Greg. Nys., *In Canticum Canticorum* 6, 130, describes an oath as a word confirming the truth through itself: ὅρκος ἐστὶ λόγος πιστούμενος δι' ἑαυτοῦ τὴν ἀλήθειαν.

---

[1] Philo uses the phrase to describe his former philosophical and contemplative life when he continually associated with divine words θεῖοι λόγοι and views (*De spec. leg.* 3.1). The reference is to his metaphysical and cosmological musings. But the phrase can also be used of the divine words which flow from God and purify the human soul (*De somn.* 1.147-8). The phrase in the singular is also found with reference to the divinely begotten Logos, e.g. *De somn.* 1.215, *De fug.* 97, 101, 108, 137.

b. Political

A military report about the location of one's opponent may be thought not trustworthy (Arrian, *Anab.* 2.7.2). Likewise also the rumour that Tiberius was responsible for Drusus' poisoning (Cassius Dio, *Hist.* 57.22.3). A report of imperial favour might not appear trustworthy (Dio Chrys. 45.3). A report might not be considered trustworthy if it fails to tally with reasonable action (Dion. Hal., *Antiq. Rom.* 9.19.3; cf. 9.21.6) or if the reasons behind the action described in it are not given (Dion. Hal., *Antiq. Rom.* 7.66.2). In all these instances the report is not believed. Conversely, a report may incorrectly be judged trustworthy if it agrees with the reporter's actions (Dion. Hal., *Antiq. Rom.* 3.23.17), or if it is difficult to question the reporter's motivation (Josephus, *AJ* 16.100-1). A report (in this instance the report of Gaius' murder) might appear trustworthy from either foreknowledge or the wishful thinking of the audience (Josephus, *AJ* 19.132).

c. Scientific

In medical contexts an explanation (λόγος) is made trustworthy and credible by proof or demonstration. See Galen (*Opera omnia*, ed. C.G. Kühn [Olms: Hildesheim 1964]) vol. 3, 387, vol. 9, 108 and 867, vol. 14, 245; cf. also vol. 4, 440 and *In Hippocr.* 6 17b.190. Plutarch (*De soll. anim.* 967a) wonders at the work of a spider in making its web. The account of its activity is trustworthy because it is confirmed by daily observation, else it would appear a myth. Explanations, for which clear evidence is lacking, can be accepted only hesitantly. Gregory of Nazianzus, for example, when talking about the types of generation of living things, hesitantly admits self-generation, 'if the account is trustworthy' (Greg. Naz., *De spiritu sancto* 10; cf. id., *Contra Iulian. imp., Orat.* 5, 16 in *PG* 35, 684, for the same expression used in relation to a report of a funeral procession).

d. Religious

The report or account of Gehenna can be said to be πιστός as it follows from Jesus' word to a healed man to sin no more (John Chrys., *In Ioann. hom.* 38 in *PG* 59, 211). The thought sequence of the apostle Paul engenders a threat and thus makes his word πιστός (id., *In epist. 1 ad Corinth. hom.* 14 in *PG* 61, 116). Christ in John's Gospel is denoted as the Word (Λόγος). As such he is πιστός because he ought to be believed (Athanasius, *Contra Arian.* in *PG* 26, 160 and 401; cf. also Origen, *Comm. in Ioann.* 2.5.46 and 51, where the Word is πιστός and ἀληθινός).

Predicative plural

a. Legal

The words of one's accusers are not to be thought πιστοί (Andoc., *Myst.* 7). By attacking the credibility of an accuser and making him appear ἄπιστος, it follows that his words cannot be πιστοί (Aristotle, *Rhet.* 1416a). An advocate might plead with the jurors to vote justly and not to believe the words of his opponents more trustworthy than his own (Isoc., *Trapez.* 58). Again, he could plead that they not think the words of slaves more trustworthy (Lysias, *Orat.* 5.3). The trustworthiness of words can also be compared with that of oaths (Isoc., *Paneg.* 81, cf. also John Chrys., *De fug. sim. spec.* in *PG* 48, 1073) or that of other witnesses (Antiphon, *De chor.* 29). The trustworthiness of words can also be compared less favourably with that of deeds or actions (Lysias, *Orat.* 7.30).

b. Political

Words might be trustworthy but not persuasive because they run counter to one's experience of fortune (Polybius, *Hist.* 15.7.1-2). Words can be compared with deeds or actions and are naturally viewed as less trustworthy (Aristotle, *EN* 1172a, Lysias, *Orat.* 34.5, Michael, *In ethica nic.* 532).

c. Religious

Action can also make words more trustworthy. Thus by practising mortification of the flesh the words about the resurrection are made more trustworthy (John Chrys., *Adv. oppug. vit. monast.* in *PG* 47, 343).

Attributive singular

a. Scientific

Galen, *Inst. log.* 1.5 and 17.7-8, differentiates propositions from axioms; the former are apprehended by perception or demonstration; the latter is a πιστὸς λόγος apprehended by thought as self-evident. Parmenides, frag. 8 *ll*.50-2, contrasts reason (λόγος) and opinion (δόξα). He had just been discussing Being and what can be apprehended about it from reason alone, i.e. that it always is, and is indivisible, motionless and complete. Now he declares that he will stop trustworthy reasoning (πιστὸς λόγος) and thought about truth. From now on the reader is enjoined to learn mortal opinions which are heard in the deceptive arrangement of words (ἐπέων).

Attributive plural

a. Scientific

Hypotheses are only to be replaced by more trustworthy explanations (Arist., *Cael.* 299a and *Lin. insec.* 969b).

b. Religious

πιστοὶ λόγοι can refer to the counsel or advice given by a friend. Eliphaz had intimated in what he at first said to Job that all humans sin and that Job must have sinned to suffer thus. In commenting on Job 6.3-4 and his response to Eliphaz, Didymus Caecus (*Kommentar zu Hiob*, eds U. & H. Hagedorn and L. Koenen [Bonn, vol. 2, 1968] 161) observes that his friend had spoken πιστοὶ λόγοι, namely, that his suffering was due to sin. Words, as in this instance, can seem credible, but they are not necessarily true. See also the commentary on Job 12.20a (*ibid.* [vol. 4, 1985] 329): διαλλάσσων χείλη πιστῶν — 'changing the speech of the trustworthy'. Didymus Caecus notes that some seem to possess credible and irrefutable words, yet God changes them. There is a contrast made between what seem credible words and the divine reality on which they rest. Conversely, the contrast can be between what is promised and what is actually said. For example, Origen, *Contra Celsum* 1.71, ponders how to reply to Celsus when he promises trustworthy words but in his argument he uses abuse and invective by calling Jesus both a wretch and a magician.

The last citation is perhaps the most interesting since we find a collocation of the two expressions, πιστοὶ λόγοι and θεῖοι λόγοι. Gregory of Naz., *Carmina quae spectant ad alios* 75-98 (PG 37, 1457-8) speaks of certain holy persons and their austere practices. One of his own flock had bound his tongue in silence and only offered praise to God in thought. Another stayed in a holy place for years in supplication and without sleep. He continues:

75	Καί τις ἀνὴρ θείοιο κατ᾽ οὔρεος, ἔνθεν ἀέρθη	And on the divine mountain, whence Christ was lifted up
	Χριστός, ὅτ᾽ ἀνθρώπους λείψε πάθος τελέσας,	when he left mankind having completed his suffering,
	Ἔνθα λόγῳ τε νόῳ τε καὶ ἄψεσιν ἀστυφέλικτος,	at that time stood a man, unshaken in word, mind and limb
	Ἑστηὼς νιφετῷ βάλλετο καὶ ἀνέμοις·	and clothed in snow and wind;
	Οὐδ᾽ ὑπόεικε λιτῆσι περισταδὸν ἄλλοθεν ἄλλων	nor did he yield to the prayers of other pious men
80	Ἀνδρῶν εὐσεβέων ἀμφὶς ἑλισσομένων,	who standing around encircled (him),
	Ἀλλ᾽ ἔχετο κρατερῶς Χριστοῦ μεγάλοιο ἄνακτος,	but he held fast to Christ, the great ruler,
	Ἔνθεν ἀναστήσας ὃν νόον ἐκ μερόπων,	thence lifting up his mind from men
	Μέσφ᾽ ὅτ᾽ ἀποψύχοντι δόμον νέον ἀμφὶς ἔθηκαν,	until they constructed round about a new abode for him as he was dying,

Οὐδ' ἐμπαζομένῳ κηδεμόνος παλάμης. — not even caring for his protector's handiwork.

85 Ἄ, φρίκος ἦλθεν ἔμοιγε· λόγοις πιστοῖσι
τετύχθαι — Ah, shivering comes over me — that with trustworthy words

Τόνδε νόμον μοναχοῖς οὔνομα καὶ
βίοτον, — the following rule has been established for monks in name and life

Οὓς πλεῖστοι μὲν ἴσασιν, ἀτιμάζουσι δὲ
παῦροι — whom most know but few dishonour as (being)

Πλεῖον θερμοτέρους ἔμφρονος εὐσεβίης, — much more headlong than rational piety.

Εὐτέ τις εὐαγέων ἀνδρῶν κείνοισι
πελάσσῃ· — When any conspicuous man approaches them,

90 Ἡμεδαποῖο νόμου μηδὲν ἐπιστάμενος, — though he know nothing of their native rule,

Πρῶτά μιν εὐμενέως μὲν ἑοῖς τίουσι
δόμοισιν, — firstly in a well-disposed manner they honour him in their abodes

Ἀμφαγαπαζόμενοι πᾶσι τύποις φιλίοις, — embracing every type of friendship,

Καὶ ψυχὰς θείοισι λόγοις, οὓς Πνεῦμ'
ἐχάραξεν, — and their own souls with the divine words, which the Spirit engraved,

Ὑψοῦσιν, φαενὴν δαῖτα χαριζόμενοι· — they exalt, offering splendid food.

95 Αὐτὰρ ἔπειτα, νόμου τις ἀπηνέος ἐν
μεσάτοισι — But then in midstream someone recalled the harsh law

Μνήσατο, καὶ τοῖον ἐξερέεινεν ἔπος, — and enquired into such a word —

Εἰ καλὸν εὐσεβέεσσι Θεοῦ πέρι πότμον
ἐπισπεῖν, — whether it is good for the pious to die for God's sake —

Ἕλκων κρυπταδίοις ῥήμασι πικρὸν ἔπος. — drawing a word bitter with secret phrases.

The context is the difference between the actual practice of monks and the fate to which they have been called. The bitter word to which they are recalled is contrary to their own actions. The rule, that monks quite inappropriately treat conspicuous persons with great honour, is established by trustworthy reports (πιστοὶ λόγοι), much to the author's fear. They even exalt themselves to acts of splendid hospitality by appeal to the divine words (θεῖοι λόγοι) of Scripture. No doubt this reference is to the numerous calls in both the Old and New Testaments to offer hospitality to strangers. But what is inappropriate is the type of person to whom the hospitality is extended and its extravagance. To conclude, it is apparent that this final instance of πιστοὶ λόγοι, although it refers to reports about the behaviour of monks and is thus categorized as religious, is little different from other uses of λόγος (singular) to refer to reports particularly of a political content.

In none of the above instances does πιστοὶ λόγοι refer to the actual words of the deity. Such words can be spoken by people about divine reality, but they are never the words of the deity himself. We have left till last a consideration of the collocations found in the New Testament. These fall into two distinct classes according to their location in the corpus, namely, usage in the Pastoral Epistles and in the Revelation.

(a)   The key to understanding usage in the pastoral epistles is Titus 1.9: A bishop is one 'who holds to the trustworthy word in accord with the teaching (τοῦ κατὰ τὴν διδαχὴν πιστοῦ λόγου), that he may be able also to encourage by sound teaching and refute his opponents'. The situation which the church faced was one of pervasive false teachings.

This was to be opposed by sound teaching and word (2.1 and 8; cf. also 1 Tim. 1.10, 6.3, 2 Tim. 1.13, 4.3). The expressions 'sound teaching' and 'sound word(s)' are interchangeable. Such words or teachings were also called 'trustworthy'. Thus in the Pastorals when the writer wishes to underline and emphasize a received teaching or saying as true he would place the phrase πιστὸς ὁ λόγος either before (1 Tim. 1.14, 3.1, 4.9, 2 Tim. 2.13) or immediately after it (Titus 3.8).

(b)   The last two collocations concern the final visions of the seer in Revelation. The vision of the new Jerusalem is seen and the voice of God from the throne heard. God's dwelling will be with mankind; everything is made new. The voice adds: 'Write that/because these words are trustworthy and true.' — γράψον ὅτι οὗτοι οἱ λόγοι πιστοὶ καὶ ἀληθινοί εἰσιν (Rev. 21.5). At first appearance 'these words' seems to refer to the voice of God, but in view of the second occurrence of the same phrase this may be doubted. Here there is a vision of the river of the water of life flowing through the middle of the city with the tree of life on either side. An angel addresses the seer: 'These words are trustworthy and true, and the Lord, the God of the spirits of the prophets, sent his angel to show to his servants what must happen soon.' — οὗτοι οἱ λόγοι πιστοὶ καὶ ἀληθινοί, καὶ ὁ κύριος, ὁ Θεὸς τῶν πνευμάτων τῶν προφητῶν ἀπέστειλεν τὸν ἄγγελον αὐτοῦ δεῖξαι τοῖς δούλοις αὐτοῦ ἃ δεῖ γενέσθαι ἐν τάχει (Rev. 22.6). Οὗτοι with the sense of οἵδε to refer to what the angel is about to say is made impossible by the paratactic καί after ἀληθινοί. 'These words' thus refers to the vision itself. What makes the vision trustworthy and true is the fact that the God of the spirits of the prophets has sent his angel to show his servants what must occur soon. What is of interest is that the vision is referred to as words. The angel is made to assume the situation of the seer as he later describes his vision and not the immediate situation as he sees the vision and hears the angel's words. Despite, or better still, because of this difficulty, it is the text of Revelation which provides the closest parallel to the wording of our inscription. The prophetic word, insofar as it gives expression to a divine vision, is described as πιστός. It is the fact that the vision is mediated to mankind generally through the agency of a prophetic person and his words that his description is trustworthy rather than divine.

In conclusion, from the references collected above it would appear that the word spoken by a deity is not so much termed 'faithful' as is that spoken for him/her by others. This may reflect the perception that, though the word of men may be either trustworthy or not, such a qualification of the deity's word is inappropriate. It is in the human sphere that there is doubt about the trustworthiness of what is spoken. It is in this sense that the expression πιστοὶ λόγοι is used by Gaurus in the opening inscription, for insofar as the words are spoken by prophets, they become faithful.

S.R. Llewelyn

§6 Quasi-divine Honours for a Severe Governor

Clarus   Pillar   61-58 BC

Ed. pr. — S. Şahin, *EA* 9 (1987) 61 no. 1; *SEG* 37 (1987) 958; Tuchelt, 165.

	ὁ δῆμος	The people (of Clarus)
	Κόϊντον Τούλλιον	(honour) Quintus Tullius
	Μάρκου υἱὸν Κικέ-	son of Marcus Cicero
	ρωνα ἀνθύπατον	(governor) with consular authority
5	εὐεργέτην ὄντα	being a benefactor
	τῶν Ἑλλήνων καὶ	of the Greeks and
	πάτρωνα τοῦ δή-	patron of the
	μου.	people.

Clarus, lying between Colophon and Notion in the Roman province of Asia (more specifically in the region of Lydia), was famous for its sanctuary of Apollo. This inscription from a white marble pillar monument was found during excavations at the site in the vicinity of the altar in front of the temple of Apollo in 1958, and published in 1987, along with others from the same site, in controversial circumstances. (For the controversy, see S. Şahin, 47-48; *SEG* 37 (1987) 956; Habicht *et al.*, 699-706. For a description of the monument, see Tuchelt, 165). Q. Tullius Cicero was governor of the province for a three-year period from 61 to 58, a term which was, according to the existing information, of unprecedented length. He was the younger brother of the more famous Marcus Cicero (cos. 63). Quintus Cicero was a cultured man, educated in part in Athens (Cic. *Fin.* 5.1). Before this office, he had held a quaestorship *c.* 68, an aedileship in 65 and a praetorship in 62. He held Asia, however, with consular authority. (See Broughton, II, 139, 158, 173, 181, 185, 191, 198 for references. For his subsequent career, *ibid.*, 205, 213, 226, 232, 239, 245, 253.)

Interest attaches to this profession of provincial goodwill because Cicero was noted for the severity of his gubernatorial behaviour. Even his elder brother chided him with the strict new standards set (Cic. *Q.Fr.* 1.1.19, 20), for his irascibility (*ibid.*, 37-39; tempered apparently in his second year, *ib.* 40) and for the 'brutally frank' way in which he articulated his displeasure with miscreants (*ib.* 1.2.6-7), not to mention his harsh punishments. Reading between the lines of the elder sibling's admonitions, one is tempted to see there a politician's overly developed concern with the goodwill of Roman business interests in the province (1.1.32-35). Q. Cicero's integrity is acknowledged (1.1.8), his avoidance of unnecessary burdens on the province (*ib.*, 9) and his genuine concern for all inhabitants of the province (*ib.*, 13; cf. 24 ['for the happiness of the governed'] and 26 [for fair taxation] as the professed ideology shared by the brothers). But M. Cicero reports complaints received from Greeks (1.2.4) as well as from Roman citizens involved in business (1.2.6). He seems to be engaged in damage control, urging his brother to shred any documents that might blot his reputation when he leaves the province (1.2.8). (For an overview of Cicero's administration, see Magie, 381-383, 1244 nn.12-14.)

Special interest attaches to the inscription because Cicero is hailed as *euergetes*, an epithet applied in the Greek east to divine rulers (cf. Luke 22.25, Acts 12.22). '*Graeca adulatio* had an important place in the system of personal relations between Greeks and

Romans. Honours commonly took the form of praise for benefaction, sometimes actually received and sometimes simply anticipated. A Roman might be called a city's benefactor, its saviour, or its founder; or, in more circumstances than is often realised, he might be assigned a cult' (Bowersock, 12; cf. Appendix 1, 150-151 for a list of republican magistrates who were offered cult). The titles 'Benefactor' and 'Saviour' (*soter*), however, do not necessarily imply divine honours (Raubitschek, 74-75; Nock). 'The East had grown accustomed to the worship of men and women. Hellenistic monarchs and rich benefactors had been accorded cults as tokens of gratitude and of political adhesion. There were many forms and titles of honour, and not all of them carried imputations of divinity ...' (Bowersock, 112). The case of Q. Cicero confirms the latter point. The Cicero brothers played with the conceit that they were (in their excellence) more than human. The provincials, M. Cicero says (*Q.Fr.* 1.1.7), will regard Q. Cicero as a deified mortal (*divinum hominem*) who has dropped into Asia from heaven, and his virtues as hallowed (*consecratas*) and counted amongst those of the gods (*ib.*, 31). But both brothers rejected cult, though a temple and monument were offered (*ib.*, 26; cf. 30 [for the opinion that unprecedented honours had been bestowed on Q. Cicero], 31; and *Att.* 5.21.7 [for M. Cicero's refusal of such worship in Cilicia]). It was the very ambiguity of such honorific terminology that would be a potent factor in what would become the imperial cult (Hillard, 197-201).

In the Acts of the Apostles the healing of people by Jesus and others is spoken of as a 'benefaction' (4.9, 10.38), and the term could even be used of the generous spirit by which servants were not to take advantage of their believing masters (1 Tim. 6.2, cf. Danker, 323-4). Winter has discussed a number of passages where Paul or others seem to advocate public generosity by believers.

On Roman patronage of a community, see the following entry.

Bibliography

G.W. **Bowersock**, *Augustus and the Greek World* (Oxford 1965). T.R.S. **Broughton**, *Magistrates of the Roman Republic* II (Cleveland 1952), III (Atlanta 1986). F.W. **Danker**, *Benefactor: Epigraphic Study of a Graeco-Roman and New Testament Semantic Field* (St Louis 1982). Chr. **Habicht**, G.W. **Bowersock**, C.P. **Jones**, 'Epigraphica Asiae Minoris rapta aut obruta', *AJPh.* 108 (1987) 699-706. T.W. **Hillard**, 'Vespasian's death-bed attitude to his impending deification', in M. Dillon (ed.), *Religion in the Ancient World: New Themes and Approaches* (Amsterdam 1996) 193-215. D. **Magie**, *Roman Rule in Asia Minor* I-II (Princeton 1950). M.J. **Mellink**, 'Archaeology in Asia Minor', *AJA* 62 (1958) 91-104. A.D. **Nock**, '*Soter* and *Euergetes*' in S.E. Johnson (ed.), *The Joy of Study: Papers presented to F.C. Grant* (New York 1951) 127-48; reprinted in *Essays on Religion and the Ancient World* (ed. Z. Stewart) II (Oxford 1972) 720-35. A.E. **Raubitschek**, 'Epigraphical notes on Julius Caesar', *JRS* 44 (1954) 65-75. J. and L. **Robert** *REG* 71 (1958) 298-99 (no. 390). S. **Şahin**, 'Epigraphica Asiae Minoris neglecta et iacentia', *EA* 9 (1987) 47-82. K. **Tuchelt**, *Frühe Denkmäler Roms in Kleinasien. Beiträge zur archäologischen Überlieferung aus der Zeit der Republik und des Augustus* I, *Roma und Promagistrate* (Tübingen 1979). B.W.**Winter** *Seek the Welfare of the City: Christians as Benefactors and Citizens* (Grand Rapids 1994).

T.W. Hillard

§7 Roman Patronal Practice in the Greek East

Clarus   Statue-base   38-35 BC

Ed. pr. — S. Şahin, *EA* 9 (1987) 62 no.5; *SEG* 37 (1987) 959; Broughton 214; K. Tuchelt 167.

	ὁ δῆμος	The people
	Μάνιον Οὐαλέριον	(honour) Manius Valerius
	Μεσσάλαν Ποτῖτον	Messala Potitus,
	ταμίαν ἀρετῆς ἕνε-	*quaestor,* on account of his virtue
5	κα καὶ πάτρωνα ὄντα τῆ[ς]	and being a patron
	πόλεως.	of the city.

For the site of Clarus, see the preceding item. The statue base formed part of an *exedra* (carrying the statues of three Roman magistrates) on the Sacred Way near the temple of Apollo (for photographs of the block *in situ*, see Tuchelt, Tables 6,2 and 7,2). For the date, J. and L. Robert, Syme, 'Potitus' 156 (= 262); with Broughton, 214, leaving a question mark. The first line, supplying the *demos* as the dedicant, is given in Robert, Syme and Tuchelt.

It has been suggested that the honorand was Potitus Valerius Messalla, later the suffect consul of 28 BC, in which case it has to be assumed that he had originally borne the *praenomen* Manius but subsequently '[yielded] to the contemporary fashion of historical or exorbitant *praenomina* ... [deciding] to transfer his second *cognomen* and use it in place of "Manius"' (Syme, *loc. cit.*). Alternatively, the honorand might be an otherwise unknown son of that man (Syme).

The inscription commemorates Messalla's first senatorial posting. At an early stage of his career an aspiring politician would seek to establish a relationship of this nature with foreign communities, often competing with earlier patrons. (See Cic. *Att.* 2.1 for Clodius' challenge, upon his return from a quaestorship in Sicily, to the more senior Cicero, whose relationship with the province had been established more than a decade earlier while also a *quaestor* in the same province.) In this case, Messalla could perhaps build upon an established family presence in the Greek East (Bowersock, 16-17). The evidence for such patronage led to the modern hypothesis that Rome originally conceived of its expanding role in the Greek world as one of *patrocinium*, transferring to its growing sphere of influence the all-pervasive concept in Roman society of patron and client (Badian, esp. 1-13, 55-83). This was countered by Gruen (158-200), arguing that no reliable early text showed the language of *clientela* being used to describe the interstate relations between Rome and the Greek East (*ib.*, esp. 159-162, 175-177) and that the personal patronage of individual Romans and their families over foreign communities ought not to be seen as a practice generated from a specifically Roman institution, since the Greeks in paying homage to the agents of a superior force were following well-established modes of Hellenistic diplomatic discourse (*ib.*, esp. 162-172, 180-184). Gruen's counterpoint perhaps went too far. Texts such as this inscription demonstrate the impact of Roman thinking. 'From the time of Sulla (i.e. *c.* 80 BC), the word *patron* emerges on inscriptions as a regular conjunct with *euergetes* and *soter*; it is a Latin word thinly disguised as Greek, and it connotes a characteristically Roman institution' (Bowersock, 12). More recently, Ferrary has sought a position 'more or less halfway between the maximalist interpretations of Ernst Badian and Erich Gruen ... The Hellenistic world had a large vocabulary for the benefactors or protectors of cities (*euergetes, soter, kedemon, ktistes, proxenos*). The introduction of the transliteration *patron* and of the derivatives *patroneia* and *patroneuein* cannot but mean that the Greeks became aware of a characteristic specific of Roman patronage' (Ferrary, 'Patronage', 105-106). It was a relationship which required a commitment by the Roman aristocrat (*ib.*, 109-110; cf. *Philhellénisme*, 117-132).

Though the term is not used, Chow has reviewed a number of passages (1 Cor. 5.1-13; 6.1-11; 10.1-22; 15.29) where Paul may be seen to be in collision with patronal conventions within his churches.

Bibliography

E. **Badian**, *Foreign Clientelae (264-70 B.C.)* (Oxford 1958). G.W. **Bowersock**, *Augustus and the Greek World* (Oxford 1965). T.R.S. **Broughton**, *Magistrates of the Roman Republic* III (Atlanta GA 1986). J.K. **Chow**, *Patronage and Power: A Study of Social Networks in Corinth* (Sheffield 1992). J.-L. **Ferrary**, *Philhellénisme et impérialisme* (Rome 1988) esp. 117-32. J.-L. **Ferrary**, 'The Hellenistic World and Roman Political Patronage' in P. Cartledge et al. (eds), *Hellenistic Constructs. Essays in Culture, History and Historiography* (Berkeley 1997) 105-19. E.S. **Gruen**, *The Hellenistic World and the Coming of Rome* (Berkeley 1984). J. and L. **Robert**, *REG* 69 (1956) 160 (no.252). S. **Şahin**, 'Epigraphica Asiae Minoris neglecta et iacentia', *EA* 9 (1989) 47-82. R. **Syme**, 'Review of A.E. Gordon, *Potitus Valerius Messalla Consul Suffect 29 B.C.*', *JRS* 45 (1955) 155-60 [reprinted in E. Badian (ed.), *Roman Papers* I, 260-70]. R. **Syme**, 'Missing Persons', *Historia* 5 (1956) 204-12 at 206 [reprinted in E. Badian, *Roman Papers* I, 315-24 at 317]. K. **Tuchelt**, *Frühe Denkmäler Roms in Kleinasien. Beiträge zur archäologischen Überlieferung aus der Zeit der Republik und des Augustus* I, *Roma und Promagistrate* (Tübingen 1979).

T.W. Hillard

§8 Her Soul Went up on High

Attica?   Gravestone   Iᵃ – IIᵖ

Ed. pr. — R.A. Moysey, E.F. Dolin, Jr, *ZPE* 69 (1987) 90-92, with alternative reconstructions by K. Clinton, *ZPE* 75 (1988) 290, and J. Bousquet, *BE* (1988) 37; *SEG* 37 (1987) 198.

['Ω ξένε, τοῦτο τὸ σ]ῆμ' 'Ατθὶς
   λάχεν· Αὐσονίη δὲ
[σῶμ' ἔσχεν, ψυ]χὴ δ' αἰθέρα
   εἰσανέβη.
[τίκτε με ‾ᵘᵘ]τεια, πατὴρ δὲ μοὶ
   'Ηρακλείδη[ς]
[πέντε δὲ καὶ δεκ'] ἔτη ζῆσα
   μετ' ἀμφοτέρω[ν].

[Friend, this] tomb Attica did win. But
Italy
[kept my body], and my soul went up on
high.
[She who bore me was ‾ᵘᵘ]teia, and my
father Heraclides;
[and for fifteen] years I lived with both.

Seven fragments of a white marble stele, presumably from Attica (assuming this is not the deceased's name, which would have been cut below the epigram), now in the University Museums of the University of Mississippi. The deceased's age is arbitrarily restored. For a student who died away from home see *New Docs* 8 (1997) 117-121. The restoration 'body' allows the epigram to invert the traditional conceit of the body as tomb of the soul (*soma/sema*).

As the first editors note, the ascent of the soul into the heavens on death is a long-standing motif of Greek tombstones. Cf. *New Docs* 1 (1981) 103; 3 (1983) 111; 4 (1987) 29, 38, 39, 46, 144. The wings of the soul are a feature of Plato's image of it as the charioteer (*Phaedrus* 254C-256E). Philo and Josephus echo Greek ideas, and most Jews probably believed in the rewards of an afterlife (Sanders, 303). But the immortality of the soul is not a New Testament concept. Jewett (449) argues that Paul followed the Old Testament usage of 'soul' as the earthly life that is lost at death (Rom. 16.4, cf. Matt. 6.25 contra 10.28), avoiding its interchangeability with 'spirit' (πνεῦμα, 1 Cor. 2.14, 15.44-5), the predominant New Testament term that is contrasted with 'body' (1 Cor. 5.3). New Testament anthropology is 'basically monistic' (Harris, 141).

Bibliography

E. **Alliez** and Michael **Feher**, 'Reflections of a soul', in M. Feher et al. (eds), *Fragments for a History of the Human Body* (Pt 2, New York 1989) 46-84. K. **Corrigan**, 'Body and soul in ancient religious experience', in A.H. Armstrong (ed.), *Classical Mediterranean Spirituality: Egyptian, Greek, Roman* (London 1986) 360-83. P. **Courcelle**, 'Flügel (Flug) der Seele', *RAC* 8 (1969) cols 29-65. F. **Cumont**, *After Life in Roman Paganism* (New Haven 1922); *id.*, *Lux Perpetua* (Paris 1949). R.H. **Gundry**, *Soma in Biblical Theology, with Emphasis on Pauline Anthropology* (Cambridge 1976). M.J. **Harris**, *Raised Immortal: Resurrection and Immortality in the New Testament* (London 1983). T.K. **Heckel**, *Der Innere Mensch: Die paulinische Verarbeitung eines platonischen Motifs* (Tübingen 1993). R. **Jewett**, *Paul's Anthropological Terms: A Study of their Use in Conflict Settings* (Leiden 1971). R.B. **Onians**, *The Origins of European Thought about the Body, the Soul, the World, Time, and Fate* (2nd edn: Cambridge 1954). E. **Rohde**, *Psyche: Seelenkult und Unsterblichkeitsglaube der Griechen* (Tübingen 1893) E.t. from 8th edition, *Psyche: The Cult of Souls and Belief in Immortality among the Greeks* (London 1925). E.P. **Sanders**, *Judaism: Practice and Belief 63 BCE – 66 CE* (corrected impression, London 1994) 298-303. R. **Sorabji**, 'Soul and self in ancient philosophy', in M.J.C. Crabbe (ed.), *From Soul to Self* (London 1999) 8-32.

E.A. Judge

§9 Excels Ancestral Honours

Carallia   Limestone statue-base   Imperial

Ed. pr. — J. Nollé, *Chiron* 17 (1987) 237-40 (ph.); *SEG* 37 (1987) 1210.

— — — — — — — — —

[ἀ]ρχιερέα διὰ βίου τῶν
   Σεβ[ασ]-
τῶν Κόνωνα Κενδεου τοῦ
καὶ Λονγείνου κατὰ τὸ ὑπο-
[γ]εγραμμένον ψήφισμα·
5 ἔδοξεν Καραλλιωτῶν τῇ βου-
λῇ καὶ παντὶ δήμωι· ἐπεὶ
   Κό-
νων Κενδεου τοῦ καὶ Λον-
γείνου, ἀνὴρ ἀγαθὸς ὢν καὶ
πρόσχημα τῆς ἡμετέρας
10 πόλεως, πᾶσαν φιλοτειμί-
αν προγονικὴν ὑπερβαλὼν
τῇ ἑαυτοῦ περὶ τὴν πόλιν σ-
[πουδῇ, οὐ μόνον - - -]
[- - - ἀλλ]ὰ καὶ διὰ τῆς τῶν
   ἠθῶν κοσμιό-
15 [τητο]ς εὐεργετῶν καὶ καθ᾽
   ἕνα καὶ πά-
[ντα τὸν δῆμον,] ἐν
   δεινοτάτοις καὶ ἐπε[ί]-
γουσιν καιροῖς μετὰ πάσης
   προθυμί-
[ας] ἑαυτὸν εὔχρηστον
   ἀπεδεί[ξ]α[τ]ο.

(honoured) as life-long priest of the
   Aug-
usti, Conon the son of Cendeas also
called Longinus, according to the following decree:.
It was decided by the council of Carallia and by the whole people: since
   Conon
the son of Cendeas also called Longinus, being a virtuous man and
an ornament of our
city, who all ancestral honour did excel
by his own zeal for the city,
not only [- - -]
[- - -] but who also from
   propriety of con-
duct benefitted individually
   and togeth-
er the people, in
   most terrible and pressing times with all
   read-
iness showed himself
serviceable.

The language of excess (ὑπερβάλλειν) typified the description of benefactors in honorific inscriptions. Benefactors 'excelled' in a range of virtues: e.g. good will (εὔνοια), benevolence (φιλανθρωπία), courage (ἀνδρεία), love of glory (φιλοδοξία) and honour (φιλοτιμία), greatness of mind (μεγαλοφροσύνη) and moderation (σωφροσύνη). Significantly, in this inscription Conon as a benefactor is said to have eclipsed the honour of his ancestors. It was as essential that the ἀνὴρ ἀγαθός replicate and surpass ancestral glory in an eastern Mediterranean context as it was for the *nobilis* in the Roman West.

Paul's attitude to ancestral honour is different. Paul does not reject the privileges resulting from his Jewish ancestry (Rom. 9.4-5; Phil. 3.4b-6). Instead he claims that the pursuit of ancestral advantage in order to outstrip competitors (Gal. 1.14) is based on misguided zeal and knowledge of God (Rom. 10.2). This quest supplants Christ's honour as soteriological benefactor and replaces it with one's own (Rom. 10.3-4; 2 Cor. 11.21b-23a; Phil. 3.7-11, cf. 2.9-11). More than this — and in contrast to the honorific inscriptions — Paul usually reserves the language of excess (ὑπερβάλλειν, ὑπερβολή) for the overflow of divine grace (2 Cor. 9.14; Eph. 2.7), glory (2 Cor. 3.10, 17), power (2 Cor. 4.7; Eph. 1.19), revelation (2 Cor. 12.7) and love (Eph. 3.19). Where Paul employs ὑπερβολή in ethical contexts, it refers to the excess of sin (Rom. 7.13; Gal. 1.13) or, more positively, the excellence of love (1 Cor. 12.31).

Paul avoids rivalry and imitation motifs in ethical contexts (Ascough, *passim*; Harrison, §7.3.1). In similar manner to our inscription, Paul employs the language of zeal. He pressures the recalcitrant Corinthians to fulfil their part of the Jerusalem collection by drawing comparisons between their lack of preparation and the generosity of their Macedonian brethren. The 'zeal' of the Macedonian Christians (σπουδή: 2 Cor. 8.8; cf. 8.1-4) should provoke the Corinthians to ensure that their initial 'readiness' (προθυμία: 2 Cor. 8.11; cf. v.10) regarding the collection comes to fruition. Nonetheless, Paul avoids the inscriptional terminology of competition (ἐφάμιλλος, ἁμιλλᾶσθαι, παραμιλλᾶσθαι). The omission is surely deliberate and points to Paul's different ethical dynamic, namely, divine χάρις (2 Cor. 8.1, 9).

Note the related discussion of ἐν καιροῖς ἀναγκαίοις (*SEG* 37 [1987] 957) in *New Docs* 9 §4).

Bibliography

R.S. **Ascough**, 'The completion of a religious duty: The background of 2 Cor 8.1-15', *NTS* 42/4 (1996) 584-99. F.W. **Danker**, *Benefactor: Epigraphic Study of a Graeco-Roman and New Testament Semantic Field* (St Louis 1982) 320-21, 326-29. J.R. **Harrison**, *Paul's Language of Grace* (χάρις) *in its Graeco- Roman Context* (diss. Macquarie 1996).

J.R. Harrison

§10 Thanksgiving to the Benefactor of the World, Tiberius Caesar

Sardis   Statue-base   AD 41-54

Ed. pr. — C. Foss in F.K. Yegül, *The Bath-Gymnasium Complex at Sardis* (Cambridge, Mass. 1986); *SEG* 36 (1986) 1092.

	Τιβέριον Καί-	Tiberius (object) Cae-
	σαρα θεὸν Σε-	sar god Au-
	βαστὸν τὸν	gustus, the
	αὐτοκράτορα τὸν Τιβερίου	*imperator*, uncle of
5	Κλαυδίου Γερ-	Tiberius Claudius Ger-
	μανικοῦ Καίσα-	manicus Caes-
	ρος Σεβαστοῦ	ar Augustus,
	τοῦ αὐτοκράτο-	the *imperat-*
	ρος θεῖον καὶ τῆς	*or*, and founder of the
10	πόλεως κτίστης (sic)	city
	καὶ εὐεργέτην τοῦ	and benefactor of the
	κόσμου εὐσεβεί-	world, out of piety
	ας καὶ εὐχαριστίας	and thanksgiving
	ἕνεκεν ὁ δῆμος	did the people (subject)
15	καθιέρωσεν	hallow,
	ἐργεπιστατήσαντος	the superintendent of works being
	Τιβ[ερίου Κλαυδίου]	Tib[erius Claudius,]
	[Δημητρίου υἱοῦ]	[son of Demetrius,]
	[Κυρείνα Ἀπολλοφάνους]	[from the Quirine (tribe), Apollophanes].

Vilified by the senatorial tradition (Tacitus), Tiberius was revered in his day in the provinces (Philo, *Leg.* 141-2). Apollophanes (identified from other inscriptions), honoured with Roman citizenship by Claudius (41-54), is presumably commemorating the restoration of Sardis by Tiberius after the earthquake of AD 17. The latter had deprecated divine honours in general, and was never deified at Rome, but on the Augustan precedent had allowed the province of Asia to incorporate him into the imperial cult. R. Seager, *Tiberius* (London 1972) 145.

Apart from its use (Acts 24.3) in flattery of the procurator Felix (freedman of Claudius, but with pretensions to royal descent), εὐχαριστία (with its verb) occurs in the New Testament exclusively towards God. It is a distinctive of the Pauline literature. Apart from Acts 3.12 (where there are textual variants), εὐσέβεια is confined to the Pastoral Epistles and 2 Peter.

E.A. Judge

§11 A Roman Road in Asia Minor

Ionia, near Smyrna   14 September, AD 92—13 September, AD 93

Ed. pr. — *I. Smyrna* 2,1.826, previously unpublished; listed without text in D.H. French, *Roman Milestones of Asia Minor*, BAR International Series, 392.i-ii (Oxford 1988) 166 no. 465.

A column (ht: 1.5 m) which once stood in a cemetery at Balçova near the road between Smyrna and Ilıca but is now lost.

	Im[p. Caesar] divi	Imperator [Caesar], of the deified
	Vespasiani f. ⟦Domiti-	Vespasian the son, [[Domitian]],
	anu̱s̱⟧ Aug. German[i]-	Augustus, Germanicus,
	cus, pont. max., t̲r̲i̲b̲	supreme pontiff, in his 12th year of tribunician
5	pot. XII, imp. XXII,	power, (hailed) imperator 22 times, consul 16
	c̲[os.] X̲[VI],	times,
	censur perpet., P. P.	perpetual censor, Father of his Country.

(*a space of 1 line*)

	Αὐτοκράτωρ Καῖσαρ θεο̱ῦ [Οὐ]-	Imperator Caesar, of the god Ves-
	εσπασιανοῦ υἱὸς ⟦Δομιτιανὸς⟧	pasian the son, [[Domitian]],
	Σεβαστὸς Γερμανικός, [ἀρχιε]-	Augustus, Germanicus, supreme
10	ρεὺς μέγιστος, δημαρ[χικῆς ἐ]-	pontiff, in the [12th] year of tribunician
	ξουσίας τὸ [ιβ΄], αὐτοκ[ρ]ά[τωρ]	power, (hailed) Imperator
	τὸ κβ΄, ὕπ[α]τ̲ος τὸ [ιϛ΄,	22 times, consul [16 times],
	τιμητὴς	perpetual
	διηνε[κή]ς, πατὴρ πατ[ρίδ]ος,	[censor], Father of his Country,
	τὰς ὁδοὺς ἐποίησεν.	made the roads.

(*a space for about 3 lines*)

15	Ἐπὶ [ἀνθυπάτ]ου Ἰουνίου	In the [proconsulship] of Iunius Caesennius
	[Κ]α̲ισ̲[εννίου]	
	Πα̲ί[τ]ου του[.] ' [. . .]υο[ ]	Paetus ...
	τ̲[. .]ε[ ]	...
	Κ̲Α̲ΤΟΥ [ ]	...
	Ε[ ]	...

6 *l.* censor

In its present state of preservation one cannot tell whether this stone was a milestone or simply a notice of construction or repair roadwork. If a measure of distance was once engraved below the text, as is typically the case with milestones, all trace of that is now lost. The format of the inscription with the official titulature of the emperor given first in Latin and then repeated in Greek is not telling in itself as it is used in either context. The presence of both Latin and Greek was not uncommon on milestones and other stones which conveyed information of an official nature from the Roman government to the local inhabitants. However, the combined use of Greek and Latin in the inscriptions of Asia Minor is not restricted to official inscriptions. It may be found on stones set up by both Greeks and Romans acting in a private capacity and is a phenomenon which merits further study for the light it throws on the impact of Roman government on the local inhabitants of Anatolia (cf. R.A. Kearsley, *Greeks and Romans in Imperial Asia*, Inschriften griechisher Städte aus Kleinasien, vol. 54 [Bonn 2001]).

The year date of Domitian's reign noted in the above inscription as that in which the roadwork was carried out is established by the total of his repetitions of the tribunician power (the tally of his consulships being lost in either case). The erasure of the emperor's personal name, Domitian, would have been carried out soon after AD 96. The condemnation of Domitian's memory was decreed by the Roman Senate after his assassination by members of his household staff in September 96 and was intended to accomplish the excision of Domitian's name wherever it appeared in official documents empire-wide. Sometimes, although it is not the case in the present instance, the erasures made as a result of this *damnatio memoriae* also include the name Germanicus which Domitian adopted in 83/84; see, for example, the statue bases commemorating the dedication to Domitian of the first temple of the provincial imperial cult in Ephesus (S.F. Friesen, *Twice Neokoros. Ephesus, Asia and the Cult of the Flavian Imperial Family* [Leiden 1993] 29-37).

The name and title of the governor of the province of Asia, L. Iunius Caesennius Paetus, is inscribed below the Greek version of the imperial titulature after a space of about three lines. The identification of the local Roman official responsible for carrying out an emperor's order, as in *ll*.15-16 of the above inscription, is something regularly found on official documents of this kind. Just as regularly, in bilingual inscriptions of this sort, it appears at the end of the Greek version of the text only. The following section of the text, which cannot be restored at all, is likely to have provided prosopographical information and, perhaps, some detail of the proconsul's earlier career.

The Roman Road Network

The construction and maintenance of roads was an important aspect of Roman government in Asia Minor for both administrative and military purposes. The first major arterial, believed to have extended from Pergamum to the Pamphylian coast in southern Anatolia, was established by Manius Aquillius as governor of Asia soon after the possessions of the Pergamene kingdom were bequeathed to the Roman people in 133 BC (S. Mitchell, *Anatolia. Land, Men and Gods in Asia Minor* vol. 1 [Oxford 1993] Map 3 at the end of the volume). A second major arterial was that built under Augustus' direction and known as the *Via Sebaste*. Built in 6 BC, this road linked the emperor's new foundations in Galatia, many of which were military colonies planted to play a part in pacifying the Pisidian region, with each other as well as with the road of Aquillius and the Pamphylian plain; for the route of the *Via Sebaste*, see D. French (ed.), *Studies in the History and Topography of Lycia and Pisidia* (London 1994) p.x, 'Map of Southwest Asia Minor'. For wide-ranging discussions on the nature and importance of the Roman roads in Asia Minor in all periods, see D. H. French, 'The Roman road-system of Asia Minor', *Aufstieg und Niedergang der römischen Welt* II, 7.2 (Berlin 1980) 698-728 and S. Mitchell, *Anatolia. Land, Men and Gods in Asia Minor* vol. 1 (Oxford 1993) 124-33; on modes of transport for persons, see S.R. Llewelyn, *New Docs* 7 (Sydney 1994), 58-92, especially 87ff with respect to the New Testament. A large collection of milestones which once stood along the course of these and later Roman roads of Anatolia is published in D.H. French, *Roman Milestones of Asia Minor*, BAR International Series, Fasc. 1-2 (Oxford 1981, 1988).

The road beside which the present inscription was found (French, *Roman Milestones* 166 no. 465, 546-47 Map 11) would have formed part of a much-used network in the countryside between the two large coastal cities of Smyrna and Ephesus. If its find spot is a rough guide, it stood beside the road running westwards between Smyrna and the famous thermal springs at the place now named Ilıca but which in ancient times lay in the territory of the city of Erythrae (G.E. Bean, *Aegean Turkey* [London 1966] 159).

Domitian and the Provinces

The veracity of Suetonius' statement (*Life of Domitian* 8) that Domitian's close supervision of provincial officials meant there were greatly improved standards of honesty and justice during his reign has sometimes been doubted, no doubt under the influence of Domitian's reputation for financial rapaciousness. P.A. Brunt, 'Charges of provincial maladministration under the early Principate', *Historia* 10 (1961) 221, for example, believes that Suetonius' judgement was formed on the basis only of an apparent lack of prosecutions for extortion. However, the discovery of epigraphic documents in the eastern part of the empire has played a large part in explaining, and verifying, Suetonius' comment regarding Domitian's energetic attitude towards good government in the provinces (H.W. Pleket, 'Domitian, the Senate and the provinces', *Mnemosyne* 14 [1961] 304-8). Among the documents found which throw light on Domitian's intervention to correct or prevent exploitation of the inhabitants of the provinces are: a letter railing against Roman officials in Syria who abused their power to requisition transport and lodgings from local people for official purposes (cf. *New Docs* 7 [1994] 75-77); an inscription protecting the provisions of an endowment bequeathed to his city by a wealthy citizen of Acmonia against embezzlement by the powerful upper class of the city; and an inscription detailing how the price of grain was to be regulated in Pisidian Antioch during a time of famine. Fuller discussion of this and other material, together with references, may be found in Pleket, *ibid.*, and in B.W. Jones, *The Emperor Domitian* (London 1992) 109-12. Such measures and others, such as the institution of the *curator civitatis*, an official appointed to individual cities to supervise their financial affairs and to ensure that they remained solvent, were necessary because the empire's revenue was dependent on the prosperity of provincial cities (A.D. Macro, *ANRW* II, 7.2 [Berlin 1980] 668-70). If left unchecked, extravagant spending of local resources by members of the local elite also weakened the financial viability of the cities. Indeed, the correspondence between the emperor Trajan and Pliny the Younger, the Roman proconsul in Bithynia-Pontus, reveals how a governor might have to intervene in the case of over-ambitious building plans and unfulfilled promises (*Ep.* 10.37-40).

The reasons for Domitian's action in these respects must surely have lain primarily in his appreciation of the link between the prosperity of Rome and of the regions subject to it from which the tax revenue was drawn. Whether or not it may be argued that Domitian's actions show a genuine desire to establish a better balance between the powerful elite families of the provincial cities and those of lesser status, some corrective certainly needs to be applied to the perception of Domitian provided by the hostile literary sources (Pleket, *ibid.*, 311-13; Jones, *ibid.*, 196-98).

Some Other Epigraphic Evidence for Domitian's Activity in the Region of Smyrna and Ephesus

Indications of roadwork are a significant pointer to both the administrative and military health of Roman government at the time (French, *ANRW* II, 7.2 [1980] 700-02), hence the road inscription above, together with another such inscription which was found north of Ephesus near the road leading towards Smyrna and dates to AD 89-92 (*I. Eph.* 3607), provide further examples of Domitian's attention to the efficiency of Roman provincial government. Within the Cayster valley which extends in a north-easterly direction from Ephesus, the boundary of the temple estate of Artemis also merited the attention of Domitian, as it had of Augustus at an earlier time, and five marker stones dating to his reign have been found (*I. Eph.* 3506-10), with two inscriptions listed under the first of these numbers. The boundary stones of all periods are discussed in D. Knibbe, R. Meriç, R. Merkelbach, 'Der Grundbesitz der ephesischen Artemis im Kaystrostal', *ZPE* 33 (1979) 139-48; see also the comments in G.H.R. Horsley, *New Docs* 4 (1987) 128-29.

Paul and Roman Roads

Paul's choice of Pisidian Antioch as the initial location for his mission in Anatolia appears an unlikely one at first due to its location well inland. However, the decision to head straight there and the failure to spend time even at the city of Perge, his first land-fall after Cyprus, may well have been due to the link he had established with Sergius Paulus, the Roman governor at Paphos, since that man's origin lay in Antioch and it might be expected that Paul would have received letters of introduction (so S. Mitchell, *Anatolia,* vol II, 5-7). Influential also appears to be the location of Jewish synagogue communities which Paul could address (S.R. Llewelyn, *New Docs* 7 [1994] 88-91).

For Paul's second journey, the itinerary has been interpreted as representing 'a shift in the travel strategy of Paul' away from the use of major paved roads. Behind this, it has been suggested, lay the desire to avoid urban centres in the provinces of Asia and Bithynia where earlier antagonism from public officials was experienced by Paul and his group (David French, 'Acts and the Roman Roads of Asia Minor', in D.W.J. Gill - C. Gempf [eds], *The Book of Acts in its First Century Setting* [Grand Rapids 1994] 49-58).

R.A. Kearsley

§12   Ephesus and Sardis Compete for the Cult of Caracalla

The first temple of the provincial imperial cult in the province of Asia was built with Octavian's permission at Pergamum in 29 BC. The *koinon* (provincial assembly) of Asia acted on behalf of individual cities in making the requests to build such temples and both the emperor and the Roman Senate had a role to play in granting approval for that action.

In the centuries that followed many other cities sought and were granted the right to build a temple for the same purpose (see R.A. Kearsley, in *New Docs* 6 [1992] 203-4). Possession of a temple of the provincial imperial cult entitled a city to be designated *neokoros* (temple warden) of the emperor/s (on this title, including its significance for the cult of Artemis at Ephesus as described in Acts 19.23-41, see *ibid.*, 205-6) and to hold the festivals which were a regular part of cultic worship.

Undoubtedly, inter-city rivalry was closely linked to the prestige gained by winning Roman permission to establish new cults of the imperial family. Being a centre of the imperial cult had a positive economic impact on the city because of the many visitors converging to take part in the ceremonies. A reflection of the impact of the temple at Pergamum on the life of Christians there has been identified in Rev. 2.13 (see C.J. Hemer, *The Letters to the Seven Churches of Asia in their Local Setting* [Sheffield 1986] 84-87). Hence, even if, as appears to be the case, participation in the cult was not compulsory at an individual level, the early Christian communities in major centres of the imperial cult would have experienced some level of conflict regarding their freedom to join in civic celebrations (1 Cor. 8.4-6 with discussion in B.W. Winter, *Seek the Welfare of the City* [Grand Rapids 1994] 125-33; for a wide-ranging survey of the relevance of inscriptions from Ephesus for uncovering the social context of the New Testament documents, see G.H.R. Horsley, *NT* 34 [1992] 105-68).

Both the inscriptions given below belong to the reign of the emperor Caracalla (early third century). This was a period when important cities such as Ephesus, Pergamum and Smyrna, which already possessed more than one temple of the provincial imperial cult, sought and obtained permission to build yet another. Caracalla appears to have been very liberal in his attitude, looking favourably on requests not only from the larger cities but from several smaller ones as well (L. Robert, *Rev. Phil.* 41 [1967] 57). He also permitted, for the first time, the formal association of local deities with the imperial cult (*ibid.*, 57) even though as early as the time of Augustus Artemis, the patron goddess of Ephesus, had been associated with the imperial cult (G.H.R. Horsley, *ibid.*, 156).

In the following inscriptions from Ephesus and Sardis something of the history of the cult in each city and of its relations with Rome is revealed. Because of the individual nature of such details the two inscriptions are treated in turn below.

Ephesus   Marble block from temple   AD 213-217

Ed. pr. — B. İplikçioğlu, 'Eine neue Ehrung für Kaiser Caracalla aus Ephesos', *EA* 9 (1987) 111-13, pl. 13; *SEG* 37 (1987) 886.

A block of blue-white marble, 0.83 (ht) x 0.45 (w) x 0.31 (d) m, found during excavation of the porch of the temple of Serapis.

[Αὐτοκράτορα Καίσαρα Μ. Αὐρήλιον]	[(Honouring) Imperator Caesar Marcus Aurelius]
['Αντωνεῖνον Εὐσεβῆ Σεβαστὸν]	[Antoninus Pius Augustus,]
Παρθικὸν μέγιστ[ον, Βρε]-	supreme Parthicus,
ταννικὸν μέγιστ[ον, Γερ]-	supreme Britannicus,
5 μανικὸν μέγιστον, 'Α[ρμενι]-	supreme Germanicus,
ακὸν μέγιστον, Νέον ["Ηλιον],	supreme Armenicus, New [Helios,]
τὸν γῆς καὶ θαλάσσης δεσ[πότην]	the lord of land and sea,
ἡ φιλοσέβαστος βουλ[ὴ]	the Augustus-loving council
τῆς πρώτης καὶ μεγίστης μ[ητρο]-	of the first and supreme metropolis
10 πόλεως τῆς 'Ασίας καὶ ιδ̣ι̣ς	of Asia and twice
[νεωκό]-	[temple-warden]
ρ[[ου[- -]ν]] τῶν Σε[βαστῶν]	[*erasure*] of the Augustuses
[[- - - ο̣ς]] 'Εφ[εσίων]	[*erasure*] of the Ephesians'
πόλεως	city, (salutes him as)
τὸν ἑαυτῆς καὶ τῆς πατρ[ίδος σωτῆρα?],	the [saviour] of itself and of its native land,
15 ἀπὸ πόρων βουλα[ρχίας]	from the funds of the president of the council,
Κλ. Τειμοκρά[τους],	Claudius Timocrates, during the
ἐκδικοῦντος Φλ. 'Ιο[υλιανοῦ β']	advocacy of Flavius Iulianus III,
υἱοῦ, ἀρχιερέως καὶ [πρυτάνεως]	high-priest, and [prytanis],
καὶ γραμματέως [τοῦ δήμου]	and secretary [of the people]
20 φιλοσεβάσ[του]	that loves Augustus.

18 *l.* υἱοῦ

The historical context of the erasure and alteration in *ll.*10-12 of this inscription is not entirely clear. According to *ed. pr.* it is due to the intense rivalry for pre-eminence which existed between the Graeco-Roman cities of Asia Minor and occurred under the following circumstances.

When Ephesus had requested a third imperial neocorate from Caracalla and Geta in 211, a temple was granted in honour of Geta. Caracalla, instead, assigned his honour to Artemis (*I. Eph.* 212). But Geta's neocorate was annulled after his death and subsequent *damnatio memoriae* in 212. The impact of these events is reflected in the coins with the legend τρίς and depicting an imperial temple which were overstruck with δίς (S. Karwiese, *Gross ist die Artemis von Ephesos* [Vienna 1995] 117-18) and by inscriptions such as *I. Eph.* 647 (see *New Docs* 6 [1992] 203). Devastated by such a loss Ephesus may have attempted to find a way to preserve its entitlement to three neocorates by proposing to Caracalla that the neocorate of Artemis be counted with the two pre-existing imperial ones. A letter from Caracalla to the city referring to it as τρίς νεωκόρος (*I. Eph.* 212 *ll.* 20-21) demonstrates it was successful in its request.

According to this view, then, by 213 Ephesus' primacy was restored by incorporating the neocorate of Artemis Ephesia to make a total of three. In 214/15, Pergamum and then Smyrna, also received third imperial neocorates from Caracalla and, as Ephesus' mixture of neocorates did not conform to the traditional usage of such titles, even the weight of imperial sanction for this formulation was not sufficient to sustain it after Caracalla's death and Ephesus was forced by the rival cities to re-word its neocorate titulature to δὶς νεωκόρος τῶν Σεβαστῶν, ἄπαξ τῆς Ἀρτέμιδος. It is this situation which İplikçioğlu suggests was the reason for the erasure and re-engraving of *ll.*10-12 in the present inscription and he suggests the text originally read:

10   πόλεως τῆς Ἀσίας καὶ ⟦[τρ]⟧ὶς [νεωκό]-
      ρ⟦ου [πρώτης, δὶς μὲ]ν⟧ τῶν Σε[βαστῶν]
      ⟦[ἄπαξ δὲ τῆς Ἀρτέμιδ]ος⟧ Ἐφ[εσίων]
      ... metropolis of Asia and three times temple-
      warden first, twice of the Augustuses
      and once of Artemis of the Ephesians

Although this inscription originally incorporated the third neocorate titulature, its function was not, at least in an overt sense, to announce Ephesus' success in this respect. As it stands the inscription honours the emperor Caracalla. Many such inscriptions honouring emperors without providing any particular reason for the occasion have been found in Asia Minor. The body initiating the decree was the city's council or *boule*, of which Claudius Timocrates was president at the time since he bears the title boularch; the fund he administered was the source of the necessary money (*ll.*15-17). The role of Flavianus Iulianus in honouring Caracalla is not specified. However, his office of *ekdikos* (public advocate) indicates that he would have acted on the city's behalf in some matter of importance. Given that he comes from a line of distinguished ancestors who, like him, held some of the city's highest magistracies (for a *stemma* of his forebears, see *I. Eph.* 3064), it is conceivable that it was he who made Ephesus' successful request of Caracalla for permission to incorporate the neocorate of Artemis with those of the emperors. The text of this inscription for Caracalla would be an entirely appropriate expression of gratitude.

Architectural details of the neocorate temples and sanctuaries at Ephesus are extremely scarce because, in each case, either human agency or earthquake played a part in their destruction in antiquity. For example, of the first neocorate temple belonging to the Flavian period, only the vaulted substructure and part of the altar are visible today at the western end of the upper *agora* (S. Friesen, *Twice Neokoros. Ephesus, Asia and the Cult of the Flavian Imperial Family* [Leiden 1993] 59-65). Even less remains of the second, Hadrianic, temple which is thought to be identical with the huge structure, known also as the Olympieion, which was built on reclaimed land near the harbour. All subsequent centres of the provincial imperial cult, dating from the early third century, were probably located in the Olympieion's mighty southern stoa after it was enclosed (Karwiese, *ibid.*, 117; S. Karwiese, 'The Church of Mary and the Temple of Hadrian Olympios', in *Ephesos. Metropolis of Asia*, H. Koester ed. [Cambridge, Mass. 1995] 314-15).

****

Sardis was one of the cities of lesser size and reputation which received permission to become an imperial *neokoros*. It lay inland from Ephesus, to the north-east in Lydia, and stood beside the Hermus River. There, excavation of a large architectural complex has produced both epigraphic and architectural evidence for the imperial cult.

Sardis	Statue base from bath complex	AD 211-17

Ed. pr. — C. Foss, in F.K. Yegül (ed.), *The Bath-Gymnasium Complex at Sardis* (Cambridge, Mass. 1986) 171 no.5, Fig. 209; *SEG* 37 (1987) 1096. (Text previously quoted in L. Robert, 'Sur des inscriptions d'Ephèse', *Rev.Phil.* 4 [1967] 48-49 n. 6).

A marble block from a shrine of the imperial cult within an open court in the bath-gymnasium complex., 0.77 (ht) x 0.67 (w) x 0.65 (d) m.

	Αὐτοκράτορα Καίσαρα	(Honouring) Imperator Caesar
	Μ(ᾶρκον) Αὐρήλιον Σεουῆρον	Marcus Aurelius Severus
	Ἀντωνῖνον Εὐσεβῆ Εὐ-	Antoninus, Pius,
	τυχῆ Σεβαστὸν ἀρχιερέ-	Felix, Augustus, supreme
5	α μέγιστον· ἡ πρωτόχθων	pontiff, the First Native
	καὶ μητρόπολις τῆς Ἀσί]-	and metropolis of Asia
	ας καὶ Λυδίας ἁπάσης κα[ὶ]	and of all Lydia and
	δὶς νεωκόρος τῶν Σεβασ-	twice temple-warden of the Augustuses
	τῶν κατὰ τὰ δόγματα τῆς ἱ-	according to the decrees of the
10	ερᾶς συγκλήτου, φίλη καὶ	holy Senate, friend and
	σύμμαχος Ῥωμαίων κ(αὶ)	ally of the Romans, and
	οἰκεία τοῦ κυρίου αὐτο-	relative of the lord Imperator,
	κράτορος ἡ λαμπροτά-	the most brilliant
	τη Σαρδιανῶν πόλις τὸν	city of the Sardians (salutes him as)
15	ἴδιον σωτῆρα καὶ εὐεργέ-	its own saviour and benefactor.
	την	

The base on which the above inscription was engraved originally supported an image of the emperor and stood within a bath-gymnasium complex at Sardis which covered a vast 20,756 square metres. The section of the structure from which the statue base is believed to have come was the Marble Court which was richly ornamented with aedicular facades in two storeys. The palaestra onto which it opened was equally impressive consisting of a large peristyle court of 100 marble columns on pedestals; the floors in the ambulatories were covered by mosaics. The Marble Court was dedicated in 211 to the emperors Caracalla and Geta, their mother, Iulia Domna, all the imperial family and the Senate and Roman people. It is believed that the Court was associated with the imperial cult of Sardis.

There appears to be a pattern of establishing 'imperial halls' as components of bath-gymnasium complexes in Asia Minor. At Ephesus, the most impressive example was within the Harbour Bath-Gymnasium. There also appear to have been lesser ones in the East Baths and the Vedius Gymnasium. Elsewhere, examples occur at Pergamum,

Hierapolis, Aphrodisias and Ancyra. It is suggested that this association may have developed out of the use of the *ephebeum* of the Hellenistic gymnasium for worship of the local ruler (F.K. Yegül, *The Bath-Gymnasium Complex at Sardis* [Cambridge, Mass. 1986] 5-7).

Although the inscription around the first-storey architrave of the building refers to Caracalla and Geta as co-emperors, the above inscription contains only the name of Caracalla. It is possible, therefore, that a separate statue of Geta was created to stand in the Marble Court also. An inscribed base for a statue of Lucius Verus reveals that the building must have been in use by the mid-second century (Yegül, *ibid.*, 12). Despite the elaborate dedication to the Severan imperial family in the Marble Court it does not appear that Sardis benefited from the family's goodwill in the same manner as Ephesus with respect to the coveted neocorates. Sardis already bore the title β΄ νεωκόρος (twice temple-warden) in the time of Verus (Foss, *ibid.*, 169-70 no. 2) and as this title also occurs in Sardis' titulature when the Marble Court was dedicated (Foss, *ibid.*, 170 no. 3) there had clearly been no gain in the city's total of neocorate temples.

'Saviour' and 'benefactor' are conventional honorific terms frequently used for deities, rulers, or for lesser mortal benefactors of communities in the Hellenistic and Roman periods. They are frequently found together, as in this inscription, and in such cases they refer particularly to deities and rulers, such as the Roman emperors. On the NT usage of the terms (eg., Luke 1.47, 1 Tim. 1.1, 2.3) see §2 above; cf. also the discussion of σωτήρ by G.H.R. Horsley, *New Docs* 4 (1987), 148. It may be suspected that its application here, and elsewhere, was as much to induce benefactions as to acknowledge their prior receipt. Sardis also emphasises the nature and the length of its good relationship with Rome in this inscription. In addition to honouring Caracalla and the imperial family, the text refers specifically to the fact that the Roman Senate had twice expressed its opinion in favour of granting Sardis permission for a provincial imperial cult. The formulaic title 'friend and ally of the Romans' refers to an even earlier period when a treaty between the city and Rome had been established. This item in particular creates an historical depth to the city's relationship with Rome which was consonant with the privilege now being accorded to it.

The bath-gymnasium building at Sardis underwent structural alterations at a later stage of its history. The most important of these occurred in the late third/early fourth century when the south wing of the palaestra was made available to the Jewish community who remodelled it for use as a large synagogue (Yegül, *ibid.*, 15).

R.A. Kearsley

Papyri

§13   A Brewer's Guarantor

Arsinoite nome   9 x 20.5 cm   IIIᵃ (second half)

Ed. pr. — K. Maresch in *Kölner Papyri*, vol. 6, eds M Gronewald, B. Kramer, K. Maresch, M. Parca and C. Römer (Opladen 1987) 198-202 (= P. Köln 268).

The papyrus is almost completely preserved. The document is a public notice which has been amended between the lines (see smaller font) to offer a fuller description of the property for sale. Cf. *UPZ* 1, 121 cited *New Docs* 8 (1998) 11-12. The back is blank.

τοὺς βουλομένους	Let those wanting
ὸ	the (property)
ὠνεῖσθαι τ⟦ὴν⟧ Κολήφιος	to purchase the (property) of Colephis,
⟦π..⟧	...
τοῦ ἐγγυησαμένου	who guaranteed
Πᾶσιν τὸν ζυτοποι-	Pasis the brewer,
Μέμφεως θεμέλιον καὶ	of Memphis, (consisting of) foundation,
5 ὸν ⟦οἰκίαν τὴν οὖσαν⟧	(consisting of a) house located
οἴκημα καὶ αὐλὴν καὶ τὰ προσ-	house, court-yard and their
κύ(ροντα) τὰ ὄντα πη(χῶν) τ ἐπὶ πή(χεις) μ̅	appurtenances, being 10 by 40 cubits
ἐν Μέμφει διδόναι	at Memphis deliver
τὰς ὑποστάσεις	their offers
Ἀπολλωνίωι τῶι	to Apollonius, the
πρὸς τῆι οἰκονομίαι	*oikonomos,*
10 καὶ Μανρεῖ τῶι τοπο-	and to Manres, the
γραμματεῖ ὡ[ς τῆς]	*topogrammateus,* in order that
κυρώσεως ἐσ[ο]μέ[νης]	ratification occur
παραχρῆμα.	immediately.
14 εὑρίσκει δὲ [?]	(The property) achieves (an offer of ...)

The document is a public notice (πρόγραμμα) which was posted by the financial officials of the administrative division to advertise the sale of property.[1] An auction of the property had already been made, and the amount of the highest bid notified at the end of the πρόγραμμα (*l.*14). Unfortunately the papyrus breaks off here and the value of the bid is lost. The purpose of the notice was to attract a higher offer by anyone else who might have been interested in acquiring the property. The offer was posted for some (10?) days afterwards to allow for further bids to be made. After this period the highest bid was ratified.

In view of the involvement of financial officials[2] and the fact that the house belonged to a guarantor of a brewer, it would seem that the sale is an attempt by the government to

---

[1] Formally similar notices are found in SB 7202 *ll.*45-49, a notice requesting bids on a tax-farming concession(?) for the island of Alexandria (third century BC), and P. Köln 219, a notice informing those wanting to register mortgages, releases of loans etc. to approach the holder of the sales-tax concession (209 or 192 BC).

[2] The *oikonomos* was vitally involved in arrangements surrounding the sale of tax-farming and monopoly concessions. See *New Docs* 8 (1998) 49-57. He also appears involved with auctions related to royal revenue. For examples see Maresch, *Kölner Papyri*, 6.201. The role of the *topogrammateus*

realise a public debt owed to it. Presumably Pasis had obtained his brewing concession from the state[3] and, as was the practice, submitted guarantors for its purchase price. On the requirement to submit guarantors for such concessions or leases see *New Docs* 8 (1998) 50-52, esp. n.19. A guarantor usually offered real property (houses, land, vineyards and gardens) under *hypotheke* (mortgage) for a defined sum. It would appear that the state suffered a loss in its arrangement with the brewer and sought recovery from the guarantor, Colephis. As he also was unable to pay the official moved to sell his pledged property. The reason for the loss is not stated; however, the editor[4] draws attention to the frequency of inflated purchase prices in this industry. Recovery was through public auction with a period left afterwards for higher bids to be submitted.

The papyrus illustrates the state's use of private capital to operate its monopolies. Administrative infrastructure, whether it be in the areas of taxation or the various monopolies, was geared to supervision rather than day-to-day operation. The latter would be sold by lease to the highest bidder. The sale price had to be guaranteed and this allowed the state to spread its risk. As our document shows, it also permitted persons of apparently small capital worth to participate in business ventures and encouraged the state's recognition of the private ownership of property.

As the brewer and his guarantor bear Egyptian names, the papyrus attests the important role that trade and commerce played in the Hellenization of the entrepreneurial classes of society. A similar phenomenon has been observed in Palestine in the same period. See M. Hengel, *Judaism and Hellenism*, vol. 1 (London 1974) 32-57. The importance of commerce and its administrative context is confirmed in the range of loanwords that went over into Hebrew and Aramaic. See E. Schürer, *The History of the Jewish People in the Age of Jesus Christ*, revised and edited by G. Vermes, F. Millar and M. Black, vol. 2 (Edinburgh 1979) 52-84.

S.R. Llewelyn

---

appears to have been to confirm the value of the property for auction and to indicate its exact location. In this instance he is also to receive over-bids.

[3] The beer monopoly was controlled by the state.

[4] Maresch, *Kölner Papyri*, 6.200.

§14 Expediting a Legal Case

Arsinoite nome   7.7 x 31 cm   III^a (second half)

Ed. pr. — K. Maresch in *Kölner Papyri*, vol. 6, eds M Gronewald, B. Kramer, K. Maresch, M. Parca and C. Römer (Opladen 1987) 196-7 (= P. Köln 267).

The papyrus is itself complete but the last lines have been erased through a washing of the ink.

	Σώστρατος	Sostratus
	Ἀπολλωνίωι χαίρειν.	to Apollonius, greeting.
	Φαμοῦνις ὁ ἀπο-	Phamounis, who is
	διδούς σοι τὴν	delivering to you this
5	ἐπιστολήν ἐστιν	letter, is
	Πτολεμαίου τοῦ	a brother of Ptolemaeus,
	παρ' ἡμῶν ἀδελ-	who is one of us.
	φός. καλῶς ποιή-	You will do well
	σεις ἐπαναγκά-	to make
10	σαι Τασῶν τὴν	Tasos, the
	Θαμῶτος θυγα-	daughter of Thamos,
	τέρα τὰ δίκαια	render to him
	αὐτῶι ὑποσχεῖν,	his legal rights
	περὶ ὧν αὐτῆι	concerning which he
15	ἐγκαλεῖ. ⟦καὶ⟧	accuses her. ⟦And⟧
	⟦. . . .ων ἄν σοι⟧	⟦... may to you⟧
	⟦προσπ . . . ηται⟧	⟦...⟧
	⟦π . λ . . πρ. . . . .⟧	⟦...⟧
	⟦αὐτόν.⟧	⟦him.⟧
20	ἔρρωσο.	Farewell.
Back	Ἀπολλωνίωι	To Apollonius.

The document is a private letter addressed by Sostratus to Apollonius asking that he use his coercive powers in a legal dispute. The dispute is between Tasos and the person to whom αὐτῷ in *l*.13 refers. As the nearest antecedent this might be taken to be Thamos, her father. If so, the matter concerns an internal family dispute. Or again the pronoun might refer to Phamounis, the person delivering the letter.[1] The latter possibility seems the better as it explains the occasion for the letter. In a dispute between persons bearing

---

[1] This is not how the editor appears to understand the antecedent of αὐτῷ. Clearly by his reconstruction of the washed portion of the text he has the woman's father in mind: ⟦καὶ περὶ ὧν ἄν σοι προσποιήσηται πάλιν πράσσειν αὐτόν.⟧ which he translates: 'und was sie, wie sie es Dir gegenüber darstellen wird, wieder von ihm einzutreiben hat'. It might be better translated: 'and concerning whatever she may pretend to you that he in turn is doing'. However, the sense and relationship of this clause to the preceding sentence is conjectural. For this reason the lines are left unrestored.

Egyptian names, one party (Phamounis) has recourse through his brother (Ptolemaeus, a Hellenised Egyptian?) to Sostratus (a Greek official?). He writes to Apollonius, the deputy of the nome *oikonomos* (i.e. principal revenue official) who was responsible for the administrative district of Polemonos Meris,[2] to help expedite the matter and gives the letter to the person who had sought his help in the first place. At the same time Sostratus uses a formula of introduction (cf. P. Sorb. 1.49, BGU 8.1871, P. Mich. 1.33) to acquaint Apollonius with Phamounis (*ll.*3-8). Phamounis has apparently accused Tasos of not giving him what was rightfully his. What this was is unclear. Naturally, if Apollonius needed further clarification, he could ask Phamounis in person.

The letter illustrates the need for self-reliance or personal initiative in matters of dispute and the importance attached to the use of persons of influence to expedite an impasse or move a case forward. A dispute often did not move to resolution unless pushed and prodded by the plaintiff. For example, in criminal cases it was the responsibility of the victims or their families to bring a charge and commence proceedings through petition. When the matter was referred between officials the victim in many cases had to follow it up or reintroduce the matter to the new official by a petition with appended copies of relevant documents. In civil cases such as distraint against a debtor creditors intervened, again through petition, at various points in the procedure in order to move it to the next stage.[3] For administrative staff the line between official duty and perceived social obligation was blurred with the result that the exercise of influence was often thought suitable and necessary to advantage a cause.[4] As such the process was also open to corruption. It is this need to intervene and the reliance on personal petition that explains the actions of the woman in the parable of the reluctant judge (Luke 18.1-8). Also relevant is the tardiness of Felix to hear the case of Paul. It is reported by the author of Acts that he was awaiting a payment by the prisoner before resolving the dispute (Acts 24.26).

S.R. Llewelyn

---

2 See ὁ πρὸς τῆι οἰκονομίαι in P. Köln 268, and Maresch, *Kölner Papyri*, 6.160.

3 See *New Docs* 7 (1994) 203-11.

4 See *New Docs* 6 (1992) 101-4 and *New Docs* 8 (1998) 25-26 for the use of official contacts to expedite the capture and return of fugitive slaves.

§15 The King as 'Living Image' of Zeus

Provenance unknown 9.5 x 10.5 cm 221-205 BC

Ed. — J.C. Shelton, *Griechische Urkundenpapyri der Bayerischen Staatsbibliothek München*, Band III, eds U. Hagedorn, D. Hagedorn, R. Hübner and J.C. Shelton (Stuttgart 1986) 3-6 (= P. Monac. III 45 = WChr 109).

The text only varies slightly from the ed. pr., U. Wilcken, *APF* 1 (1901) 480-84. Changes have been made in the light of two subsequently-found fragmentary versions of the same titulature, *SEG* 8.504a and *SEG* 18.633 = *SB* 10039. Breaks are filled by comparison with these texts and the royal title on the Rosetta stone (*OGIS* 90 = *SB* 8299).

[βασιλεὺς ὁ νέος ὁ ἰσ]χύων, ὧι ὁ
 π[ατὴρ ἔδωκεν]
[τὴ]ν βα[σιλεί]αν, κύριος βασιλ̣ειῶν,
 μεγαλόδο-]
[ξος, εὐσ]εβὴς τὰ πρὸς θεούς,
 ἀνθρώ[πων σωτήρ,]
[ἀντι]πάλων ὑπέρτερος, ὁ τὴν
 Α[ἴγυπτον καταστη-]
5 [σάμενος,] τὰ ἱερὰ ἐπανορθώσας καὶ
 τ[οὺς νόμους τοὺς]
[τεθέντας ὑπὸ τοῦ μεγίσ]του καὶ
 μ[εγίστου Ἑρμοῦ]
[βεβαι]ῶν, [κύριος] τριακοντετη[ρίδων
 καθάπερ ὁ]
['Ήφαιστος] ὁ μέγας, βασιλεὺς
 καθάπερ [ὁ Ἥλιος, μέγας βασι-]
[λεὺς τῶν τε ἄ]νω καὶ τῶν κάτω
 χωρ[ῶν, ἔκγονος θεῶν]
10 [Εὐεργε]τῶν, ὃν ὁ Ἥφαιστος
 ἐδοκ[ίμασεν, ὧι ὁ Ἥλιος ἔδω-]
[κεν τὸ κρ]άτος, εἰκὼν ζῶσα τοῦ
 Δι[ός, υἱὸς τοῦ Ἡλίου,]
[Πτολεμαῖ]ος αἰωνόβιος, ἠγαπ[ημένος
 ὑπὸ τῆς "Ισιδος]
[?]... υλυρων[?]

[The young king, the mi]ghty one, to
 whom his [father gave]
[th]e ki[ngdom,] lord of kingdo[ms,
 magestic,]
[pi]ous in matters of the gods,
 [saviour of] men,
victorious over his [riv]als, who
 [stabilised Egypt,]
restored the temples and [secured the
 laws]
[ordained by the great]est and
 g[reatest Hermes,]
[lord of]thirty-year [festivals
 like] the
great [Hephaestus,] king
 like [the Sun, great king]
[of the up]per and lower regions,
 [child of the Benefactor gods,]
of whom Hephaestus appr[oved,
 to whom the Sun gave]
[his po]wer, living image of
 Ze[us, son of the Sun,]
[Ptolemae]us, living eternally,
 lov[ed by Isis] ...
 ...

The text of the papyrus is different from comparable titulature (i.e. *SEG* 8.504a, *SEG* 18.633 = *SB* 10039 and *OGIS* 90 = *SB* 8299) in its use of the nominative case. This suggests to the editor that it may have introduced an edict, or perhaps a solemn letter. The solemnity of the title lies in the use of Egyptian divine names to describe Philopator (who reigned 221-205 BC) and is perhaps indicative of the growing Egyptian influence on the Ptolemaic throne at the time. However, besides the Rosetta stone, it is the only known Greek translation of an Egyptian royal titular. The titles are as follows:

(a) Horus: [βασιλεὺς ὁ νέος ὁ ἰσ]χύων, ὧι ὁ π[ατὴρ ἔδωκεν] [τὴ]ν
                  βα[σιλεί]αν,

(b) Nebty: κύριος βασιλ[ειῶν, μεγαλόδοξος, εὐσ]εβὴς τὰ πρὸς θεούς,
                  ἀνθρώ[πων σωτήρ,]

(c) Golden Horus: [ἀντι]πάλων ὑπέρτερος, ὁ τὴν Α[ἴγυπτον καταστησάμενος,]
                  τὰ ἱερὰ ἐπανορθώσας καὶ τ[οὺς νόμους τοὺς] [τεθέντας
                  ὑπὸ τοῦ μεγίσ]του καὶ μ[εγίστου Ἑρμοῦ] [βεβαι]ῶν,
                  [κύριος] τριακοντετη[ρίδων καθάπερ ὁ] ['Ἥφαιστος] ὁ
                  μέγας, βασιλεὺς καθάπερ [ὁ Ἥλιος,

(d) Praenomen: μέγας βασιλεὺς τῶν τε ἄ]νω καὶ τῶν κάτω χωρ[ῶν,
                  ἔκγονος θεῶν] [Εὐεργε]τῶν, ὃν ὁ Ἥφαιστος ἐδοκ[ίμασεν,
                  ὧι ὁ Ἥλιος ἔδωκεν τὸ κρ]άτος, εἰκὼν ζῶσα τοῦ Δι[ός,

(e) Nomen: υἱὸς τοῦ Ἡλίου,] [Πτολεμαῖ]ος αἰωνόβιος, ἠγαπ[ημένος
                  ὑπὸ τῆς Ἴσιδος]

For a detailed commentary on the titulature the editor points to H.J. Thissen, *Studien zum Raphiadekret* (Beitr. zur Klass. Philol. 23, 1966), esp. 10-11 and 27-42. Of interest to the present study is the cluster of concepts and terminology associated with the Ptolemaic throne and its propaganda. The concepts of dynastic power and legitimacy, legal and social stability, piety in matters religious and benefaction in the human sphere, and divine authority and favour are all covered by the terminology. One notes the idea, for example, of secure foundation in the choice of participles to describe the king's rule under (c). In the New Testament a similar note is struck when describing the role of scripture in the education of the believer; see 2 Tim. 3.16 — 'All scripture is God-inspired and beneficial for teaching, reproof, restoration (ἐπανόρθωσις), instruction in righteousness'. The expression 'living image' finds resonance also. The metaphor uses the vehicle of the stamped resemblance on a coin or the likeness of a statue; it presupposes the use of images to portray the deity, but by the addition of 'living' applies this to the person of the king himself. His life becomes the image of the deity.

The same participle 'living' is used with a number of nouns and with various senses in the New Testament. For example, the sense of 'life-giving' is found in such uses as 'living water' (John 4.10, 7.38) and 'living bread' (John 6.51); but cf. 'living water' at John 7.38 which refers to the Spirit. The expression 'living word(s)' is variously attested. At Acts 7.38 it refers to the words spoken to Moses by an angel on Sinai. The sense appears to be 'spoken word' which is opposed tacitly to the written word which was then handed down by Moses. One is reminded of the notion of oral law which lies behind the traditions of the Talmud. Heb. 4.12 contains a predicative use; the word of God is 'living and active'. I take this to be a case of hendiadys. 1 Pet. 1.23 speaks of believers having been begotten anew by the 'living and abiding word of God'. Paul can speak of offering one's body as a 'living sacrifice' (Rom. 12.1), i.e. a life lived in a manner holy and pleasing to God. Again, Paul states that Adam became a 'living soul', i.e. a living being, whilst Christ became a 'life-giving spirit' (1 Cor. 15.45). The entry to the Holy Place through the body and blood of Jesus is described as a 'new and living way' (Heb. 10.20). The sense seems to be that Jesus' sacrifice, unlike that of the priest's offering of the blood of bulls and goats, is efficacious, i.e. it truly cleanses from sin. The author of 1 Peter can speak of a 'living hope' (1 Pet. 1.3) into which the believer is begotten anew through the resurrection of Jesus from the dead. The participle is chosen in part for the play that it affords between the concepts of life and resurrection. He also calls Christ and his believers, who are built into a spiritual house, 'living stones' (1 Pet. 2.4-5). The sense of the participle is to underline the metaphor; the stones are people. It is perhaps this last example which comes closest to the use of the expression 'living image' in the above titular; for both entail the use of an inanimate object as a metaphor for a person or persons, and this metaphorical use is underlined by the choice of 'living' to qualify it.

The use of 'living image', as stated, presupposes the use of divine images made of inanimate material. For authors in the Judaeo-Christian tradition the notion that an image made of stone, wood, metal or whatever could represent God was abhorrent. For this reason when a person or persons are described as the image of God, the noun is never qualified by 'living'. Thus Paul in his argument for the veiling of women describes the male as the image of God (1 Cor. 11.7). The allusion here is to the story of creation, where God is said to make man in his own image (Gen. 1.26-7). But also for Paul the condition of mankind is fallen and the image in consequence is subject to renewal (1 Cor. 15.49, 2 Cor. 3.18, Col. 3.10). More importantly for the apostle it is Christ who is the image of God (2 Cor. 4.4, Col. 1.15). Interestingly, for New Testament writers it is not the image which is 'living', but God himself. Various uses of the participle have already been listed above; however, by far the most common use applies to God, i.e. 'the living God', Matt. 16.16, 26.63, Acts 14.15, Rom. 9.26, 2 Cor. 3.3, 6.16, 1 Thess. 1.9, 1 Tim. 3.15, 4.10, Heb. 3.12, 9.14, 10.31, 12.22, Rev. 7.2, 15.7; cf. also John 6.57. The extent of usage over the range of New Testament literature is surprising and indicates that the phrase encapsulated a congenial concept, namely, the idea that other gods are but stone and wood. This transfer of the participle from the image to its subject reflects the all-pervasive force of the second commandment against making images of the deity.

S.R. Llewelyn

§16 Calendar Variation

Arsinoite nome   30.5 x 11.5 cm   9 March 213 BC

Ed. pr. — K. Maresch in *Kölner Papyri*, vol. 6, eds M Gronewald, B. Kramer, K. Maresch, M. Parca and C. Römer (Opladen 1987) 170-72 (= P. Köln 260).

The papyrus is in five fragments and written *charta transversa* (↓). Its right edge is lost.

Μητρόδωρος 'Απολλωνί[ωι χ]αίρειν.	Metrodorus to Apollonius, greeting.
παρεσόμεθ[α πρ]ὸς τὴ[ν]	We will be present at the
πρᾶσιν τῶν ὠνῶν καὶ τ[ὰς	sale of tax-farming contracts and their
συ]ντάξεις τῆι κϛ ...[.]...[?]	arrangements on the 26th ...
ἅμα τῆι ἡμέραι εἰς 'Οξύρυγχα.	at day-break in Oxyrhyncha. Therefore
συνάγαγε οὖν τὰ ἔθνη εἰς τὴν	collect the guilds at the
προγεγραμμένην κώμην τῆ[ι κ]ϛ,	aforementioned village on the 26th, that
ὅπως μὴ κωλυώμεθα	we not be hindered
5 τὰς συντάξεις ποιεῖσθαι.	in making the arrangements.
ἔρρωσο. (ἔτους) θ̄, ὡς δ' [αἱ]	Farewell. (Regnal) year 9, or fiscal
πρ(όσοδοι) (ἔτους) [ι Τῦβι ..]	year 10 [Tybi ...]

On the back with the fibres (→)

(m.2) [*c.* ?] (ἔτους) ι Τῦβι κϛ, Μητρόδωρος	[...] Year 10, Tybi 26, Metrodorus
[?] ὠνῶν πράσεως	[...] of the sale of tax-farming contracts
[?]κον	[...]
10 (m.1) 'Απολλω[νίωι]	To Apollonius.

From the surviving documentary evidence, it appears that Metrodorus was the *oikonomos* responsible for the whole of the Arsinoite nome, whereas Apollonius was his subordinate (ὁ πρὸς τῆι οἰκονομίαι in P. Köln 268, §13 above) with responsibility for the Polemonos Meris alone.[1] In this papyrus Metrodorus writes to his subordinate to inform him of his impending presence at the auction of tax-farming contracts. The reference to the gathering of guilds or associations (τὰ ἔθνη, *l.*3)[2] indicates to the editor that the sale concerned the leasing of a state monopoly. On the presence of a large number of people at such sales see P. Cairo Zen. 3.59371, where the writer requests the delivery of further supplies of fragrant wine which was in high demand by the crowd who had come to bid. On the sale of tax-farming contracts, the types of arrangements

---

1 See Maresch, *Kölner Papyri*, 6.160.
2 The use of the term ἔθνος to denote a guild or association is variously attested in Greek. For example, Plato refers to various types of trade or social groupings as ἔθνη, i.e. doctors, shipbuilders, citizens, soldiers, bandits, thieves and any other association (ἄλλο τι ἔθνος). See *Gorgias* 455b and *Resp.* 351c. OGIS 90 *ll.*16-17, P. Petrie 3.59(b) *l.*4 and P. Tebt. 1.6 *l.*24 refer to sacred guilds of priests. P. Ryl. 2.65 *l.*3 speaks of members of an association of grave-diggers (οἱ ἐκ τοῦ ἔθνους νεκροτάφοι), and P. Petrie 3.32(f) recto *l.*2 and verso col.2 *l.*11 of a guard tax on associations and factories (τὸ φυλακιτικὸν ἔθνων καὶ ἐργαστηρίων).

entailed, and the role of the *oikonomos* in this process see *New Docs* 8 (1998) 49-57. The process is rather involved with fixed periods set aside for overbids to be made and guarantees to be lodged. It is this complicated procedure which, no doubt, is alluded to by the reference to arrangements (συντάξεις, *ll.*2 and 5).

Metrodorus advises Apollonius of his arrival on the 26th. The ink has been washed off the remaining portion of the text so the month is not clear. However, the letter is docketed as received by Apollonius on the 26th of Tybi. The editor thus suggests that Metrodorus was to arrive the following month and restores *l.*2 to read: τῇ κϛ [τοῦ μ]ηνὸς Μεχείρ]. It is then that the sale of contracts was to occur. Two documents concerning the sale of tax-farming contracts (P. Rev. Laws 57.4 and *UPZ* 1.112 col. 1 *l.* 2) date from the third century like our document, and have Mesore as the month of sale. It has been argued that the date of sale was tied to a six-month cycle in the financial year, the first six months of the financial year running from Mecheir to Epeiph, and the second from Mesore to Tybi.[3] Two papyri confirm the sale of contracts in Mecheir: 8th in P. Cairo Zen. 3.59371 (239 BC), and 15th in P. Lugd. Bat. 20.30 *ll.*13-4, 23 (242/1 BC). P. Köln 260 appears to record a sale in the same month. The auction was to begin 26 days after the financial year had started. Due to the delay in finalising all arrangements (10 days for making overbids and 30 days to lodge guarantees) the contract will not have been settled until well into the financial year.

Of further interest is the fact that P. Köln 259 and 260 are dated to the ninth regnal year but tenth financial year. For the two years to be different requires the interposition of the beginning of a new financial year.[4] As both documents were written in Tybi, the month prior to Mecheir, the editor[5] concludes that the financial year here had already begun a month earlier. Bingen had earlier noticed a similar discrepancy between a number of petitions of the year 221 BC. They were all written in chronological proximity in the month of Tybi but dated by different fiscal years (year 1 and 2 variously). Rather than accept an error, he postulated a loose practice of anticipating the change of fiscal year in the month of Tybi.[6] He understands this as symptomatic of the growing discord between the Macedonian calendar of 354 days on the one hand and the fiscal calendar of 365 days on the other. When established by Ptolemy II the new year for both was the same; however, with every intervening year the calendars had further diverged. By 202/1 BC the situation was remedied by aligning the Macedonian calendar fully with the Egyptian.

The issue of multiple calendars in the ancient world is of some relevance to the area of New Testament studies. In a religious system where the celebration of rituals and

---

[3] U. Wilcken, *UPZ* 1, pp.502-3. In the third century there were three calendars in operation in Egypt: the Macedonian eponymous calendar of 354 days, the Egyptian calendar of 365 days which began with Thoth, and the fiscal calendar which ran according to the Egyptian months but began with Mecheir. The Macedonian calendar fell into disuse from 202/1 BC when it was synchronized with the Egyptian calendar, the Macedonian month of Dystros being equated with the Egyptian month of Thoth. At the same time the fiscal calendar also lapsed, as it was only required so long as there were two conflicting calendars in use. See H.-A. Rupprecht, *Kleine Einführung in die Papyruskunde* (Darmstadt 1994) 26-29.

[4] Reckoning by the Egyptian calendar, a new year or fiscal year began with every advent of its first month after the ascension of the king. The result was that the first year was invariably shorter than a full calendar year. However, the new regnal year by the Macedonian calendar began on the anniversary of the ascension. This different method of calculation explains the year difference in our papyrus.

[5] Maresch, *Kölner Papyri*, 159-160.

[6] J. Bingen, 'La canephore Nymphaïs et le calendrier sous Philopator', *Chr. d'Ég.* 50 (1975) 246-48.

festivals was dictated by the calendar, the presence of two systems for reckoning time was bound to cause schism. One has only to think here of the different calendars in use by the priests of the Jerusalem temple (a lunar calendar of 354 days with an intercalated month approximately every three years) and the sectarians at Qumran (a solar calendar of 364 days). On the theological, political and social implication of the pursuit of a divergent calendar see S. Talmon, 'The Calendar Reckoning of the Sect from the Judaean Desert', in C. Rabin and Y. Yadin (eds), *Scripta Hierosolymitana* (Jerusalem 1965) 162-199.

The confusion which could arise from the lack of a universal dating system is attested in the New Testament. Luke seeks to place the gospel events in a time-frame which could be understood by his readers. Thus he dates the birth of Jesus to the reign of Augustus at the time of the first census when Quirinius was governor of Syria (Luke 2.1-2), i.e. AD 6/7. The baptism of John began in the fifteenth year of Tiberius Caesar when Pontius Pilate was governor of Judaea, AD 28/29. Unfortunately, the Lukan attempt to supply a meaningful time-frame has led to confusion.[7] The birth of Jesus appears more sensibly to have occurred in the last years of Herod the Great who died in 4 BC (Matt. 2.1, 3; Luke 1.5, 26, 39-41). Moreover, if Jesus began his ministry in or soon after the fifteenth year of Tiberius (AD 28/9) and at age 30 (Luke 3.23), then even allowing for variation caused by approximation of age,[8] the internal evidence of Luke himself points to a birth earlier than AD 6. For alternative explanations of the matter see P.W. Barnett, 'Bethlehem and the Census', in *Jesus and the Rise of Early Christianity* (Downers Grove 1999) 97-99.

                                                                S.R. Llewelyn

---

[7] See *New Docs* 6 (1992) 123-32.
[8] See *New Docs* 6 (1992) 31.

§17 A Tax-Bureaucrat Humiliated in a Bath-house

Arsinoite nome   26 x 15 cm   March 195—192 BC

Ed. pr. — H. Zilliacus, *Papyri Helsingienses I, ptolemäische Urkunden* (Helsinki 1986) 23-25 (= P. Hels. I 2).

From mummy cartonnage. Margins of 2.5 cm above and left. On the right the text is written up to the edge. The bottom is broken off with 1 or 2 lines lost. The surviving papyrus is in two fragments with the resulting loss of line 12. A narrow strip is lost from the left margin of the upper fragment. The writing is in relatively large letters which are rubbed in places. There is a *kollema* 6.5 cm from the left edge of the sheet. Back is blank.

Φίλωνι ἀρχιφυλακίτηι παρὰ	To Philon the chief-guard from
Διονυσίου τοῦ Ζωίλου τοῦ	Dionysius son of Zoilus who
ἀντιγραφομένου παρ' οἰκονόμου	acts as *antigrapheus* to the *oikonomos*
τὴν ἀπόμοιραν τῶν περὶ Θεογονίδα	for the revenue of the regions around
5 τόπων. τῆι τῇ τοῦ ἐνεστῶτος	Theogonis. On the 18th of the present
μηνὸς Φ[αμε]νὼθ ἤδη λύχνων	month of Phamenoth when already the
καομένων	lamps were burning
λουομένου μου ἐν τῶι καλουμένωι	and I was washing in the new
Ἀριστοδήμου καινῶι βαλανείωι	bath-house called Aristodemus'
καὶ χρωμένου σικύαι ἀρυταίνηι	and was using a calabash bowl,
10 περιεσπάσθην ὑπὸ Φίλωνός τινος	I was dragged off by Philon, one
τῶν στρατιωτῶν ὡς παραχύτην	of the soldiers, as a bath-attendant
.. με [c. 15 εἰ]-	... [(though) having said (nothing)]
πόντος προσπηδήσας μοι	he set upon me
μετ' ἄλλων, ὧν τὰ ὀνόματα	with others, whose names I
15 ἀγνοῶ, ἔτυπτόν με πυγμαῖς τε	know not, and struck me with punches
καὶ λακτίσμασιν εἰς ὃ τύχοι μέρος	and kicks to whatever part of my body
τοῦ σώματος καὶ ἐκσπάσαντές	was available. They dragged me
με ἐκ τοῦ βαλανείου ἦγον ὡς ἐπὶ	from the bath-house and led me to the
τὴν κατὰ τὸ Σαμοθράικιον πύλην.	gate in the vicinity of the Samothracian
20 ἐπιφανέντων δὲ τινῶν φυλακιτῶν	temple. When certain guards appeared,
παρέδωκάν με αὐ[τοῖς]. ἐπεὶ	they handed me over to them. Since
[ο]ὖν	therefore
κλεινοπετής εἰμι, ἀξιῶ συντάξαι	I am bed ridden, I ask (you) to order
ἀσφαλίσασθαι τὸν Φίλωνα καὶ τοὺς	the arrest of Philon and his
μεθ' αὑτοῦ μέχρι τοῦ ἐπιγνωσθῆναι	fellows until my complaint is
25 τὰ κατ' ἐμέ. τούτου δὲ γενομένου	investigated. When this happens
...	...

11 The editor tentatively recontructs: [θεραπεύειν κελεύοντος. ἐμοῦ δ' οὐδὲν εἰ]πόντος or ἀπει]πόντος **22** κλινοπετής **26** The ending of petitions is generally formulaic, e.g. [τεύξομαι τῆς παρὰ σοῦ βοηθείας].

Of interest in the above papyrus is the mention of a Samothracian temple in the Arsinoite nome. In view of the widespread nature of the mystery cult of the Cabiri in the Hellenistic period and the patronising of its centre at Samothrace by the Ptolemies one might be inclined to agree with the editor who suggests that this temple was also associated with the Μεγάλοι Θεοί. But as noted (ed. pr., 25 n. 19) evidence for the cult in Egypt is sparse. The only other places where Samothrace is referred to are Philadelphia and Coptus, but a local cult is not implied. See S.G. Cole, *The Cult of the Great Gods at Samothrace* (Leiden 1984) 168-69.

The editor lists four other instances of assault occurring in bath-houses. The venue, naturally enough, offered the assailants a number of advantages. More than likely the victim would be unarmed and unattended by friends or family. It also might offer a better chance of escape, should the attack fail, as the victim and any helpers might be loath to enter the chase given the absence of attire. It is also of interest to note that in Greek legal systems the location of a crime affected the type of legal remedy or procedure pursued and the severity of the penalty awarded. For example, under Athenian law a theft committed in a public place such as a bath was considered a greater threat to the social order; it was thus prosecuted by public suit (γραφή rather than δίκη) and punished more severely. See *New Docs* 7 (1994) 150-51. There were also other factors which aggravated a crime. In Ptolemaic Egypt the time that a crime was committed (i.e. if at night) and the number of perpetrators were aggravating factors (Taubenschlag, *Laws* ... 441). Interestingly in the above papyrus both factors are noted. The assault was committed after dark when the lamps were lit (*l*.6) and by Philon acting with accomplices (*ll*.14-5).

The plaintiff in the petition gives his occupation as 'the *antigrapheus* to the *oikonomos* for the revenue of the regions around Theogonis'. In the Ptolemaic administrative system the *oikonomos* was the nome official responsible for matters of taxation. And in this he was assisted by an *antigrapheus*. They administered such matters as the sale of taxes, the acceptance of guarantees from and the administering of oaths to tax-farmers and their associates, the staffing of the collection procedure, the recording of all tax transactions, and the annual reconciliation and dispersion of profit or loss to the parties. See *New Docs* 8 (1998) 49-57. An important role which the *oikonomos* and his *antigrapheus* played was to control the potential excesses of tax-farmers in their efforts to turn a profit. As such they were not involved in the direct collection of taxes, apart from arrears. It is therefore unlikely that they would have met with the same level of opprobrium as the tax-farmers themselves.

The reason for the soldiers' assault is unexplained. The editor suggests that it was an act of revenge against a much-disliked class of person, namely, the tax-collector. Seeing Dionysius with a calabash bowl in hand they toyed with him and asked him to serve them as a bath-attendant. When he declined, they set upon him. But caution is required in interpreting the soldiers' motives. First, as outlined above, the *antigrapheus* was not so much a tax-collector as part of the control mechanism governing tax-collection. The distinction is an important one, though tax-payers may not have always respected it. Other reasons for their actions can be suggested. For example, soldiers were not above acting as thugs. See B. Baldwin, 'Crime and criminals in Graeco-Roman Egypt', *Aegyptus* 43 (1963) 259. Second, the loss of *l*.12 makes any reconstruction of motives difficult. Indeed, that the soldiers handed Dionysius over to the guards (*ll*.20-1) poses some difficulty for the editor's reconstruction. Why would they do this, if they were acting out of personal spite towards a tax-bureaucrat? It is also worth considering that a petition only presents one side of the story. If there was actually provocation on the part of Dionysius, he would be reticent to disclose it.

Whatever the reason for the assault, one senses that Dionysius was deeply humiliated by it. The humiliation arose from the dissonance between the office he held in the nome and his treatment as a common bath-attendant and assault at the hands of the soldiers. A similar sense of humiliation was, no doubt, experienced by the apostle Paul when he, as a Roman citizen, was assaulted and attacked on his travels (2 Cor. 11.23-25). But whereas our petitioner sought redress for the injury through a judicial procedure, Paul inverted his humiliation into a mark of honour, an indicator that he was a better attendant or servant of Christ. The choice of the term διάκονος in v. 23 is significant. It is as servant that his humiliation was to be borne.

S.R. Llewelyn

§18 Changing the Legal Jurisdiction

Arsinoite nome 28 x 18 cm 194/93—180 BC

Ed. pr. — H. Zilliacus, *Papyri Helsingienses I, ptolemäische Urkunden* (Helsinki 1986) 18-22 (= P. Hels. 1.1).

The papyrus, taken from mummy cartonnage, has margins above (2.5 cm) and on the left (2 cm). The text is written to the right edge. On the upper right portion a piece of approx. 12.5 x 5 cm is missing and at the bottom about 2 cm. Original dimensions of the papyrus are estimated at 30 x 20 cm. Two *kollemata* are visible, 4 cm from the left edge and along the right edge of the papyrus. Above the text there is a horizontal line of short curves. The hand is regular and careful. The back is blank.

[βασιλεῖ Πτ]ολεμαίωι καὶ	[To king Pt]olemaeus and
β[α]σι[λ]ί[σ]ηι Κλεοπάτραι τῆι	queen [Cleopatra, his
ἀδελφῆι]	sister,]
[Θεοῖς Ἐπι]φανέσ[ι] καὶ	[to the gods man]ifest and
Εὐ[χ]αρ[ίσ]τοις [χαίρειν 10 *vac.* ?]	blessed, [greetings]
[π]αρ᾿ Ἀσκληπι[ά]δου. ἀδ[ικοῦμαι	from Asclepiades. [I am wronged by
ὑπὸ Πεταῦτος *c.* 8 ἐκ]-	Petaus ...]
[λα]βόντος γὰρ μοῦ μετ᾿ ἄλλων τὴν	since I with others contracted the six[th-
ἕκ[την τῶν παραδείσων ? τῆς]	part (tax) on gardens for]
5 [Δι]καίου τοῦ Ἀρσινοίτου νομοῦ	Dikaiou (Nesus) in the Arsinoite nome
τῶι (ἔτει) ι[. καὶ Πεταῦτος τοῦ]	in the 10th year [and Petaus, the]
[π]ρογεγραμμένου μετέχοντός μοι	aforementioned, shared with me the
τῆ[ς αὐτῆς ὠνῆς πρὸς τὸ τέ]-	[same sale to a fo]urth
[τ]αρτον μέρος, περὶ ὧν καὶ ὅρκον	part, concerning which we
ἐγραψάμεθ[α καὶ ὑπεκεχειρο]-	wrote an oath [and]
[γ]ράφει ἕκαστος ἡμῶν τοῖς ἰδίοις	each of us signed (it) with his own
γράμμασι, κ[αὶ τούτου μὲν]	letters, and [this (Petaus), however,]
[ο]ὐχ ὑπομένοντος διεγγυῆσαι τοῦ	did not submit to give security for the
ἐπιβ[άλλοντος αὐτῶι]	fourth
10 μέρους τετάρτου, ἀλλὰ κελεύοντος	part [which fell to him,] but he told (us)
πα[ρ᾿ αὐτοῦ δανείζεσθαι ?]	[to borrow from himself,] for
οὗ ἂν ἐγγυήσηται καὶ πραχθῆ	whom [my wife Aynchis] should give
ὑπὲρ ἡμ[ῶν Ἀῦγχις ἡ γυνή	security and be made actionable for
μου,]	us,
περὶ ὧν καὶ ἐγραψά[μ]ην αὐτῶι	concerning which I wrote for him a
συγγραφὴ[ν δανείου χαλκοῦ]	contract [for a loan of]
(ταλάντων) ζ, καὶ τούτο[υ	7 [bronze] talents and, this
τετε]λεσμένου τὸ διε[γγύημα	done, we established
αὐτοῦ κατ]-	[his surety]
εστήσαμε[ν ......]ν καὶ ἄλλων	... and other
ἀντ[ὶ *c.* 14]	instead of ...

15 ἐ......[......]..... σὺν τῆι αὐτοῦ   ... with his
    ἀπομ[ο]ί[ραι ....]   portion ...
    [.....]....[......] χαλκοῦ   ... of 5 bronze
    (τάλαντα) ε ´Γωκη, ὥστε   (talents), 3828 (dr) so that
    ἀπέχε[ιν]   he repay
    [τοῦτο]. νυνὶ δὲ ἡ[μᾶς   [this.] But now
    δια]σευόμενος καὶ συκοφαντῶν   intimidating and falsely accusing
    πεποί-   [us]
    ηται καταβόησιν ἐπὶ τῶν λαοκριτῶν   he has laid a charge before the *laokritai*
    κατ' Αύγχιος τῆς   against Aynchis,
    γυναικός μου φάμενος ταύτην   my wife, saying that she had become
    ἔγγυον γεγενῆσθαι, διὰ τῆς   the one giving surety, by the
20 τοῦ δανείου συγγραφῆς ἧς   contract of loan which
    ἐγραψάμην αὐτῶι μετὰ τῶν   I wrote for him with my
    μετόχων,   partners,
    τοῦ ἐπιβάλλοντός μοι μέρους   for the third part which falls to me.
    τρίτου. ἐπεὶ οὖν τὸ δάνειον   Since, therefore, the loan, which
    ὃ ἀπαιτεῖ τὴν ἄνθρωπόν μου ἀντὶ   he demands from my woman against
    τῆς ἐγγύης ἧς ἐνεγύησα κ[α]-   the surety which I guaranteed,
    θ' ἡμᾶς (?) ἐστιν ἣν καὶ   is against us, which also he has
    κεκόμισται, ἐπισυκοφαντῶν δὲ   received, and falsely accusing
    καθέστακεν ταύτην ἐπὶ τοὺς   has stood her before the *laokritai*, I
    λαοκρίτας, ἀξιῶ ὧν συν-   request, since I
25 επείγων καὶ καθήκο‹ν›τός μοι ἐπὶ   am eager and it is appropriate for me
    τῶν τὰ προσοδικὰ κρινόντ[ων]   before the *chrematistai* who judge
    χρηματιστῶν τὸ δίκαιον λαμβάνειν   matters of revenue to receive and give
    καὶ διδόναι, καὶ ἔστιν   justice — and the
    τὰ προγεγραμμένα ἀπὸ τῆς   aforewritten is from the revenue (of the
    προσόδου τῆς Φιλαδέλφου,   village) of Philadelphia —
    ἀποστεῖλαι μοῦ τὸ ὑπ[ό]μνημα ἐπ'   to send my petition to them, that
    αὐτούς, ὡς ἂν χρηματί-   deliberating
    σαντες αὐτὸ εἰς κρίσ[ι]ν   on this they might summons Petaus to
    ἀνακαλέσωνται τὸν Πεταῦν,   judgement,
30 καὶ ἐὰν ἀποδείξωμεν μετεσχηκότα   and if we demonstrate that he shared
    ἡμῖν τὴν ἕκτην   with us the sixth-part (tax)
    καὶ ἀπέχοντος αὐτοῦ τὸ διεγγύημα   and received the surety
    ὑπὲρ οὗ καὶ ἐγραψά-   for which we wrote
    μεθα αὐτῶι τὴν προγεγραμμένην   for him the aforementioned
    δανείου συγγραφὴν   contract of loan
    συνκρίνωσιν οἱ χρηματισταὶ   the *chrematistai* might conclude
    ἀποτεῖσαι αὐτὸν .....]   that he repay ...

[. . . . . . . τὸ ἐπι]βάλλον αὐτῶι μέρος ... the fourth part which falls to him ...

τέταρτον [c. 8]

35   [   ]ν προσδέχουσι δ[... they accept ...

      ]

      [τὴν τοῦ] δανείου   ... [the] contract of loan ...

      συγγραφὴ[ν   ]

      [   ]. .[. . .]. .[...

      ]

17 δια]σειόμενος

The text is a petition addressed to Ptolemy V Epiphanes and Queen Cleopatra. It was usual Ptolemaic practice to address petitions to the king. The personal jurisdiction of the king for the most part was concerned with matters of fiscal governance and state security, but it also took a direct part in legal matters from the private domain. H.J. Wolff, *Das Justizwesen der Ptolemäer* (Munich 1962) 8, alleges that such a role belonged to Hellenistic royal theory where the monarch was not only the unlimited divine master of his subjects but also their protector and helper. But from the second half of the third century the addressing of petitions to the king became a mere formality as they were submitted to the office of the *strategos* and were directly dealt with there (*ibid.* 10). A direct participation of the king was by this time exceptional.

The essence of the above dispute between Asclepiades and Petaus is somewhat difficult to understand in view of the gaps in the text. However, it would appear that Asclepiades was the head of a partnership formed to collect taxes for the village of Dikaiou Nesus. It was usual for the collection of taxes to be sold for discrete areas, village by village. An individual won the contract from the government to collect the tax (ἀρχώνης), but he then drew in others as partners (μέτοχοι). The contract from the government's point of view devolved on the ἀρχώνης, but the partners could participate in the business by widening the property base and security of the sale. However, they were not active participants in the actual collection of taxes. As U. Wilcken, *Griechische Ostraka aus Aegypten und Nubien* I (Leipzig 1899) 590, surmises, they were strictly distinguished from the tax-farmer in the Revenue Laws and do not appear in any of the business documents of the Ptolemaic period to have themselves been called tax-farmers (τελῶναι).

A partnership (κοινωνία) was fixed by an agreement between its members. The agreement was termed a μετοχή and was often in the form of a ὁμολογία or acknowledgement. On the ὁμολογία see *New Docs* 6 (1992) 32. Such agreements typically defined the duration of the partnership (e.g. P. Corn. 8 *ll.*11-12, P. Amh. 94 *l.*4 and P. Bour. 13 *ll.*1-2), and the division of rights (P. Rev. Law col. 34 *ll.*14-17, P. Corn. 8 *ll.*14-16, BGU 4.1123 *ll.*4, 8-9, and P. Bour. 13 *l.*6) and obligations (P. Corn. 8 *ll.*10-14, BGU 4.1123 *ll.*5, 10-11, and P. Bour. 13 *ll.*3-6), usually expressed as fractions of the concession, which arose under the agreement. The conditions of the agreement were binding for the duration of the partnership and partners were hindered from harming each other (e.g. BGU 4.1123 *l.*11) with penalties set for any breach (*l.*12) or a right of action established in favour of one of the partners (e.g. P. Bour. 13 *ll.*7-8), presumably the ἀρχώνης. In the present case the agreement involved, besides the subscription of each partner, an oath (*ll.*7-8). Such an oath is otherwise unattested in partnership agreements. Since the sale of taxes was an annual event, one may suppose that the duration of the partnership was limited to one year.

> The terms μετοχή and μέτοχος are found severally in the New Testament. The latter term can be used to indicate, as in the LXX (Pss 45.7, 119.63, Eccl. 4.10) one's fellow or social equal (Heb. 1.9). The term can also be used metaphorically to refer to one's share or participation in Christ or his benefits (Heb. 3.1, 14, 6.4 — the benefit may even include discipline, Heb. 12.8). At 2 Cor. 6.14 Paul warns believers against associating with unbelievers. The injunction relies on a metaphor based on the opposites righteousness/iniquity and light/darkness. Just as there is no μετοχή or κοινωνία between righteousness and iniquity or light and darkness, so there should not be any association between believers and unbelievers. The discussion by Hanse (*TDNT* vol. 2, 830-2) indicates a strong affinity between metaphorical uses in the New Testament and the use of similar terminology in philosophical discourse. The underlying idea is that of participation or sharing, often in an entity or state belonging to a higher plane. The only use in the New Testament that approaches that found in our papyrus occurs at Luke 5.7 (cf. also 5.10). Here a partnership of fishermen (Simon Peter, James, John and others) is indicated by the evangelist.

The failure of Petaus to submit a guarantee for his fourth share in the partnership (*ll.*8-10) and the nature of the loan made between the parties (*ll.*10-17) are problematic. After the sale of the right to collect a tax the contractor was required to submit the written declarations (σύμβολα) of all guarantors for the purchase price within thirty days to the relevant nome officials (P. Rev. Laws col. 34 *ll.*2-4, *UPZ* 112 col. 1 *l.*13 - col. 2 *l.*2). Guarantees secured by *hypotheke* or mortgage against real property were occasionally endorsed by a royal oath (P. Petrie 2.46 a and b). But these were uttered by the guarantor rather than the contractor or his partners. More importantly, it is unclear whether a μέτοχος (as distinct from the ἀρχώνης) was actually required to submit guarantees for himself. As M. Rostovtzeff, *Geschichte der Staatspacht in der römischen Kaiserzeit*, in *Philologus, Supplementband* 9 (1904) 348-49, notes, the μέτοχοι of the tax-farmer may actually have been his guarantors and as such were naturally not required to offer guarantors of themselves. However, it might be noted that the function of the partners was viewed differently depending on where one's interest lay. For example, the μέτοχοι were considered as guarantors of the state in case of a deficit but associates of the tax-farmer in the matter of a partnership's profit. In the former case each partner was liable to the portion which he guaranteed (P. Rev. Law col. 34 *ll.*17-19). But the matter was not so clear-cut for in this same instance it also appears that the state could exact the debt of one partner, should he fail to pay, from another (UPZ 112 col. 6 *ll.*14-15). As Rostovtzeff observes, 'in the case of a deficit by one of the partners the whole partnership is responsible'. Be that as it may, Wilcken, *Griechische Ostraka* 548, does entertain the possibility that guarantees might be extended in the private contract between the tax-farmer and his partners, though, as noted above, there is no evidence for this in actual partnership agreements. Nor does the present document offer any support for this hypothesis, for it appears that the signed agreement establishing the partnership (*ll.*7-8) was quite distinct from the obligation which appears to arise under it to submit a guarantor (*ll.*9-10).

In the present document, instead of submitting a guarantee the partner Petaus appears to have made a loan to Asclepiades and his other partners. The proportion stated in *ll.*10 and 21 implies that the association consisted originally of four equal partners, Asclepiades, Petaus and two others. The loan of seven talents was formalised in a written agreement (συγγραφή) and guaranteed by Asclepiades' wife. Thereby his guarantee, presumably to the state, was established (*ll.*13-14). In other words, it appears that Petaus sought and entered into partnership but did not wish to guarantee his portion. Instead, he made a loan to the partnership to the value of his share which was guaranteed by Aynchis, the petitioner's wife. It was this guarantee which in place of his own functioned, perhaps through assignment, to secure the purchase price of the tax. Why he should want to do this is unclear. Perhaps he thought that he might be able by this procedure to limit his liability to the state for any shortfall in collection (cf. *UPZ* 112 col. 6 *ll*.14-15). If so, Asclepiades was justified in his fear, for in *ll*.16-17 we learn that only 5 talents 3828 drachmae were repaid. The editor rightly supposes that this represents the actual amount collected from the tax. In other words, there was a shortfall of 1 talent 2172 drachmae between the value of the guarantee (seven talents) which secured a fourth portion of the purchase price and the amount collected. Even so, in view of the signed agreement of association it is unclear whether such a ploy by Petaus would necessarily have relieved him of his obligations under the partnership. Asclepiades appears to have thought that it did not, for he applied only 5 talents 3828 drachmae to the loan and considered the loan repaid. After all as a partner he was responsible for the shortfall. But in response Petaus pressed his case and sought distraint against Asclepiades' guarantor for his portion of the loan, an amount (a third part of the value of the loan, i.e. 2 talents 2,000 drachmae, *l*.21) which would more than cover his loss.

Interestingly, in *l*.22 Asclepiades states that he made the guarantee. This raises a question over the nature of the property and its legal relation to the husband and wife. In a Greek marriage the husband had full rights of disposal over the dowry (φερνή) that his wife brought into the marriage. But as G. Häge, *Ehegüterrechtliche Verhältnisse in den griechischen Papyri Ägyptens bis Diokletian* (Köln-Graz 1968) 40-61, points out the dowry is unlikely to have included the type of property used to guarantee security, i.e. land and slaves. Also our papyrus attests that the wife acted as guarantor presumably using her own property as security. In view of the amount secured the woman must have possessed considerable means. Be that as it may, the property of Aynchis does not appear to have been at the complete disposal of her husband. As such the property must have stood in relation to the woman much as the later προσφορά might do (Häge, 270). It would seem that the property belonged to the woman independently of her marriage settlement and that her husband's legal involvement was limited to that of acting as her guardian (κύριος — See Häge, 23-6, 270 and J. Modrzejewski, 'La structure juridique du mariage grec', in *Scritti in onore di Orsolina Montevecchi* [Bologna 1981] 247-58, 264-67). However, insofar as he was her guardian he could be said to have guaranteed the loan (*l*.22).

> An Egyptian marriage might also be considered here. The dowry in such marriages was an alimentation capital paid to the husband for the maintenance of his wife. In consideration of this capital the husband made fixed yearly payments in cash and/or grain to his wife. All the property belonging to the husband was pledged as security for both the alimentation capital and payments (P. Tebt. 3.776). The notion present in the Egyptian practice, where an alimentation capital was given for the duration of the marriage and as consideration for fixed yearly alimentation payments in accord with the given capital, was foreign to the Greek idea of a dowry. It is of interest to note that the alimentation capital is described in P. Tor. 13 as a loan (cf. δεδανεικέναι 1.8). As such a designation is not found in the demotic papyri, U. Wilcken, *UPZ* 1.118, 550, concludes that the term was adopted by the Greek translators as a fictive description of the demotic transaction. That a capital sum was handed over which in return required fixed maintenance payments suggested to the orderly and legal thinking of the Greeks that the transaction was like both a dowry and a loan (so Häge, 123). Now should a marriage in conformity with Egyptian law be thought to

underlie the relationship between Asclepiades and Aynchis, then two possibilities arise. Either the property belonged to the husband but was pledged to the wife, for example, by a fiduciary sale as security for her alimentation capital (see P. Tebt. 776 *ll.*10-13, P. Oxy. 237 col. 8 *ll.*22ff., and P.W. Pestman, *Marriage and Matrimonial Property in Ancient Egypt* [Leiden 1961] 41-2, 116, 140-2), or it was property owned independently by Aynchis. Both, however, have difficulties. The problems are: (a) in the former case, should the husband enter into a transaction which might prejudice the claim of his wife, the woman's consent in the form of a statement-of-no-title was usually sought and not a guarantee as envisaged in our papyrus. See P. Tebt. 776 *ll.*21-22, and Pestman, 44, 133-5; and (b) should the woman own property independently of her husband, she was free to administer it and to enter into legal transactions as she saw fit; the assistance of her husband was unnecessary. It is only later under the influence of Greek law that the validity of such transactions required the husband's interposition as guardian to validate such acts. See Pestman, 151-2.

One is reminded here of the important role that women of means played in the early churches. Although women could take a very active and direct role in the mission of the church (cf. B. Witherington, *Women in the Earliest Churches* [Cambridge 1988] 104-117, 151-4, or ibid., *Women and the Genesis of Christianity* [Cambridge 1990] 180-190, 218-20; A. Weiser, 'Die Rolle der Frau in der urchristlichen Mission', and G. Dautzenberg. 'Zur Stellung der Frauen in den paulinischen Gemeinden', in *Die Frau im Urchristentum*, ed. by G. Dautzenberg, H. Merklein and K. Müller [Freiburg 1988] 175-9 and 184-8 respectively), the provision of hospitality and a place to meet was a ministry which fell especially to the well-to-do; it is here that we find a number of wealthier women playing an important and leading role in their congregations. Mary, the mother of John Mark, in Jerusalem (Acts 12.12), Lydia in Philippi (Acts 16.15 and 40) and Nymphas in Laodicaea (Col. 4.15) provided meeting places for their local congregations. Or again it appears that Tabitha provided for the material needs of widows in Lydda (Acts 9.36-42). See further Weiser, 'Die Rolle der Frau ...' 167-75, L.F. Massey, *Women and the New Testament* (Jefferson NC 1989) 41-57, Witherington (1988) 143-57 and (1990) 210-24. We are also left to ponder the roles which other named women played in their communities, e.g. Phoebe in Cenchrea (Rom. 16.1-2), Chloe in Corinth (1 Cor. 1.11), Euodia and Syntyche in Philippi (Phil. 4.2-3) and Mary, Tryphaena, Tryphosa, Persis and Rufus' mother in Rome/Ephesus (Rom. 16.6 and 12-3), or again the well-to-do women who were converted at Thessalonica (Acts 17.4) and Beroea (Acts 17.12). Women in company with their husbands or other males also appear to offer accommodation, e.g. Priscilla and Aquila in Corinth (Acts 18.3), in Ephesus (1 Cor. 16.19) and later in Rome or perhaps still in Ephesus (Rom. 16.5); Philemon and Apphia in Colossae (Phlm. 1-2); and Philologus and Julia in Rome or Ephesus (Rom. 16.15). The role of providing hospitality and a meeting place was significant, for the house-church was the fundamental structure of the early church's mission and no doubt exercised an influence on the nature of this new belief.

Legal Systems

The above papyrus touches on the issue of the competing jurisdictions of the indigenous Egyptian court and the Greek court. The action of Petaus was initiated before the enchoretic court of the *laokritai*. But the petitioner seeks to have it transferred to the Greek court of the *chrematistai*.

The three Greek cities of Ptolemaic Egypt had their own legal systems much as the legal systems in operation in the other cities of the Hellenistic empires. However, most of the territory of Egypt (i.e. the *chora*) fell outside the areas of these cities. Here two legal systems, one Greek and the other Egyptian, were valid. An integrated legal system under the supreme authority of the king was probably achieved by means of the issuance of a set of royal *diagrammata* (*c.* 270 BC under Ptolemy II Philadelphus) which principally regulated procedural matters. These regulations set up the *dikasteria*, courts of *laokritai* and the *koinodikion* for the inhabitants of the *chora*, both Greeks and Egyptians.

> The *dikasteria* or Greek courts (consisting of perhaps ten judges) were set up for the non-indigenous population of the *chora*. Unlike the court of the *chrematistai* who were appointed by the king, the members of these courts were probably chosen by their constituents, i.e. that section of society over which they were to have jurisdiction. Judgement was in terms of Greek law, i.e. the royal διαγράμματα, προστάγματα and πολιτικοὶ νόμοι.

> The *laokritai* were a board of Egyptian judges, whose membership need not necessarily have been priestly. Their court was in all probability a permanent and professional institution administering justice for the indigeneous population. In the Fayum the court had its own building (λαοκρίσιον); members were probably paid an honorarium; and courts were provided with a skilled staff (e.g. for recording proceedings). Proceedings were conducted in the vernacular and, if not over-ruled by a royal διάγραμμα or πρόσταγμα, judgement was issued in conformity with the enchoric law (οἱ τῆς χώρας νόμοι).

> Evidence for the function of the *koinodikion* is largely wanting. Taubenschlag, *Law*, 483, suggests that it 'was competent for civil cases (contracts, private delicts) between Greeks and Egyptians'. In other words, whereas disputes between Greeks were heard by the *dikasteria* and disputes between Egyptians by the *laokritai*, disputes between parties of different nationalities were settled by the *koinodikion*.

The *chrematistai* were a travelling *collegium* of judges appointed by the king for the purpose of giving direct royal relief to those in the *chora*. As opposed to other courts they were a royal judiciary. In time they began to usurp the functions of the other courts. At the beginning of the second century BC (by which time evidence for the continued existence of the Greek *dikasteria* ceases) local boards of *chrematistai* were set up in each administrative district or nome as a permanent authority, applying the substantive laws of the Greek *dikasteria*, i.e. the royal διαγράμματα, προστάγματα and πολιτικοὶ νόμοι. The court of the *laokritai* continued to function until the early first century but increasingly under the encroachment of the *chrematistai*. For further discussion of the legal systems of Ptolemaic Egypt see H.J. Wolff, *Das Justizwesen der Ptolemäer* (Munich 1962).

Wolff argues that the individual was not assigned to a legal system on the basis of his or her racial origin as such, but rather each system was attached to a particular court by the will of the king. Individuals, however, tended to litigate in accord with their ethnic laws and thus before the court which respected them. But this was not always possible for the mixed populations of Egypt where persons of different ethnicity became parties to all forms of legal relationship. Also, at the same time as the growing encroachment of the court of the *chrematistai,* the documentary evidence shows the distinctions between the legal systems being blurred. One finds contracting parties at will availing themselves of legal documents and practices of either Greek or Egyptian provenance. Noting this phenomenon R. Taubenschlag, 'Le droit contractuel', *Opera Minora II* (Warsaw 1959) 458, observes: 'persons of different nationality were able to contract in one or other form according to their free agreement'. In the event of a dispute and trial, it further appears that a party was not constrained to argue the case within one particular legal system but might actually draw on rules from various legal systems (e.g. *UPZ* 2.162 col. 4 and 7).

The *prostagma* P. Tebt. I 5 *ll*.207-220 deals in part with disputes between contracting parties of differing nationality. It can be seen as an attempt to protect the jurisdiction of the court of the *laokritai* against the escalating encroachment of the *chrematistai* in that it regulates the competence of the Egyptian and Greek courts in matters of contracts. Here, the nature of the deed (i.e. whether it was itself Greek or Egyptian) was signficant in suits between parties of mixed nationality. If an Egyptian brought a suit against a Greek and the contract was Greek, the case was to be heard before the Greek court or *chrematistai*. If a Greek brought an action against an Egyptian and the contract was Egyptian, the case was to be heard by the *laokritai*. In other words, in suits between parties of mixed nationality the contract's type determined which court was competent to decide – if a Greek contract, then the decision lay with the *chrematistai*; if a demotic document, then the *laokritai*. As J. Modrzejewski, 'Chrématistes et laocrites', *Le monde grec* (Brussels 1975) 705, observes: 'in mixed lawsuits, the language of the contract is the decisive criterion whatever the status of the litigants.'

Why in P. Hels. 1 did the plaintiff seek to change the court? The petition, insofar as it describes the contract of loan as a συγγραφή, implies that the type and language of the document may have been Greek. However, some caution is required here since it is the plaintiff who describes the contract and in terminology that could be understood by a Greek. Even so, the ethnicity of the parties may still have been the reason for the complaint's initial court of lodgement. See Modrzejewski, 'Chrématistes et laocrites', 699-708. Petaus presumably thought the indigenous court the appropriate forum as both he and the guarantor, Aynchis, were Egyptian, to judge by their names. But ethnicity is not the ostensible basis for Asclepiades' appeal to transfer the case. The stated reason is founded on the fact that the court of the *chrematistai* dealt with matters of state revenue (οἱ τὰ βασιλικὰ καὶ προσοδικὰ καὶ ἰδιωτικὰ κρίνοντες, P. Tor. 13 *l*.6 and P. Amh. II 33 *ll*.9-10). Asclepiades relies on this to justify his appeal: καθήκο‹ν›τός μοι ἐπὶ τῶν τὰ προσοδικὰ κρινόντ[ων] χρηματιστῶν τὸ δίκαιον λαμβάνειν καὶ διδόναι, καὶ ἔστιν τὰ προγεγραμμένα ἀπὸ τῆς προσόδου τῆς Φιλαδέλφου, (*ll*.25-7) — 'it is appropriate for me to receive and give justice before the *chrematistai* who judge matters of revenue — and the aforewritten is from the revenue (of the village) of Philadelphia'. This explanation further supports the doubtful reading in *ll*.22-3, κ[α]θ᾽ ἡμας ἐστιν — 'the loan is against us'. The petitioner makes the point that the contract of loan was really with him and his other associates in the tax-collecting partnership. In other words, it is inextricably tied to the business for which the partnership was formed.

The complexity of multiple legal systems is relevant to the historical study of early Christianity, especially insofar as one considers the overlapping jurisdictions of Roman governors and the indigenous Jewish court, the Sanhedrin. The issue is of considerable importance to any understanding of the hearings of Jesus and Paul.

Matthew and Mark record two trials of Jesus, one at night before the Sanhedrin in the house of the high priest, and the other the next day before Pilate, the Roman procurator. There has been much dispute over whether the night hearing before the Sanhedrin actually occurred or whether it is just a creation of the second evangelist. A number of factors are considered. For example, Luke does not record a night hearing and may be following a more reliable source. There are irregularities in the time and location of the trial. Hearings before the Sanhedrin were conducted during the day and it had its own building within which to determine matters. Mark's account of a second convening of the Sanhedrin in the morning (Mark 15.1) also demonstrates apparent difficulties:

(i)   There is no reference to the earlier meeting;

(ii)   There is no notice as to its location;

(iii)   The sentence had already been passed during the night session (Mark 14.64). What then was the purpose of this second meeting?

(iv)   No reason is given for the handing over of Jesus to Pilate.

A further issue is the competence of the Jewish court in capital matters. If the court was not competent to sentence a prisoner to death, one can well understand why Jesus might be handed over to the Roman governor to decide his fate once he had been found guilty by the Sanhedrin. But it is precisely this lack of competence which is questioned. As evidence that the Sanhedrin could hear, decide and execute a penalty of a capital nature P. Winter, *On the Trial of Jesus* (Berlin, 1974) 18-19, cites *m. Sanh.* 2.3 (*b Sanh.* 48b), 5.2 (*b Sanh.* 9b, 41a), 7.2; Philo, *Leg. ad Gaium* 307; the temple inscription; Paul's execution of Christians (Acts 26.10, cf. also 5.33); the stoning of Stephen and James (Josephus, *AJ* 20.200-203 — the crime of Ananus was not the execution as such but the convening of the Sanhedrin without notification in the period of an interregnum); and Festus' attempt to have Paul tried before the Sanhedrin (Acts 25.9-11).

It is in the debate over jurisdiction in the instance of Paul's arrest that the competing nature of multiple legal systems comes most clearly into focus. After a disturbance in Jerusalem Paul is arrested by the Roman tribune, Claudius Lysias (Acts 21.33), who proceeds to examine him under torture (22.24). Paul appeals against such treatment on the basis of his Roman citizenship (22.25) and the examination then proceeds by a hearing with accusers in attendance (22.30). The latter seek to have Paul moved under the pretext of trying him before the Jewish court (23.15). When the tribune learns that this may not have been their real intention, he has the prisoner moved to Caesarea for a hearing before the Roman governor (23.23). In his accompanying letter the tribune writes that the charges against Paul involve matters of Jewish law (23.29). In the hearing before the governor Paul's accusers charge him with disturbing the peace and attempted profanation of the temple (24.2-8). Paul disputes these charges and instead seeks to make the issue a doctrinal dispute over the resurrection of the dead (24.18-20). The governor, Felix, postpones his decision until the evidence of the tribune could be heard, no doubt in order to assess the truth of the charges made against Paul by his accusers. On the change of governors the Sanhedrin again sought the transfer of the prisoner to their jurisdiction (25.3), but the governor refused. However, in his hearing of Paul the governor proposed a relocation to Jerusalem, apparently in view of the nature of the charges. Still the hearing was to be before the governor (25.9) rather than the Sanhedrin. Paul saw such a move as a concession to his accusers and equivalent to the surrender of himself to them (25.11 and 20). Such a relocation would prejudice the fairness of his hearing and in consequence Paul appeals to Caesar. There is here a clear contest over jurisdiction.

S.R. Llewelyn

§19 Lost Sheep

Heracleopolite nome   29.5 x 10 cm   7 August 160 BC

Ed. pr. — P. Hohti, *Papyri Helsingienses I, ptolemäische Urkunden* (Helsinki 1986) 131-33 (= P. Hels. I 31).

The papyrus (taken from cartonnage) is in three fragments. The middle portion has lost the upper layer of papyrus with the subsequent loss of 2 lines fully (*ll.*19-20) and 3 lines partly (*ll.*17-18, 21). The top of the papyrus is also broken off. Here the ticketing or receipt of the petition (ἐλήφθη) may have been marked. The black ink is well preserved except in the middle where it has faded. The lettering is in a small to middle-sized hand. The back is blank.

[?] [?]
Στράτωνι οἰκονόμωι
παρὰ Διοδώρου τοῦ Αὐτο-
μένου Μακεδόν[ος τοῦ τῶν]
Νεοπτολέμου [*c.* 8]
γεωργοῦ τοῦ Μελανθίου κλ(ήρου)
βασιλικοῦ· πλειόνων
φθορῶν γενομένων ἐν ἧι
γεωργῶ γῆι ἐκ τοῦ διασα-
φ[ουμ]ένου κλήρου χ..
συνέβη διαπαρατηρουμένωι
καταλαβεῖν πρόβατα οὐκ ἄρα
σ... καλὰ εὑρόμενα ἐν τῆι
τεθηκοπομένηι δι᾽ ἐμοῦ
χορτον..νι καὶ ὀλύραι,
ὧν νομεῖς Πανετβεῦις
...ατος καὶ .. [*c.*5]..ς
[*c.* 6].υφου καὶ Πα..α-
Lost upper papyrus layer
Lost upper papyrus layer
Traces
ἃ καὶ βουλόμενος ....
ἐξεβιάσαντο οἱ νομεῖς τὰ πρόβατα σὺν ἑτέροις. ἐπεὶ οὖν
πεπόηκαν φθορὰν (ἀρουρῶν) ιβ ὧν
ἐκφόριον ἀνὰ (πυροῦ) (ἀρτάβην) α
ἀξιῶ προσκ[λ]-
ηθῆναι, ὡς τῶν κτηνῶν καὶ
τῶν διασαφουμένων νομέων
ἀναχθέντων ταῦτα μὲν πραθῆι
οἱ δὲ νομεῖς τύχωσιν ἁρμοζόντως
ἵνα μηθὲν ἐλάττωμα τῆι γῆι

...
To Straton, the *oikonomos*,
from Diodorus, son of Automenes,
a Macedonian, [soldier of the troop]
of Neoptolemus ...
farmer of Melanthius' royal
allotment. After much
destruction occurred in the
land which I farm from the
indicated allotment ...
it happened whilst tending (my land)
that I seized some sheep, not as it seems
... in a good state, which were found in
    the hay and fodder
    stored by me,
whose herdsmen (are) Panetbeuis
son of ... and ...
... and ...
...
...
which he also wishing ...
the herdsmen forcibly led off the
sheep with some others. Since therefore
they have devastated 12 arouras for
which the tax-in-kind is 1 artaba of
    wheat, I ask that they be
summoned that after the animals and
indicated herdsmen have been
produced, these (sheep) might be sold
and the herdsmen meet with suitable
(punishment) that upon the land no loss

ἀναφέρηται.   be brought.

(ἔτους) κα Ἐπείφ ι   Year 21, Epeiph 10

14 τεθηκοποιημένηι   **25** πεποίηκαν

The petition of Diodorus, a soldier and cleruch, is directed to the *oikonomos*, Straton. The subject of the complaint is the actions of the herdsmen whose names are now mostly lost in the middle section of the papyrus. Two charges are made against them. The first concerns the loss of fodder which was stored on the petitioner's allotment and which the sheep had apparently eaten. The second is the forcible removal of the same sheep after they had been seized by the petitioner. Diodorus probably intended to sell the sheep to cover his loss (cf. *l.*29) but was prevented by the herdsmen's action. Accordingly, the petitioner now asks for the sheep to be sold to recompense him for the loss and for the herdsmen to be punished. The latter request refers probably to the penalty attendant on forcible acquisition which was quite independent of the action for recovery in Hellenistic law. In the Ptolemaic period a penalty of 5 bronze talents was established by royal ordinance and paid to the injured party. See *New Docs* 7 (1994) 132. The petition is directed to the *oikonomos* (principally a tax official) as the loss to Diodorus directly affected the revenue paid to the government (*ll.*24-6).

The real or potential use of force was constitutive of the Greek concept of theft. It was the presence of this element which distinguished theft from fraud. See *New Docs* 7 (1994) 151-2. Because the presence of force could be either real or potential, one finds that the actual object of a forcible act could either be a person or his property. In other words, in the above petition the act of forcible removal need not imply an actual use of force against Diodorus. Indeed, from his silence on the issue of personal injury one can reasonably infer that the act was committed in his absence. The act, nevertheless, is forcible since it involves the entry to property without the owner's consent with an attendant potential for violent confrontation should the parties meet.

Βία and its cognates are met variously in the New Testament. The use of force by persons against property (in this instance of the Kingdom of God) is encountered in the problematic verses Matt. 11.12 par. Luke 16.16; see *New Docs* 7(1994) 152-62. The use of force by persons against persons is found in a number of confrontations recorded in Acts (Acts 21.35 and 24.7; cf. also Acts 5.26). There is also one instance where force involves the interaction of two objects. Acts 27.41 concerns the shipwreck of Paul and reads: 'But striking a shoal they grounded the ship; the bow, having become stuck, remained unmovable, but the stern was being loosed by the force of the waves' (ὑπὸ τῆς βίας τῶν κυμάτων). The use of the genitive with ὑπό (i.e. the agent) rather than an instrumental dative is somewhat unusual. Interestingly, it is such events as storms at sea which in Greek legal terminology were considered acts of God (θεοῦ βία). See *New Docs* 6 (1992) 82-6. In other words, to the Greek mind force was essentially a quality exerted or used by an agent rather than an object.

In the parable of the lost sheep (Luke 15.4-7 par. Matt. 18.12-14) we have a story of a shepherd who leaves his 99 sheep to look for the one lost sheep. The story, like the parables generally, is drawn from everyday life in Palestine. It has a single point of comparison; in this instance its purpose is to vindicate Jesus' association and sharing of table fellowship with sinners. Here the context and audience of the Lukan account is no doubt the more original (J. Jeremias, *The Parables of Jesus* [London 1972] 38-40). The moral of the parable is the joy of the shepherd in finding the lost sheep. This is the point of comparison; it is like the joy of God over the sinner who repents. As parables were drawn from everyday practice and experience, Jeremias (133-4) is at pains to stress that the shepherd would not have left his 99 sheep to themselves. They would have either been given into the care of other shepherds or if there was no-one to help, then the sheep would have been enclosed, perhaps in a cave. As our petition informs us, the risk of leaving the sheep unattended might not only entail their loss but also a claim for compensation for any damage they might cause.

S.R. Llewelyn

§20 Escaping the Birth of a Daughter

Provenance unknown   13 x 18.5 cm   II^a

Ed. pr. — R. Hübner, *Griechische Urkundenpapyri der Bayerischen Staatsbibliothek München*, Band III, eds U. Hagedorn, D. Hagedorn, R. Hübner and J.C. Shelton (Stuttgart 1986) 23-25 (= P. Monac. III 57).

The letter is probably written by the sender or some private assistant and not by a professional scribe, for the letters are formed clumsily and without ligature. There survive traces of an earlier letter written on the back of the papyrus.

	ἡ μήτηρ [.] ρηκ[.]α . . ι Πτόλ-
	λι Νικάνδρωι Λυσιμάχωι
	Τρυφαίνηι χαίριν. εἰ ἔρρωσ-
	θε, ἦ ἄν, ὡς ‹θέλω›. τοῖς θεοῖς
	εὔχομαι
5	εἰδῖν ὑμᾶς ὑγιαίνοντας. ἐκο-
	μισάμεθα τὸ παρὰ σοῦ ἐπιστό-
	λιον ἐν ᾧ διεσάφις τετοκέ-
	ναι. τοῖς θεοῖς εὐχόμ⟦α⟧ην
	καθ' ἡμέραν ὑπὲρ σοῦ· νυν-
10	εἰ δὲ ἐκπεφευγέας σου τὴν
	μεγίστην εὐφροσύνην δι-
	άξωι. ἀπέσταλκά σοι ἐλαίου
	φακὸν πλήρηι καὶ εἰσχάδων
	μνᾶς . [.] . ους· καλῶς ποιή-
15	σις ἐκκεν[ώσ]ασα τὸν φακὸν
	καὶ ἀποστίλασά μοι αὐτὸν ἀσ-
	φαλῶς διὰ τὸ κεχρῆσθαί με
	αὐτὸν ὧδε. μὴ ὄκνι ἐπι-
	λέγειν Κλεοπάτραν τὴν μ[ι]-
20	κρὰν ὡς σαυτ[ῆ]ς θυγάτριον

Their mother to ... Ptollis,
Nicander, Lysimachus and
Tryphaena, greeting. If you are well,
it would be as I wish. I pray to the
    gods
to see you well. We
received your letter
in which you told that you had given
birth. I was praying to the gods
daily for your sake. Now
that you have escaped
I will be most exceedingly happy.
I send you a flask
full of olive oil and
... minas of dried figs. Please
empty the flask
and return it to me safely
as I have need
of it here. Don't hesitate to
call the little one Cleopatra
as your very own daughter ...

3 χαίρειν **4** εἴη **5** ἰδεῖν **7** διεσάφεις **9-10** νυνί **10** ἐκπεφευγυίας or ἐκπέφευγας σύ· τὴν κτλ. **12** -άξω **13** πλήρη, ἰσχάδων **14-5** ποιήσεις **16** ἀποστείλασα **18** ὄκνει

The document is a letter written by a mother to her children. The name of the mother is not known. Either the writer omitted it, which is itself unusual (it was more usual for the relationship to be stated in the naming of the addressees), or it was given in the lost portion of the first line. However, the ending in iota before Ptollis makes it more probable that the lost portion contained the name of another of her children. The names of only four children survive: three sons, Ptollis, Nicander and Lysimachus, and one daughter, Tryphaena.

Of interest is the change from the plural address in *ll.*1-5 to the singular address from *l.*6. The letter is addressed in the first instance to all her named children and the writer expresses here the usual wish for their health and well-being. However, from *l.*6 the writer turns to her daughter who, she has just learned by letter, has given birth to a daughter. The new mother's identity is not certain. The editor assumes that it was

Tryphaena who had just given birth, and dismisses the possibility that the name of another daughter was cited in the lost portion of *l*.1. Justification for this assumption is not provided. Against this view it is to be noted that as the news of the birth gave occasion to the letter, the letter may perhaps have been addressed in the first instance to the new mother. Be that as it may, the writer expresses her joy at the birth, sends gifts of olive oil and dried figs, and then tenders advice on the naming of the child. The letter, no doubt, accompanied the delivery of the gifts. The request that the oil flask be returned might suggest that the conveyors of the letter and gifts were on a return voyage. Of interest is the fact that they are not introduced. Perhaps they were already known to the addressees. However, the phrase ἀποστίλασά μοι αὐτὸν ἀσφαλῶς in *ll*.16-7 indicates that the responsibility for the flask's return rested with the writer's daughter, and not with any person making a return journey. The text breaks off as the writer appears to give a reason for accepting the name Cleopatra. However, the use of μὴ ὄκνει indicates that the letter informing our writer of the birth hesitantly considered the naming of the child and asked for advice.

Another point of interest is the emotional journey that the writer expresses. Before the birth she was praying daily to the gods. Implicit in this is the fear and apprehension surrounding the birth of a child in antiquity, an event which was life-threatening to both mother and child. The same ominous sense is communicated in the choice of word to describe the successful birth. The new mother had 'escaped' it (*l*.10). Though one can speak of escaping death or illness, there is no other documentary evidence, as far as I am aware, that uses ἐκφεύγω of childbirth. Safe delivery now became a source of the greatest joy.

The image of childbirth finds several expressions in the New Testament. Paul uses the expectation of it to describe the state of the created world as it awaits deliverance from the present corruption (Rom. 8.22). The present is a time of lamenting and travail. Again Paul describes his trouble and concern over his communities as a work of childbirth (Gal. 4.19). In Revelation there is the image of the woman Israel crying out in pain whilst giving birth to the Messiah. The child is safely delivered and taken up to the throne of God (Rev. 12.1-6), whilst the mother flees into the wilderness for the period designated by the prophet Daniel. Perhaps the best parallel to the mood of the mother in our papyrus letter is afforded by John 16.21. There Jesus offers a comparison between the pain of the woman in travail and the joy felt after a safe delivery. After the birth she no longer even remembers the suffering she had gone through for the joy of the newborn. The images all involve the element of pain, but discount the notion of possible death for the reason that this aspect of childbirth did not fit the metaphor. There is only one New Testament passage which countenances this eventuality. The context is the day of the Lord which will come secretly upon all like a thief in the night. The apostle Paul continues: ὅταν λεγῶσιν, Εἰρήνη καὶ ἀσφάλεια, τότε αἰφνίδιος αὐτοῖς ἐφίσταται ὄλεθρος ὥσπερ ἡ ὠδὶν τῇ ἐν γαστρὶ ἐχούσῃ, καὶ οὐ μὴ ἐκφύγωσιν — 'when they say, Peace and safety, then suddenly destruction is at hand just like the pain of childbirth to the pregnant woman, and they will certainly not escape' (1Thes. 5.3). Of interest is the fact that both our papyrus letter and 1Thes. 5.3 typify delivery as an escape. In the light of the above papyrus letter it is now clear that Paul avails himself in this passage of a term covering both senses of delivery, i.e. delivery from childbirth and from destruction.

S.R. Llewelyn

§21 Paying the Last Farthing

Heracleopolis   9.5 x 16.5 cm   II^a

Heracleopolis   9.5 x 16.5 cm   II[a]

Ed. pr. — D. Hagedorn, *Griechische Urkundenpapyri der Bayerischen Staatsbibliothek München*, Band III, eds U. Hagedorn, D. Hagedorn, R. Hübner and J.C. Shelton (Stuttgart 1986) 16-8 (= P. Monac. III 52).

The papyrus is complete except for the bottom. Dated by script to the second half of the second century BC.

Διοσκουρίδει ἡ[γ]εμόνι καὶ	To Dioscurides, commander and
φρουράρχωι παρὰ Πετεχῶντος	head-guard, from Petechon,
ἐνπόρου τῶν ἀπὸ τοῦ Ὅρμου.	merchant, resident at the port.
ἀδικοῦμαι ὑπὸ Στοτοήτιος	I am wronged by Stotoetis
5 οἰνοκαπήλου τῶν ἐξ Ἡρα-	the wine retailer from
κλέους πόλεως· ὀφείλων	Heracleopolis; for, owing
γάρ μοι πρὸς τιμὴν οὗ ἠγο-	me for the price of
ράκη παρ' ἐμοῦ οἰν[ο]ν	wine he bought from me, (namely) 40
χαλκοῦ (τάλαντα) μ Δυο. ὧν καὶ	(talents) and 4470 (dr.) in bronze, for
10 χ.. χειρόγραφον αὐτοῦ ἔχω,	which also I have his note-of-hand,
ταύτας ἀπα[ι]τούμενος	though he is demanded for payment of
πλεονάκις ο[ὐ]χ ὑπομένει	these often, he does not submit
ἀποδιδόναι, ἀλλὰ διαπλανᾷ με.	to repay, but fobs me off.
διὸ ἀξιῶ, ἐὰν φαίνηται,	Wherefore I ask, if it seems (right),
15 συντάξαι [ἀ]σφαλίσασθαι	to order his arrest
αὐτὸν μέχρι τοῦ τὴν ἀπό-	until he makes
δοσίν [μ]οι αὐτὸν ποήσασθαι.	repayment to me.
...	...
Verso with the fibres	
[?] Μεσ[ορ]ὴ κε Πετεχῶντος ...	... Mesore 25 (from) Petechon
[?]τος περὶ οἴνου	... concerning wine

17 ποιήσασθαι

Petechon, a merchant, had sold a large consignment of wine to a retailer called Stotoetis on credit and states that he has in his possession the note of indebtedness written by the same. But though frequent demands were made, the debt was not repaid and it had become apparent that the debtor had no intention to pay. Frustrated Petechon now writes to the local head-guard to arrest and imprison the debtor. The purpose of this was not to punish non-payment but to coerce payment by imprisonment. One notes that the creditor did not act unilaterally. He could not just take the law into his own hands and apprehend the debtor.[1] Rather he must seek the assistance of the relevant official to effect the arrest

---

1 Self-help was predominantly confined to actions within dependent, familial relationships, e.g. father / child, husband / wife, master / slave. See R. Taubenschlag, *Opera minora* vol. 2, 135-141. But there is also evidence for self-help with the seizure of pledges and hypothecated property. The fictive generic 'Persian of the *epigone*' may also have permitted a creditor to act unilaterally against a debtor so designated. See J.F. Oates, *The Status Designation*: Πέρσης, τῆς ἐπιγονῆς (*YCS* 18, 1962).

and imprisonment. But one also notes that he proceeds to execution against the person of the debtor without a judicial decision, for surely if he had obtained one, it would have been mentioned in the petition. See also *UPZ* 1.124 where the official appears able to proceed to imprisonment once the debt is acknowledged by the debtor.[2] In P. Monac. 52 a *cheirographon*, an unofficial (unregistered) document, seems to be sufficient to establish the debt. Presumably the deed of debt had a clause permitting execution against the person of the debtor. The debtor was, no doubt, placed in a δεσμωτήριον (P. Hib. 1.34 *l*.2, and 73 *l*.8) with his release dependent on the authority of the individual who ordered his imprisonment in the first place, or by his superior.[3] The condition of release is stated as the repayment of the debt.

The interest in the document is that together with *UPZ* 1.124 (176/5 or 165/4 BC) it attests in Ptolemaic times the use of official imprisonment for a private debt. Of interest is the fact that though prisons fell within the administrative competence of the nome *strategos*, in both P. Monac. 52 and *UPZ* 1.124 it is his subordinates (*phrourarchos* and *epistates*, respectively) who were approached in writing by the creditor to effect imprisonment. It would appear that the process could be expedited at the village level. A petition (ἔντευξις) to the nome *strategos* was not required, but rather the creditor could directly notify by a ὑπόμνημα the relevant local official. Such delegation engendered certain risks to debtor classes, but on the evidence of *UPZ* 1.124 Wilcken[4] suggests a number of safety features in the procedure:

(a) execution against the person of the debtor was only exercised by an official;

(b) the debtor had to first acknowledge his debt before that official; and

(c) the debtor or his family had a remedy of petitioning the *strategos*, if there was any abuse of power.

From the evidence of P. Hib. 1.34 and 73 (243 BC: both petitions concern the same matter, the imprisonment of a certain Callidromus in order to effect the return of a donkey to its owner or, failing that, payment of its value) it would appear that the procedure of personal execution was regulated by royal *diagramma*. See the wording of P. Hib. 1.73 where after stating that his superior had released the prisoner, the petitioner continues: ὥστε μὴ δύνασθαι ἡμᾶς τὴν πρᾶξιν ποιήσασθαι κατὰ τὸ διάγραμμα — 'so that we are unable to effect execution in accord with the *diagramma*'. It should be noted that the petitioner has corrected ἐκ τοῦ σώματος to read κατὰ τὸ διάγραμμα in this line. In other words, his first thought is to state that he was unable to exact execution 'against the person' due to his release, but he amends this to read 'in accord with the *diagramma*'. From P. Hib. 1.34 we learn that the *diagramma* or *diagrammata* also regulated release from prison and the penalty which applied in the case of wrongful release. One assumes that it also prescribed penalties for wrongful imprisonment.

Imprisonment for personal debt was a coercive measure applied by officials and not based on a judicial decision. As such it was a practice which often ran against the interests of the state. An imprisoned debtor might satisfy the demands of his creditor,

---

2 Execution to recover a private debt proceeded either against the property or person of the debtor, and it is a matter of some dispute as to the extent to which a creditor might be able to avoid a judicial decision to effect recovery. See *New Docs* 7 (1996) 215-20. P. Monac. 52 and UPZ 1, 124 seem to suggest that imprisonment could be employed against a debtor once the local official was satisfied of the debt and its non-payment.

3 P. Hib. I, 34 *ll*.4, 7-8 and 73 *ll*.9-11. Also R. Taubenschlag, *Opera minora* vol. 2, 713-9.

4 See U. Wilcken, *UPZ* 1 pp.584-8.

but whilst incarcerated, he could not meet the various fiscal and personal demands placed on him by the state. It is for this reason that one finds a tendency to exclude execution against the person of the debtor and replace it by execution against his property only. Thus in 118 BC Ptolemy Euergetes II (P. Tebt. 1.5 *ll.*221-47 and 255-64) prohibited personal execution against cultivators of public land, weavers, byssus manufacturers and other classes of tax-payers. Instead, any debt was to be exacted from their other property which was not necessary to their trade or work: τὰς δὲ πράξεις τῶν ἐν αὐτοῖς γενέσθαι ἐκ τῶν ἄλλων ὑπαρχόντων τῶν μὴ ἀνειργομένων διὰ τοῦ προστάγματος. Officials were restrained from imprisoning such persons for private debt (ἴδιον ὀφείλημα) or other wrong. Remedy for the creditor was through appointed magistrates who would decide the matter in accord with the royal edicts, i.e. execution against the property of the debtor. Euergetes II did not completely prohibit execution against the person of the debtor, but as Modrzejewski observes,[5] such classes of person as were exempted from it formed the vast bulk of the population of Egypt. The Roman prefect T. Julius Alexander through an edict of AD 68 (*OGIS* 669 *ll.*25-34) expressly prohibited imprisonment for private debts. The focus of the edict is the practice of creditors shifting debts from the private sphere to the public purse and thereby effecting imprisonment. The practice is prohibited. Exaction was to be from the property not the person of the debtor: ἵνα αἱ πράξεις τῶν δανείων ἐκ τῶν ὑπαρχόντων ὦσι καὶ μὴ ἐκ τῶν σωμάτων. Imprisonment is to be used only against criminals (κακοῦργοι) and debtors of the public purse. In other words, the state reserved the right of personal execution for itself alone.

The practice of execution against the person of the debtor is referred to in the Q material of Matt. 5.25-26 and Luke 12.58-9. But here one notes that a judicial decision is required for imprisonment to occur. The debtor is advised to be reconciled with his adversary lest he hand him over to the judge and the latter then decide to have him imprisoned. However, in an interesting parallel to the wording of P. Monac. 52 *ll.*16-7 (μέχρι τοῦ τὴν ἀπόδοσίν [μ]οι αὐτὸν ποήσασθαι; cf. μέχρι τοῦ τὰ δίκαια αὐτὸν ποῆσαι, *UPZ* 1.124 *ll.*23-4) the gospel writers state that the prisoner will not be released until he has paid the last cent (ἕως ἂν ἀποδῷς τὸν ἔσχατον κοδράντην / ἕως καὶ τὸ ἔσχατον λεπτὸν ἀποδῷς). Release from a debtor prison was conditional upon payment of the sum owed, and as *UPZ* 1.124 *ll.*12-3 makes clear, this might include also the 50% penalty which applied in cases of default.

S.R. Llewelyn

---

5 J. Modrzejewski, 'Servitude pour dettes ou legs de créance', *Rech. Pap.* 2 (1962) 80-1.

§22 Invitation to a Wedding

Oxyrhynchus?   7 x 2.5 cm   II or IIIP

Ed. pr. — K. Maresch, *Kölner Papyri*, vol. 6, eds M Gronewald, B. Kramer, K. Maresch, M. Parca and C. Römer (Opladen 1987) 247 (= P. Köln 280).

Written against the fibres. The back is blank. As most surviving invitations come from Oxyrhynchus the editor tentatively suggests this provenance. The text has been restored following the editor's suggestions.

ἐρω[τ]ᾷ σε Πασίων [ ].[?]	Pasion [...] asks you
δειπνῆσαι εἰς γά[μ]ους τῶν τέ-	to dine at the wedding of their
κνων αὐτῶν ἐν [ ]	children at [...]
Ὥ[ρο]υ αὔρι[ον] .[?]	of Horus tomorrow [...]
5 ...	[...]

The editor suggests reading: (a) [καὶ Ὥ]ρ[ος] in the first line, the name being prompted by αὐτῶν in *l.*3 and inferred from its occurrence in *l.*4; and (b) ἐν [τῇ οἰκίᾳ τοῦ] at the end of *l.*3. The first suggested reading is unusual in so far as all extant wedding invitations are issued by a single host even when the papyrus refers to the marriage of children (plural; cf. P. Oxy 111 and 524). One also notes that the verb of invitation here suggests a single host. But the difficulty is αὐτῶν in *l.*3, as a comparison with P. Oxy 111 and 524 shows. The suggestion that the celebration was to occur at another's house is unsurprising and does not justify the supposition that the invitation was issued in two names; indeed in three other invitations (P. Fay. 132, P. Fuad I Univ. 7, P. Oxy. 524) we find invitations to the house of an individual who is not the host. How then is the space at the end of the first line to be explained? Perhaps the simplest and most straightforward explanation is the hypothesis that the lost portion contained the alias of Pasion. Such an alias is given in P. Oxy. 1486.

The second suggestion relating to the reading at the end of *l.*3 might also be queried. We have two invitations to a temple (P. Oxy. 2678 and SB 11652) and another to the λόχιον (P. Oxy. 181). This location is found in only one other papyrus, an invitation to a cult meal of Sarapis (P. Coll. Youtie 51 also from Oxyrynchus). Its identification is uncertain. However, Gilliam[1] plausibly suggests that the λόχιον was a birth-house associated with the cults of Isis and Sarapis, the parents of the divine Horus, and located in the Serapeum at Oxyrhynchus. If so, one is tempted to read instead ἐν [τῷ λοχίῳ τοῦ] in *l.*3.

The editor also suggests restoring *ll.*4-5 as follows: αὔρι[ον ἥτις ἐστὶν (date with or without the name of the month) ἀπὸ ὥρας x (mostly ὥρας θ). The evidence indicates that when αὔριον is mentioned the tendency naturally enough is to drop the name of the month, though the date is retained. The evidence also indicates that the 8th hour (rather than the 9th) is also just as likely a candidate for the starting time. See below for further details.

There are fourteen extant invitations to a wedding including our text. They are P. Fay. 132, P. Fuad I Univ. 7, P. Köln 280, P. Oxy. 111, 181, 524, 927, 1486-7, 1579-

---

[1] See commentary on P. Coll. Youtie 51.

80, 2678, SB 7745 and 11652. They show the following format, the rounded brackets indicating occasional omission:

(1)   The invitation: ἐρωτᾷ or καλεῖ σε + name of host

(2)   The occasion: (δειπνῆσαι) εἰς τοὺς γάμους (+ relationship of the person marrying to the host)

(3.a) (Where)

(3.b) When

(4)   (Farewell: διευτύχει)

A farewell is found in only one invitation (P. Oxy. 2678) and therefore should not properly be considered a formal element of the invitation. The location of the reception is not always stated. In three instances it is a temple (P. Oxy. 181, P. Oxy. 2678 and SB 11652). One invitation appears to name a λύκανον as the location, though its identity is unknown and the preposition missing.[2] On other occasions it is the home or property of an individual, either presumably the host (P. Oxy. 111, 1579, SB 7745) or a named third party (P. Oxy. 524, P. Fuad I Univ. 7 and P. Fay. 132). Are these third parties related to the persons marrying? Unfortunately, one cannot tell from the invitations themselves. One most readily thinks of the father of the other party, but if so, why is the invitation not made in his name? In three instances (P. Oxy. 927, 1487 and 1580) the location is not given at all. In such cases one may reasonably assume that the location was the host's house. Time appears always to be stated, usually from the 8th (P. Fuad I Univ. 7, P. Oxy. 1486-7, 1580, SB 11652) or 9th hours (P. Fay. 132, P.Oxy. 111, 927, 2678, SB 7745). In P. Oxy. 181 the time is from the 10th hour.[3] The time is lost in three (P. Köln 280, P. Oxy. 524, 1579). The numeral date is mentioned in nine papyri with the month or intercalated day in four of these. If αὔριον is used to indicate the day, it is usual for the name of the month to be omitted (once with day and month, five times with just day and once without either day or month). There are three instances where just the hour is mentioned. The details in our papyrus are lost. In all texts the invitation is issued by just one host. The relationship between the host and those marrying can vary as the table below shows.

The usual practice appears to be for the male head of the family to invite guests to the wedding of dependent females. There are two instances of a mother issuing the invitation.[4] Presumably their husbands had died. There is only one clear example of an invitation being to the wedding of the host's son. On the other hand, there are seven examples of invitations to the weddings of presumably dependent females (daughters and sisters). The three examples of invitations to children's weddings should be interpreted in the light of these figures. Interestingly the two invitations issued by women state the

---

[2] U. Wilcken, *APF* 6, p.424, suggests that the reading might be the vocative of the name Λυκάνων. Unfortunately, in none of the other invitations is the guest named. In view of the use of other cultic venues Judge suggests that the term might be associated with the Egyptian cult concerned with the jackal. (D.M. Doxey, 'Anubis', *Oxford Encyclopedia of Ancient Egypt* I [2001] 97-98.) Again we may just have a scribal error caused by a lapse in concentration whilst making multiple invitations.

[3] One might compare here the reference to Ptolemy Philopator's banquet at 3 Macc. 5.14-16. The official in charge of the event is forced to wake the king towards the middle of the 10th hour, when the guests had already assembled and the time of the banquet was already passed. However, as the invitation does not concern a wedding, it is not considered in the figures above.

[4] See also WChr 382, a petition concerning an assault which took place at a wedding held at the house of the plaintiff's sister. Due to the legal nature of the document it is likely that the plaintiff would name the true owner of the house where the assault took place.

location as their home. When the invitation was issued by a brother for his sister the location is unstated. The one other instance of an unstated location involves the invitation by a male to the marriage of an unstated relative. Is it also to the marriage of his sister? It would be interesting to have a larger number of examples to test the associations between the variables indicated in the table.

Table of Invitations to a Wedding

Papyrus	Host	Marriage of	Location	Time
P. Fay. 132	father	daughter	property of 3rd party	from 9th hour
P. Fuad I Univ. 7	father	daughter	house of 3rd party	tomorrow, 16th from 8th hour
P. Köln 280	father	children	[...] of Horus	?
P. Oxy. 111	mother	children	at home	tomorrow, 5th from 9th hour
P. Oxy. 181	?	daughter	the birth house (in the Serapeum?)	from 10th hour
P. Oxy. 524	father	children	house of 3rd party	tomorrow, 30th from ? hour
P. Oxy. 927	male	not stated	not stated	tomorrow, 29th from 9th hour
P. Oxy. 1486	bridegroom	self	λύκανον (?)	22nd Pharmouthi from 8th hour
P. Oxy. 1487	brother	sister	not stated	tomorrow, 9th Tybi from 8th hour
P. Oxy. 1579	mother	daughter	at home	tomorrow, 18th from ? hour
P. Oxy. 1580	brother	sister	not stated	tomorrow, from 8th hour
P. Oxy. 2678	father	son	temple of Sabazius	14th Mesore from 9th hour
SB 7745	father	daughter	at home	5th intercalated day from 9th hour
SB 11652	male	not stated	temple of Aphrodite	from 8th hour

Invitations were not just issued to weddings. They are extant for various other occasions, e.g. cult meals (see G.H.R. Horsley, *New Docs* 1 [1981] 5-9), *epikriseis* and guest meals. Persons issuing invitations usually bear Greek or Roman names, and probably belonged to the better-off strata of society. The invitations themselves date from the second and third century and most come from Oxyrhynchus. U. Wilcken, *Grundzüge* 419, argues that they were delivered in person by a messenger possibly supplied with a guest-list. In support of this contention he notes that:

(a) the guest is not named;

(b) the host's name is only given in the briefest form; and

(c) mostly they have no address on the back.

I would also add that since the guests are not named but only addressed by the second person pronoun, invitations were produced in bulk for the occasion and given to the messenger to deliver. Wilcken further notes that most invitations were issued the day before or even on the day itself, e.g. P. Oxy. 1486 is issued for a wedding to take place 'today'. He concludes that most hosts appear not to have reckoned on the possibility of conflicting social obligations among their guests. The conclusion assumes that they had not been informed of the occasion earlier and overlooks the possibility that these invitations might only have functioned as reminders.[5] His conclusion, however, might be seen to be supported by a Lukan parable.

Luke 14.16-24 records the parable about a dinner to which various guests were invited by 'a certain individual' (ἄνθρωπός τις, 14.16). The parable informs us that the guests had already been invited (κεκλημένοις, 14.17) when the slave was sent out to call them at the appointed time of the meal (τῇ ὥρᾳ τοῦ δείπνου, 14.17). On the basis of the papyrological evidence it seems that the earlier invitation may well have been written and delivered the previous day. Note also that the words of his propertied guests, as each makes his excuse for not coming, reflect the wording of our invitation (ἐρωτῶ σε, 14.18 and 19). However, the parable perhaps plays on the precarious nature of such invitations at short notice. In the end the invited guests cannot come and the host has to resort to asking guests who presumably could come because they were unlikely to have had conflicting engagements. Thus in the parable the poor, the crippled, the blind and the lame are invited as the unexpected guests.

The image of the wedding feast is strongly represented in the New Testament, especially in the parables of Jesus, but also in one miracle story and one apocalyptic image.

(1) At Luke 12.36-8 Jesus addresses his disciples telling them to be ready for the return of the Son of Man. They are likened to slaves awaiting the return of their master from a wedding feast. The master is apparently not the bridegroom in this parable. The issue of the parable is that the master might return home late, at the second or third watch. Those awake to receive him are designated 'blessed'. There is no indication in the parable as to who issued the invitation or where the marriage feast took place.

(2) The second parable (Luke 14.7-11) concerns those guests invited to a wedding who choose for themselves places of honour at the banquet. The parable assumes that the invitation was issued by a male, but there is no indication as to his relationship to the married couple. The location of the banquet is also not specified, though the parable assumes that there was a hierarchical seating arrangement. Of interest, however, is the wording of v.8 which reflects the wording of the wedding invitation: ὅταν κληθῇς ὑπό τινος εἰς γάμους par. καλεῖ σε ὁ δεῖνα εἰς τοὺς γάμους.

---

5 Cf. J.F. Gilliam, 'Invitations to the Kline of Sarapis' in *Collectanea Papyrologica* I, ed. A.E. Hanson (Bonn 1976) 318.

Matthew's gospel also contains two wedding parables, but these, narrated under a tendency to allegorize, present details which are more fanciful.

(3) Matt. 22.1-14 is an allegorized version of Luke 14.16-24. The invitation to a dinner becomes an invitation by a king to his son's wedding. The location of the banquet is a νυμφών (bridechamber?, v.10). But it is hazardous to deduce much from the details of the story. For example, the issuing of multiple invitations probably only reflects the attempt to parallel the repeated sending of prophets to Israel. Some invited guests even kill the messengers and are in turn destroyed by the king's army and their city burned (parallel to the destruction of Jerusalem). Of interest, however, is Matthew's special material (vv.11-14) added at the end of the parable. It concerns a person found at the wedding feast without wedding clothes and assumes a particular mode of dress at such functions. Be that as it may, the closing verses reiterate what the image of the wedding feast symbolizes for Matthew, namely, the separation of the elect from the damned (cf. Matt. 8.11-12, 25.10 and 12).

(4) Matt. 25.1-13 contains a parable similar to Luke 12.36-8. The message is that one must be awake and prepared for the coming of the Lord (cf. Matt. 24.42-51). However, the details have changed. The master is now the bridegroom and those waiting are ten virgins. The bridegroom comes in the middle of the night after the lamps had been burning some time. Those who had not brought a reserve supply of oil had to go off to purchase more. In the meantime, the bridegroom and the prudent virgins enter upon the wedding feast and the doors are locked. When the others return, they are refused entry and recognition of them denied. Again, the strong allegorizing tendency of the story warns against putting too much trust in details. A wedding feast at midnight! Again, also we note that the parable is told to illustrate the separation of the elect and damned.

(5) John 2.1-10 records the miracle performed by Jesus at a marriage feast in Cana of Galilee. Of interest is the presence of a head waiter and the dialogue between him and the bridegroom. The former detail implies that the wedding arrangements were fairly formal; the latter that the provision of wine at such functions was the responsibility of the bridegroom. Cf. P. Oxy. 3646 where the father appears to be responsible for the wine at his son's wedding. See also SB 12854. It is also of interest to note that the guests included Mary and Jesus, as well as his disciples.

(6) The last example is the image of the marriage of the Lamb at Rev. 19.7-9. The occasion is a joyous one and emphasis is placed on the bride's apparel (a metaphor for the righteousness of the saints). The seer is commanded to write: μακάριοι οἱ εἰς τὸ δεῖπνον τοῦ γάμου τοῦ ἀρνίου κεκλημένοι — 'Blessed are those called to the wedding feast of the Lamb'.

In reviewing the uses of the marriage feast as an image in the New Testament it is striking that Matthew's emphasis is negative rather than positive. He stresses the exclusion of guests and not the blessedness of those invited. Perhaps the reason lies in the evangelist's greater use of allegory. For him it is not enough that a guest accept the invitation; he must also prepare himself and be ready to enter the marriage feast. Entry requires more than just passive acceptance. To make this point he must stress the exclusion of certain guests who are not prepared appropriately.

S.R. Llewelyn

§23 The Ecumenical Synod of Dionysiac Artists

Oxyrhynchus   Archival roll   26 July AD 288

Ed. pr. — J.R. Rea, P.Oxy. XXVII (London 1962) 2476, re-edited by P. Frisch, *Zehn agonistische Papyri*, Papyrologica Coloniensia XIII (Opladen 1986) 3, 52 (= P. Oxy. 2476).

13 ἀπὸ τῆς οἰκο[υμένης περὶ τὸν
    Διόνυσον τεχνῖται κ]αὶ ἡ ἱερὰ
    μο[υ]σι[κ]ὴ περιπολιστικὴ
    οἰκουμεν[ι]κὴ [Διοκλητιανὴ
    Μαξι]μιανὴ εὐσ[ε]βὴ‹ς› εὐτυχὴ‹ς›

... [artists] from the inhabited world [who support Dionysus] and the sacred musical inter-city ecumenical [Diocletianic] Maximianic loyal successful

14 σεβαστὴ με[γάλη σύνοδος τῶν περὶ
    τὸν Διόνυσον τεχ]νιτῶν
    ἱερονι[κ]ῶν στεφαν[ι]τῶν τοῖς ἀπὸ
    τῆς α[ὐτῆς συνόδου τεχνί]ταις
    ἱερονίκα[ις στ]εφανίτα[ι]ς

august grand [synod] of the world-champion gold-medallist artists [who support Dionysus] to the world-champion gold-medallist artists of the same [synod]

15 χαίρειν. γι[νώσκετε (?)
    καταταγέ]ν[τα εἰς τὴν ἱερὰν]
    μουσικὴν [.. π]εριπολειστικὴν
    οἰκουμενικὴν Δ[ιοκλητιανὴν
    Μ]αξιμ[ι]ανὴν μ[ε]γάλην σύνοδον

send greetings. Take notice that there has been [admitted into the sacred] musical inter-city ecumenical Diocletianic Maximianic grand synod

16 Αὐρήλιον Ἁ[τ]ρ[ῆν Πετε]ησίου
    Νεχ[θενίβιος ἀρ]χιερέα
    Ὀξ[υ]ρυ[γ]χεί[τ]ην καὶ
    ἀποδεδωκότ[α] τὸ κατὰ τὸν νόμον
    β[ασιλικ]ὸν [ἐν]τάγιον πᾶν ἐκ
    πλήρους (δηνάρια) ωῦ

Aurelius Hatres (son) of Peteesis (grandson) of Nechthenibis, high priest, of Oxyrhynchus, having paid in full the whole fee as required by imperial law of 850 denarii

17 καὶ τὰ εἰς τὰ ἱ[ε]ρὰ σ[ε]βαστὰ
    τελέσματα. ἐ[γράψαμ]εν ὑμεῖν ἵν’
    ἰδῆται. ἐρρῶσθαι.

and the dues for the Augustan sacrifices. We have written to inform you. Farewell.

This is the latest-dated document of the ecumenical synod of Dionysiac artists (the date is that at which the dossier was sent on to Oxyrhynchus from Panopolis, where Hatres had been installed as the high priest of the VIIth four-yearly Great Festival of Pan). Under imperial patronage they had developed into an empire-wide association of victors in the major international musical contests, alongside the parallel association of athletes (known respectively as the 'thymelic' and 'xystic' synods). Because world-champions (lit. 'sacred victors') who had won gold medals (lit. 'crowns') had to be regularly on the move around the international circuit, entitlement to membership was certified on behalf of the central synod in Rome (in this case by three delegated *archontes*) to the synod of the new member's home city, which secured for him the coveted tax-exemption and other privileges. As our excerpt shows, membership privileges could also be won by undertaking a costly magistracy. A few years later (between 293 and 305) Diocletian tightened the rules, requiring three actual victories at world-champion level before admission (P.Lips. 44 = Mitteis, Chr. 381 = *CPL* 241, a private copy taken down at the reading of the rescript later condensed as *Cod. Iust.* 10.54.1).

The joint ecumenical synod seems to have been the only civil body in the empire to act internationally. (The financial houses of the *publicani* had long been marginalised, *New Docs* 8 [1997] 58-9.) It treated with cities through its own ambassadors, but like them was totally dependent upon imperial patronage. The political significance of its special status, structure and function deserves further exploration, along with that of the apparent parallel with the ecclesiastical synods (cf. *New Docs* 8 [1997] 144). The term is first used of a church council for the 60 bishops who met in Rome in 251 (Eus. *HE* 6.43.2-4, 21-22). Aemilianus, acting for the governor, forbade Dionysius of Alexandria in 257 to hold synods (*HE* 7.11.10). In the year 338 the epithet 'ecumenical' is first added (in reference to the Nicene Synod of 325) both by Eusebius (*Vit. Const.* 3.6f.) and by Athanasius (*Apol. c. Arianos* 7.2). Chadwick takes this as 'borrowed', perhaps for the sake of tax-exemption. Ammianus Marcellinus (ob. 395), a Greek writing in Latin, twice (15.7.6f, 21.16.18) feels obliged to note that *synodos* is a term Christians use (he perhaps did not know that it had passed into Latin centuries before, *OLD*, s.v. *synhodus*, and had been used by Diocletian). Ammianus displays elaborate distaste for synodical activism, describing it (self-consciously) in militarist terms (as indeed Eusebius had proudly done).

As for the analogy between civil and ecclesiastical provincial systems, any conscious or causative connection once contemplated (c.f. Abbott & Johnson, 175f.) now faces the objection that the term 'synod' was never used of the imperial provincial councils (Deininger, 187f). By and large the civil currency of what became key ecclesiastical terms (*ecclesia, episcopus, presbyterus, diaconus, anagnostes*) seems to have fallen away prior to public recognition of their ecclesiastical use. The matter should be clarified by the steadily accumulating documentary evidence.

Bibliography

F.F. **Abbott** and A.C. **Johnson**, *Municipal Administration in the Roman Empire* (Princeton 1926). C. **Andresen**, *Die Kirchen der alten Christenheit* (Stuttgart 1971) 186-191. R.S. **Bagnall**, review of Frisch (with list of other agonistic papyri), *Gnomon* 60 (1988) 42-45. W. **Brashear**, *Vereine im griechisch-römischen Ägypten* (Konstanz 1993). J. **Deininger**, *Die Provinziallandtage der römischen Kaiserzeit von Augustus bis zum Ende des dritten Jahrhunderts n.Chr.* (Munich 1965) 186-187. H. **Chadwick**, 'The origin of the title "Oecumenical Council"', *JTS* 23 (1972) 132-135. Ecole française de **Rome**, *L'Association dionysiaque dans les sociétés anciennes* (Rome 1986). P. **Foucart**, *De collegiis scenicorum artificum apud Graecos* (Paris 1873). E. **Herrmann**, *Ecclesia in Re Publica: Die Entwicklung der Kirche von pseudostaatlicher zu staatlich inkorporierter Existenz* (Frankfurt 1980). A.H.M. **Jones**, *The Greek City from Alexander to Justinian* (Oxford 1940) 231, 280. E.A. **Judge**, 'Contemporary political models for the inter-relations of the New Testament churches', *Reformed Theological Review* 22 (1963) 65-76. J.A.O. **Larsen**, *Representative Government in Greek and Roman History* (Berkeley 1966). A. **Lumpe**, 'Zur Geschichte des Wortes σύνοδος in der antiken christlichen Grätität', *Annuarium Historiae Conciliorum* 6 (1974) 40-53. F. **Millar**, *The Emperor in the Roman World* (London 1977) 456-463 ('The synods of athletes and performers'). F. **Perpillon-Thomas**, *Fêtes d'Égypte ptolemaïque et romaine d'après la documentation papyrologique grecque* (Louvain 1993). A.W. **Pickard-Cambridge**, *The Dramatic Festivals of Athens* (2nd edn: London 1968) 279-321 (dossier of texts) 336 (bibliography). F. **Poland**, 'Technitae', *RE* 2. Reihe, 10. Halbband (Stuttgart 1934) cols 2473-2558 (with complete list of documents). M.B. **Poliakoff**, review of Frisch, *Journal of Roman Archaeology* 2 (1989) 295-298. C. **Roueché**, *Performers and Partisans at Aphrodisias* (London 1993) 49-60 ('The organisation of performers'), 223-237 ('The activities of the synods'). A.J.S. **Spawforth**, 'Dionysus, artists of', *Oxford Classical Dictionary* (3rd edn: Oxford 1996) s.v. I. **Stefanes** (Stephanis), *Dionysiakoi technitai* (Heraklion 1988) listing 3023 artists known across 1000 years. P. **Stockmeier**, review of Herrmann, *Byzantinische Zeitschrift* 76 (1983) 89-91.

E.A. Judge

JUDAICA

§24 The Elders and Rulers (Archons) of the Jews

Heracleopolis   13 x 8.5 cm   II^a

Ed. pr. — D. Hagedorn, *Griechische Urkundenpapyri der Bayerischen Staatsbibliothek München*, Band III, eds U. Hagedorn, D. Hagedorn, R. Hübner and J.C. Shelton (Stuttgart 1986) 8-10 (= P. Monac. III 49).

The text on the recto runs across the fibres whilst the address on the verso runs with the fibres and thus parallel, though upside down, to the text proper. Top and bottom edges are complete but the text is broken on both sides. Three different hands are evident: (a) the document proper (*ll.*2-5); (b) the docketing (*l.*1) and additions in *ll.*6 and 7; and (c) the verso (*ll.*8-9). The reading of the location at *l.*8 is problematic due to the uncertainty of the signs of abbreviation employed. It is also possible that other addressees may have been included in the lost portion at the end of *l.*8.

	(*m.1*) [ἐλ(ήφθη) (ἔτους) . ᾿Ε]πεὶφ ιθ̄	Received year ... Epeiph 19
	(*m.2*) [τοῖς ἐν] Τεβέτνοι πρεσβυτέρο[ι]ς	To the elders of the Jews in
	τῶν [᾿Ι]ουδαίων π[αρα ?]	Tebetnu from
	[?] λθημι........ητη..[.].ου.... [...	
	c. ?]	
	[?]ακέναι ἐνωπίωι ουκα...τη[.].. ἐπι.	to have ... (to N.N.?) in person
	.[?]	... ...
5	[?]αν τυχεῖν ἐφ' ὑμᾶς αυυπερβ....[.].	... to chance against you ...
	τῆι ιᾱ [?]	on the 11th (day) ...
	(*m.1*) [?] ⟦...⟧	...
	[?]ν κε̄ ἑωρ(α) αυυωι	... 25 I have seen ...

Verso with the fibres

8	(*m.3*) τοῖς [ἐ]ν ῾Ηρ(ακλέους) πό(λει)	To the archons of the
	ἄρχου[σι ?]	Jews
	τῶν ᾿Ιουδαίων [?]	in Heracleopolis

The nature of the document and its contents is unknown due the poor state of the papyrus' preservation. We do not know the name or identity of the sender, and whether he was a fellow Jew or outsider. We do not know the matter which necessitated the communication. Was it cultic, legal, financial or some other concern? This is to be regretted as the document might have afforded some insight into the organisation of a Jewish community in the Ptolemaic *chora*.

The document does, however, attest the use of two titles for the leadership of the community:

(a) πρεσβύτεροι (*l.*2): The title is given to members of the Jerusalem Sanhedrin or of a local *gerousia*. The editor cites a number of examples, Judith 6.16, 21 passim, Luke 7.3 and SEG VIII 170 (= CIJ II 1404 *ll.*9ff. [pre-AD 70]: the well-known dedication by Theodotus of a synagogue and lodgings in Jerusalem recording that the synagogue was established by his ancestors as well as by the elders and Simonides). But this papyrus is the earliest documentary evidence for the term's use in the diaspora. Further, the editor concludes from the observation that the document is addressed to the elders as a group with no further designation that they were a well-defined board associated with the Jewish community. Of further interest is the fact that a village (Tebetnu) has its own *gerousia*.

(b) ἄρχοντες (*l*.8): This title for Jewish officials is better attested. The editor cites as examples John 3.1 and P. Lond. III 1177 (=WChr. 193, CPJ II 432 *l*.57 [AD 113]: a report of income and expenses by the administrators of Arsinoe's water system recording among its receipts payment by the archons of a synagogue and by the *eucheion*). The archons formed the executive board of the *gerousia*. The term could also be used of the leaders of a synagogue, Luke 8.41.

The document does not make clear the relationship of the different addressees in the body of the document and on the verso. The editor entertains two possibilities:

(i) The back of the document may have formed the address for delivery purposes. Letters were usually written on one side then folded so that the blank verso stood on the outside. The address was then written on this. If this suggestion is correct, then the two addressees are one and the same. After all, the archons, as the executive board, were also members of the *gerousia*. The suggestion is interesting in that it envisages a distinction between a more general addressee in the prescript of the document (*l*.2) and a more specific addressee in the address proper (*l*.8). If such a practice can be attested, then it would warn against any simple assumption from the abstract nature of the address, say, in the prescript of James 1.1 ('James the servant of God and the Lord Jesus Christ to the twelve tribes in dispersion, greeting') to the undeliverability of the document. (Such a feature is used in part to argue that James was not a letter.) But the editor rejects the possibility that the two bodies are one and the same.

(ii) In view of the fact that two different place-names appear to be mentioned in *ll*.2 and 8, i.e. Tebetnu and Heracleopolis respectively, the editor prefers to see the address on the back as a redirection of the document. This explains the change of hands in the address. If so, the elders may have formed a local *gerousia* in the village, whilst the archons were a higher body resident elsewhere with competence for a larger administrative district, perhaps the whole nome (Heracleopolis was the capital of the Heracleopolite nome and Tebetnu[1] a village in that nome) or several nomes.

Other reasons for the difference in those named in the prescript and address might also be suggested. For example, the document may have been sent to the archons in Heracleopolis in the first instance for them to relay on to the elders in Tebetnu. Such a practice is attested elswhere in the addresses of letters. See *New Docs* 7 (1996) 38-41. But the difficulty with the suggestion is that one might have expected the address to be in the same hand as the letter itself. For this reason alone it seems preferable to accept the editor's second explanation as the better solution.

Applebaum[2] offers a useful discussion of the organisation of Jewish communities and in particular the functions of the elders and archons in such communal structures. Naturally enough organisational arrangements change from location to location and across the span of time. However, on the basis of evidence from the *Letter of Aristeas*,

---

[1] See A. Calderini, *Dizionario dei nomi geografici e topografici dell' Egitto greco-romano* vol. 4, 4 (Milan 1986).

[2] S. Applebaum, 'The Organisation of the Jewish Communities in the Diaspora' in *The Jewish People in the First Century*, vol. 1, eds S. Safrai and M. Stern (Assen 1974) 464-503.

Philo and Josephus, Applebaum (pp.473-6) argues that the Jewish community or *politeuma* of Alexandria was led by a *gerousia* of elders and that it acted as an umbrella organisation over the several synagogues there.[3] He supposes its powers to be notorial (supervision of contracts), judicial (settlement of disputes) and administrative (application of government legislation to Jewish courts). However, the powers of the *gerousia* were not limited to these spheres; it might also police dissent within the community, send envoys to a ruler to represent its interests and vote honours to a benefactor.[4] The presence of archons is also shown by the evidence. The question arises as to the relationship of these officials to the *gerousia* of elders. It is Applebaum's contention (pp.491, 493-5) that where there is evidence that they formed a distinct group from the elders of the *gerousia*, they were the executive committee or board within it. In particular, they were responsible for secular aspects of a synagogue's business, e.g. signing contracts, paying dues to civil authorities, attending to repairs and maintenance of communal structures and buildings etc.

In discussing P. Lond. III 1177 (= WChr. 193, CPJ II 432 *l*.57) Kasher[5] holds that there were two synagogues in Arsinoe, one belonging to Jews from the Theban nome and the other (the *eucheion*) belonging to local Jews, and that water levies for both were paid by the archons. If so, he argues, we have here a federal system with an umbrella organisation covering the administration of the Jewish community and its two synagogues. Our editor's second interpretation of P. Monac. 49 can be made consistent with such an organisational structure, if we assume that each synagogue or local Jewish community had its own council of elders, and that a federation of councils had a common executive board or committee, the archons. The advantage of such a system would be to give each community a larger collective voice and more effective representation at the centres of regional administration.

The collocation of archons[6] and elders is met variously in Jewish sources. There is a fragmentary votive mosaic from Spain dedicated by the archons and elders (CIJ 1.663). At Judith 7.23 and 8.10-11 the terms appear to be used synonymously. Here the Jewish community in a town despair of Ozian and its archons/elders. The precise relationship between the two titles is perhaps made clearer at Josephus, *AJ* 11.105; in this passage Darius confirms Cyrus' decision to assist the Jews and writes to his officials

---

3 Applebaum (p.485) argues that an umbrella role was also played by the *gerousia* of Antioch; however, he doubts its existence in Rome (pp.500-1). He credits this difference to the cities' policies of access to citizenship. As the Greek city and its organisational structure jealously protected and limited access to citizenship, it had to allow the development of complementary organisational structures for non-citizen inhabitants. In Rome where access to citizenship, especially through manumission and military service, was easier, there was no overarching need for a larger organisational structure. Representation might be through citizen membership of the synagogues.

4 Berenice in Cyrenaica appears to have possessed a council which consisted entirely of archons (Applebaum, 486-8, 491-2). Within its competence lay such matters as the collection of taxes, exemption from liturgies and the maintenance of buildings and synagogues.

5 A. Kasher, *The Alexandrian Jews in Hellenistic and Roman Egypt* (Tübingen 1985) 140-1.

6 One must bear in mind that in most instances the archons would have been priests or synagogue leaders. Cf., for example, Mark 5.22 with Matt. 9.18 and Luke 8.41, John 7.45 with 7.48, and Acts 4.5 and 8 with Acts 4.23. See also Matt. 16.21, 21.23, 26.3, 47, 27.1, 3, 12, 20, 41, Luke 14.1, 23.13, 24.20, Acts 3.17, 13.27, 14.5, 23.14, 24.1, 25.15. One must ask why an author might choose to describe these officials by a term used as a Greek civic title rather than by terms like priest or synagogue leader which better connote the office.

accordingly, who then assist the 'elders of the Jews and the archons of the *gerousia*'.[7] Though one might be inclined to think that the elders formed the *gerousia* and the archons were an executive committee within it, this is not stated by the text which seems to see the elders and *gerousia* as separate bodies. The same separation is implied by 3 Macc. 1.8. However, the situation is not clear and any dogmatic position is dangerous given the potential for geographical and chronological variation between Jewish communal structures. Thus we find that Acts (4.5 and 8) describes the Jerusalem Sanhedrin as consisting of archons, elders and scribes. Despite this variation 1Macc. 14.28 and Ezra 10.8 and 14 are particularly suggestive of a separation based on a local/regional basis. The latter concerns an assembly of all Israel called to address the issue of intermarriage. The assembly is convened by the archons and elders under the threat of excommunication to those who do not attend. A decision is reached. The archons are to represent the whole national assembly in a matter which could not be settled there and then, and those who had married foreign wives together with their town/village elders and judges were to seek reconciliation with the deity. A similar dichotomy between a central body of archons and local bodies of elders is found in the wording of 1Macc. 14.28. Here are listed the people called to witness the conferral of the high-priesthood on Simon. Among those listed are the archons of the nation and elders of the countryside (ἄρχοντες ἔθνους καὶ οἱ πρεβύτεροι τῆς χώρας). It is in these last two references that one finds the closest parallels to the federal system alleged to operate in P. Monac. 49.

S.R. Llewelyn

---

[7] Interestingly, the term archon is absent in the parallel passages Ezra 6.14 and 1Esdras 7.2.

§25 Jews, Proselytes and God-fearers Club Together

Aphrodisias   Marble stele (pilaster?)   IIIP?

Ed.pr. — J. Reynolds, R. Tannenbaum, *Jews and Godfearers at Aphrodisias* (Cambridge 1987) pp.5-7; *SEG* 36 (1986) 970.

Face *a* (left side)

m.3		θεὸς βοηθὸς πατέλλα? δρ [. 1 or 2 .]	God, helper of those who offer food.
m.2		Οἱ ὑποτεταγμέ-	Those set out below
		νοι τῆς δεκαν(ίας)	from the decury
		τῶν φιλομαθῶ[ν]	of the lovers of learning
	5	τῶν κὲ παντευλογ(ούντων)	known too as constant in blessing
		εἰς ἀπενθησίαν	for prevention of sorrow
		τῷ πλήθι ἔκτισα[ν]	founded (it) for the community
		ἐξ ἰδίων μνῆμα	at their own expense as a memorial.
Σα-		ʼΙαηλ προστάτης	Jael (m. ?), patron,
μου-	10	*v.* σὺν υἱῷ ʼΙωσούᾳ ἄρχ(οντι?)	with son Joshua, rul(er?).
ηλ		Θεόδοτος παλατῖν(ος?) σὺν	Theodotus, (former?) official, with
πρεσ-		*v.* υἱῷ ʿΙλαριανῷ *v.*	son Hilarianus (*sc.* Isaac?).
βευ-		Σαμουηλ ἀρχιδ(έκανος?) προσήλ(υτος)	Samuel, archd(ean?), prosel(yte).
τῆς		ʼΙωσῆς ʼΙεσσέου *v.*	Joses (*sc.* Joseph), (son) of Jesse.
Περ-	15	Βενιαμιν ψαλμο(λόγος?)	Benjamin, psalm(singer?).
γε-		ʼΙούδας εὔκολος *v.*	Judas (the) good-natured.
ούς		ʼΙωσῆς προσήλυ(τος)	Joses, prosely(te).
		Σαββάτιος ʼΑμαχίου	Sabbatius, (son) of Amachius.
Sam-		ʼΕμμόνιος θεοσεβ(ής) *v.*	Emmonius, God-fear(er).
uel,	20	ʼΑντωνῖνος θεοσεβ(ής)	Antoninus, God-fear(er).
en-		Σαμουηλ Πολιτιανοῦ	Samuel, (son) of Politianus.
voy		Εἰωσηφ Εὐσεβίου προσή(λυτος)	Joseph, (son) of Eusebius, prose(lyte),
from		κα[ὶ] Εἰούδας Θεοδώρ(ου)	and Judas, (son) of Theodorus,
Perge		καὶ ʼΑντιπέος ʿΕρμή(ου?)	and Antipeus, (son) of Hermi(as?),
	25	καὶ Σαβάθιος νεκτάρις	and Sabathius (the) sweet-tempered,
		⟦[?κα]ὶ Σαμο[υ]ηλ πρεσ-	and Samuel, en-
		βευτὴς ἱερεύς⟧	voy (and) priest.

The remaining three-fifths of face *a* is blank except for a graffito

1 πατελλάδω[ν] van Minnen   3 τῆσδε καν(ονίδος) Bowersock   5 *l.* καί.

Face *b* (front)

[? first line completely lost]

m.1 [?.. *c*.8.. Σ]εραπίωνος *v.* [*v.*]   [... of S]erapion.

[third line completely erased]

[᾽Ιωση]φ Ζήνωνος *v.*   [Jose]ph, (son) of Zeno.

5   [Ζή]νων ᾽Ιακωβ *stop* <u>Μανασῆς ᾽Ιωφ</u> *sic*   [Ze]no, (son) of Jacob. Manasses,
                                                                 (son) of Job.

    ᾽Ιούδας Εὐσεβίου *v.*   Judas, (son) of Eusebius.

    ῾Εορτάσιος Καλλικάρπου *v.*   Heortasius, (son) of Callicarpus.

    Βιωτικός *stop* ᾽Ιούδας ᾽Αμ<u>φιανοῦ</u>   Bioticus. Judas, (son) of Amphianus.

    Εὐγένιος χρυσοχόος *v.*   Eugenius, goldsmith.

10 Πραοίλιος *stop* ᾽Ιούδας Πραοιλίου *v.*   Praoelius. Judas, (son) of Praoelius.

    ῾Ροῦφος *stop* ᾽Οξυχόλιος γέρων   Rufus. Oxycholius (the) elder.

    ᾽Αμάντιος Χαρίνου *stop* Μύρτιλος   Amantius, (son) of Charinus. Myrtilus.

    ᾽Ιακω προβατον(όμος?) *stop* Σεβῆρος *v.*   Jaco(b), sheepf(armer?). Severus.

    Εὔοδος *stop* ᾽Ιάσων Εὐόδου *v.*   Euodus. Jason, (son) of Euodus.

15 Εὐσαββάθιος λαχα(νοπώλης?) *stop*   Eusabbathius, green(grocer?).
    ᾽Ανύσιος   Anysius.

    Εὐσαββάθιος ξένος *stop* Μίλων   Eusabbathius (the) foreigner. Milo.

    ᾽Οξυχόλιος νεώτερος *v.*   Oxycholius (the) younger.

    Διογένης *stop* ᾽Ευσαββάθιος   Diogenes. Eusabbathius, (son) of
        Διογέν(ους)   Diogen(es).

    [᾽Ιού]δας Παύλου *stop* Θεόφιλος *v.*   [Ju]das, (son) of Paul. Theophilus.

20 [᾽Ι]α[κ]ωβ ὁ κὲ ᾽Απελλί(ων?) *stop*   [Jac]ob, also called Apelli(o?).
        Ζαχαρίας μονο(πώλης?)   Zacharias, mono(?).

    [Λε]όντιος Λεοντίου *stop* Γέμελλος   [Le]ontius, (son) of Leontius.
                                                                 Gemellus.

    [᾽Ιο]ύδας ᾽Αχολίου *stop* Δαμόνικος *v.*   [Ju]das, (son) of Acholius.
                                                                 Damonicus.

    Εὐτάρκιος ᾽Ιούδα *stop* ᾽Ιωσηφ Φιληρ(?)   Eutarcius, (son) of Judas. Joseph,
                                                                 (son) of Philer(?).

    Εὐσαββάθιος Εὐγενίου *v.*   Eusabbathius, (son) of Eugenius.

25 Κύρυλλος *stop* Εὐτύχιος χαλκο(τύπος?)   Cyrillus. Eutychius, bronze-(smith).

    ᾽Ιωσηφ παστι(λλάριος?) *stop* ῾Ρουβην   Joseph, confe(ctioner?). Reuben,
        παστ(ιλλάριος?)   conf(ectioner?).

    ᾽Ιούδας ῾Ορτασί(ου) *stop* Εὐτύχιος   Judas, (son) of Hortasius. Eutychius,
        ὀρν(ιθοπώλης?)   poul(terer?).

    ᾽Ιούδας ὁ κὲ Ζωσι(?) *stop* Ζήνων   Judas, also called Zosi(?). Zeno, re-
        γρυτ(οπώλης?)   c(ycler?).

    ᾽Αμμιανὸς χιλᾶς *stop* Αἰλιανὸς   Ammianus, stockfeeder(?). Aelianus,
        Αἰλια(νοῦ)   (son) of Aelianus.

30 Αἰλιανὸς ὁ καὶ Σαμουηλ	Aelianus, also called Samuel.
Φίλανθος	Philanthus.
Γοργόνιος Ὀξυ(χολίου) *stop*	Gorgonius, (son) of Oxy(cholius).
Ἑορτάσιος Ἀχιλλέ(ως)	Heortasius (son) of Achilles.
Εὐσαββάθιος Ὀξυχ(ολίου) *stop*	Eusabbathius, (son) of Oxych(olius).
Παρηγόριος	Paregorius.
Ἑορτάσιος Ζωτικοῦ Συμέων	Heortasius, (son) of Zoticus. Symeon,
Ζην(?)	(son) of Zen(?).

c. 6 lines blank

Καὶ ὅσοι θεοσεβῖς *stop* Ζήνων	And the following God-fearers. Zeno,
βουλ(ευτής)	coun(cillor).
35 Τέρτυλλος βουλ(ευτής) *stop* Διογένης	Tertullus, coun(cillor). Diogenes,
βουλ(ευτής)	coun(cillor).
Ὀνήσιμος βουλ(ευτής) *stop* Ζήνων	Onesimus, coun(cillor). Zeno, (son) of
Λονγι(ανοῦ?) βου(λευτής)	Long(ianus?), coun(cillor).
Ἀντιπέος βουλ(ευτής) *stop* Ἀντίοχος	Antipeus, coun(cillor). Antiochus,
βουλ(ευτής)	coun(cillor).
Ῥωμανὸς βουλ(ευτής) *stop* Ἀπονήριος	Romanus, coun(cillor). Aponerius,
βουλ(ευτής)	coun(cillor).
Εὐπίθιος πορφυρ(ᾶς) *stop* Στρατήγιος	Eupithius, purple(-seller). Strategius.
40 Ξάνθος *v.* Ξάνθος Ξάνθου *v.*	Xanthus. Xanthus, (son) of Xanthus.
Ἀπονήριος Ἀπον(ηρίου) *stop*	Aponerius, (son) of Apon(erius).
Ὑψικλῆς Μελ(?) *stop*	Hypsicles, (son) of Mel(?).
Πολυχρόνιος Ξάν(θου) *stop*	Polychronius, (son) of Xanthus.
Ἀθηνίων Αἰ(λιανοῦ?)	Athenion, (son) of Ae(lianus?).
Καλλίμορφος Καλ(λιμόρφου?) *stop*	Callimorphus, (son) of Cal(limorph-
ΙΟΥΝΒΑΛΟΣ	us?). Junbalus (*sc.* Jubal?).
Τυχικὸς Τυχι(κοῦ) *stop*	Tychicus, (son) of Tychicus.
Γληγόριος Τυχι(κοῦ) *v.*	Gregorius, (son) of Tychicus.
45 Πολυχρόνιος βελ(?) *stop*	Polychronius, mis(sile-maker?).
Χρύσιππος	Chrysippus.
Γοργόνιος χαλ(κοτύπος ?) *stop*	Gorgonius, bron(ze-smith?). Tatianus,
Τατιανὸς Ὀξυ(χολίου?)	(son) of Oxy(cholius?).
Ἀπελλᾶς Ἡγε(μονέως?) *stop*	Apellas, (son) of Hege(moneus?).
Βαλεριανὸς πενα(κᾶς?)	Valerianus, tab(let-maker?).
Εὐσαββάθιος Ἡδ(υχρόος?)	Eusabbathius, (son) of Hed(ychrous?).
?Μανικιος Ἀττά(λου?) *v.*	Manicius, (son) of Atta(lus?).
Ὀρτάσιος λατύ(πος?) *stop* Βραβεύς *v.*	Hortasius, stone-ca(rver?). Brabeus.
50 Κλαυδιανὸς Καλ(λιμόρφου?) *stop*	Claudianus, (son) of Cal(limorphus?).
Ἀλέξανδρος πυ(?)	Alexander, bo(xer?).
Ἀππιανὸς λευ(?) *stop* Ἀδόλιος	Appianus, pla(sterer?). Adolius,
ἰσικιάριος	mincer.

Ζωτικὸς ψελ(λός) *stop*	Zoticus, arm(band-maker?).
Ζωτικὸς γρύλλος	Zoticus, comedian(?).
Εὐπίθιος Εὐπι(θίου) *stop*	Eupithius, (son) of Eupithius.
Πατρίκιος χαλκο(τύπος)	Patricius, bronze-(smith?).
Ἐλπιδιανὸς ἀθλη(τής) *stop* Ἡδυχροῦς *v.*	Elpidianus, athle(te?). Hedychrous.
55 Εὐτρόπιος Ἡδυχ(ρόος) *stop*	Eutropius, (son) of Hedychrous.
Καλλίνικος *v.*	Callinicus.
Βαλεριανὸς ἀρκά(ριος?) *stop* Εὕρετος	Valerianus, treasu(rer?). Heuretus,
Ἀθηναγ(όρου)	(son) of Athenagoras.
Παράμονος ἰκονο(γράφος?) *stop v.*	Paramonus, portrait-(painter?).
Εὐτυχιανὸς γναφ(εύς) *stop* Προκόπιος	Eutychianus, fuller. Procopius,
τρα(πεζίτης?)	mon(ey-changer?).
Προυνίκιος γναφ(εύς) *stop* Στρατόνικος	Prunicius, fuller. Stratonicus,
γναφ(εύς)	fuller.
60 Ἀθηναγόρας τέκτω(ν) *v.*	Athenagoras, carpenter.
Μελίτων Ἀμαζονίου *v.*	Meliton, (son) of Amazonius.

The remaining third of face *b* is blank

The 2.8m. tall, rectangular stone was provided with margins on three sides, the fourth being only roughly dressed. It is slightly tapered, being designed probably to stand against a wall with the three sides available for inscriptions. Face *c* however remains blank.

Face *a* has two plug-holes half-way down, from which presumably something was to be hung (a door, suggests G.W. Bowersock cited by Feldman, *Jew and Gentile* 575, n.116). Reynolds and Tannenbaum (= R. & T.) envisaged it standing to one's left on approach. As one passed it one might then view face *b*. The text here is cut with more skill and symmetry than that of face *a*, and in a different hand. We have called the hand of face *b* *m.1* to allow for the possibility that it was cut first. R. & T. considered this, along with the possibility that face *a* was cut much later. But they decided to apply *m.1* to the hand of face *a* since face *b* lacks room for a proper heading (though they allowed this could have been on a superimposed stone, or on an adjacent one). Moreover, face *a* does refer to the founding of a monument (*ll.* 7-8), which seems odd if face *b* belonged to a separate statement of such a kind. Botermann, Bonz and others have however given more weight to the palaeographic and philological differences that point to a later date for face *a* (IV, V or even VI) and an earlier one for face *b* (late II). It is safer to keep open the implications of the surviving evidence rather than accommodate it to an 'economical' (R. & T.) reconstruction.

Face *a*, *l.*1, has been assigned to a third hand (*m.3*). G.W. Bowersock judged this line at least to be 'much later' (V?), using photographs that were clearer than those reproduced by R. & T. (Feldman, *Jew and Gentile* 577, n.138). Its sloping alignment contrasts awkwardly with that of *m.2*. (J.H.M. Strubbe, *SEG* 1994, 1753, challenges this however.) Several other additions (some made soon after the basic text, but in other hands) are shown in our text by underlining. Other entries were made over erasures (face *b*, *ll.* 15, 20, 32, 39, 48). Samuel's entry (face *a*, *ll.* 26, 27) had also been erased, presumably so that he could be moved up to the more prominent but inelegant position in the margin alongside the opening entries. Apart from face *a, ll.* 1 and 5, we have kept the text of R. & T., though sometimes reflecting in the translation conjectural restorations they had offered in their discussion.

The mix of ways in which individuals are identified is common in Greek documents, patronymics being given in many cases, occupations in some, personal characteristics in a few (some of which could be construed as second names), while others are given no identification at all beyond their proper name. The total lack of Roman *nomina* (legal family names), which became the official norm in AD 212 when Caracalla conferred citizenship on the whole free population of the empire, enrolling the new citizens in his own *gens Aurelia*, suggests a date either in the half-century before that point (since face *b, ll.* 29, 30, implies a date not earlier than Hadrian, whose *nomen* supplies Aelianus), or well after it once the strict use of Aurelius had been relaxed (though it need not have been enforced in a non-official document). R. & T. discuss the significance of each name (except Valerianus) individually.

The purpose of the list remains unclear. But the grouping of nine *bouleutai* (city councillors) at the head of the section beginning with face *b, l.* 34, and the fact that in its initial form the first occupation given is purple-seller (*l.* 39) and the last fuller (*l.* 59), implies the men were ranked on a basis reflecting their wealth, presumably the size of their donations to the building where the stele stood. Taking the texts from all of our three numbered hands as relating to the same purpose, R. & T. tentatively identify it as a communal welfare institution. Others (cf. McKnight 158, n.64) prefer to take it as a funerary monument. Our translations are deliberately made to leave these options open. The full discussions of R. & T. (R. primarily on epigraphic matters, T. on the historical interpretation) are models of caution, and must be carefully weighed before any conclusion is pressed. To promote this we have chosen to highlight alternatives to their preferred ones, where they have been advanced by others.

1) The main list (*m.1*, face *b*) is clearly divided into two sections (of 55 and 52 men respectively) marked off by the six-line gap after *l.* 33, and the heading of *l.* 34 'And the following God-fearers'. The second section has no biblical names and only a small proportion (one in eight) of Greek names favoured by Jews. The nine councillors can hardly have been pious Jews given their necessary involvement in the public cults of the city (from which Jews were officially excused under Septimius Severus and Caracalla, AD 196-211, *Dig.* 50.2.3.3). It is virtually impossible therefore to construe the classificatory term *theosebeis* in this case as identifying a category of particularly observant Jews. It must surely indicate Gentiles whose piety inclined them towards Judaism, or at least, as Lieu argues (497), who were honoured in such terms by the Jewish community in recognition of their financial support. By contrast the names in the first section are overwhelmingly (three in four) either of Hebrew origin or Greek ones favoured by Jews. One must therefore suppose either that we have lost a heading, 'The following Jews', for this section, or that the context in which the list was originally displayed (e.g. in connection with a synagogue) made it clear that it was a list of people identified as members of the Jewish community.

2) The briefer (and later?) list (*m.2*, face *a*) includes two *theosebeis* whose names are Graeco-Roman (though the rare Emmonius of *l.* 19 may echo the Hebrew *'emun*, 'faithful') and three 'proselytes' with biblical names, like most of the ten others who must all be taken as Jews by birth, together with the patron (*l.* 9) and his(?) son (*l.* 10), and the son (*l.* 12) of the leading member. They constitute a formal association

who have paid for a 'memorial' (*l.* 8) that is to benefit the general community. The association appears to be a *dekania* (*l.* 3), or company of ten ('decury'). If so, the first ten named after the patron (and omitting the two sons of *ll.* 10, 12) will have been the original founders, five of them being explicitly Gentiles by birth, and five (by implication of their names) born Jews. The head of the decury is a Gentile by birth (*l.* 13). Given the fact that proselytes are explicitly so identified (even though as Jews now they are presumably fully observant), it seems improbable that the *theosebeis* in this list are so called as being Jews of distinctive piety (the proposition of Bonz) rather than as being sympathetic Gentiles as in face *b*. It seems indeed that we have a consciously planned partnership between Gentile sympathisers, proselytes and Jews for specified ends.

The possibility (cited from G.W. Bowersock by Feldman, *Jew and Gentile* 575, n.116) that face *a*, *ll.* 2, 3, should read Οἱ ὑποτεταγμένοι τῆσδε καν(ονίδος) ('Those set out below on this door frame') should be discarded since it would have been otiose for the text to say it was on a door-frame when everyone could see that it was, and improbable that such a dedicated fraternity should have celebrated the munificence of only certain of its members. 'Decury' is needed in any case to avoid having to take the following genitives as partitive.

The members are known for two commitments. They are first 'lovers of learning' (*l.* 4), most probably 'a private adult education society' (R. & T. 34) for the study of the law. Secondly, they are 'constant in blessing' (*l.* 5), that is presumably in reciting the 'eighteen benedictions' of the synagogue liturgy (or meeting privately for prayer). Being a decury may imply that they supplied the quorum for synagogue services (R. & T. 37). But they will also have had beneficent or funeral activities, as is implied by the memorial they now create 'for prevention of sorrow' (*l.* 6), whether bereavement or destitution.

3) The subsequent invocation of *l.* 1 (*m.3*, face *a*) does not necessarily refer to the decury of *ll.* 2-8, but if it does the balance is tipped in favour of poor relief as the purpose on this occasion – the Latin loan-word *patella* is best construed here as 'plate' or 'offering dish'. It passed also into Hebrew. R. & T. interpret it as the equivalent of the Talmudic *tamhui*, and thus as a charity 'soup-kitchen' (27). Taking the case as dative, they then envisage the letters δο as indicating some form of 'giving' (whether noun or verb), and read the line as having two separate grammatical elements, the invocation of God as helper followed by a plea or statement about donations to charity. They judged this more likely (26) because they found no attestation for a noun πατελλᾶς (-άδος) which would have permitted the two elements to be integrated as shown in our text. It was possible, however, to read the last extant letter as omega (8), but this would have created a conceptually difficult name for a body with which the following decury was to be linked.

Now that such a link may be set aside (on the grounds that *l.* 1 was written separately and later), the matter should be re-opened. Van Minnen (257) cites an inscription (first published in 1904 in the journal of the Russian archaeological institute at Constantinople) from the tomb of Constantina, daughter of Georgios πατελλᾶ, of the province of Pisidia. The first editor took the word as a patronymic but van Minnen plausibly construes it as the genitive singular of an occupational noun πατελλᾶς, plural πατελλᾶδες, which he suggests might mean *Imbissinhaber* ('snack-bar holder'). Such a formation is well attested from this period in Asia Minor, as well as in this inscription: *b*, 28 χιλᾶς, 39 πορφυρ(ᾶς), 47 πενα(κᾶς?), 50 v.l. πυ(ρηνᾶς). See C.D. Buck and W. Peterson, *Reverse Index of Greek Nouns and Adjectives* (Chicago 1949) 12. Our translation is intended to keep the options open.

What bearing does the Aphrodisias inscription have on the debate over the 'God-fearers' in the Acts of the Apostles? The adjective *theosebeis* is not used there, but similar-sounding participial phrases refer to people linked with the Jewish community as 'fearing' (*phoboumenoi*) or 'revering' (*sebomenoi*) God. Those 'fearing' are Cornelius at Caesarea (10.2) and the ones addressed by Paul at Pisidian Antioch (13.16, 26). Those 'revering' are the 'proselytes' (13.43) and 'women of high standing' (13.50) there, Lydia at Philippi (16.14), others at Thessalonica (17.4) and Athens (17.12), and Justus at Corinth (18.7). It had been widely assumed that these were Gentiles who were attracted to Judaism, but without necessarily becoming proselytes. The Roman authors of the time repeatedly comment on such an interest. Arthur Hertzberg wrote of 'an increasing number, perhaps millions by the first century', *Encyclopaedia Judaica*, X (1971) 55.

In 1981 Wilcox (115) argued that the 'God-fearers' of Acts 'ought not without further external evidence be interpreted as referring to a class of Gentile synagogue adherents rather than to members of the Jewish community, whether Jewish by birth or by conversion'. Kraabel went further, arguing that they were a tendentious fiction on the part of the author of Acts, who dropped them (hence the 'disappearance' of Kraabel's title) once he had made the point that 'Christianity had become a Gentile religion legitimately and without losing its Old Testament roots' (p.127 in the 1992 reprint). There was 'no clear independent record of them in the material evidence from the classical world'. With reference to the Miletus inscription (*CIJ* II 748), Robert had declared that *theosebes* 'ne peut désigner un païen judaïsant' (45). In 1996 Levinskaya demonstrated that the Panticapaeum inscription (*CIRB* 71) also could not be emended to yield 'God-fearers' in this sense (75). But she accepted fully the implications of the new Aphrodisias inscription, seeing it as the later formalisation of the widespread interest in Judaism attested for the first century (80).

Kraabel had safeguarded himself against this by asserting that 'one clear inscription' would not be enough to disprove his hypothesis that 'there never was a circle of God-fearers associated with ancient Judaism' (128). It need only attest the particular case. We do not know whether the Aphrodisias inscription was linked with a synagogue building. Kraabel's study of the known synagogues has shown no parallel to it. But R. & T. are not inclined to be very surprised by the high proportion of God-fearers in their text. 'We know from the Book of Acts that there were God-fearers in many of the synagogues ... it is entirely possible that the discrepancy in numbers between God-fearers in Aphrodisias and elsewhere is an epigraphical one ... the inscriptional evidence elsewhere is from individual epitaphs and donations ... the proportion of God-fearers to Jews in Aphrodisias may not be atypical' (89). Most of the many discussions of the matter since have supported this assumption. In the weighty opinion of Feldman (1993, p.363) the caution of R. & T. over its significance to the history of Christianity is 'excessive'. Stanton identifies the 'companions' of Trypho in Justin Martyr's *Dialogue* as God-fearers. Lieu traces the ambiguities and polemics in the use of the term in second-century Christian literature. Finally, Mitchell has revived the proposition of Schürer: the cult associations of 'the Highest God' represent the God-fearers (cf. R. & T. 64-65, and for the ambiguities see now also Marek).

Bibliography

B.B. **Blue**, in D.W.J. Gill and C.H. Gempf (eds), *The Book of Acts in its Graeco-Roman Setting* (Grand Rapids 1994) 178-183. M.P. **Bonz**, 'The Jewish donor inscriptions from Aphrodisias: are they both third-century, and who are the *theosebeis*?', *HSPh* 96 (1994) 281-299 H. **Botermann**, review of R. & T., *ZRG* 106 (1989) 606-611; 'Griechisch-jüdische Epigraphik: zur Datierung der Aphrodisias-Inschriften', *ZPE* 98 (1993) 184-194. B. **Brooten**, 'Iael προστάτης in the Jewish donative inscription from Aphrodisias', in B. Pearson (ed.), *The Future of Early Christianity: Essays in Honor of Helmut Koester* (Minneapolis 1991) 149-162. S.J.D. **Cohen**, 'Crossing the boundary and becoming a Jew', *HThR* 82 (1989) 13-33. L.H. **Feldman**, 'The omnipresence of the God-fearers', *BAR* 12.5 (1986) 58-63; 'Proselytes and "sympathizers" in the light of the new inscriptions from Aphrodisias', *REJ* 148 (1989) 265-305; *Jew and Gentile in the Ancient World: Attitudes and Interactions from Alexander to Justinian* (Princeton 1993) 342-382, esp. 362-369 and 577; J.G. **Gager**, 'Jews, Gentiles and synagogues in the Book of Acts', *HThR* 79 (1986) 91-99. C.H. **Gempf**, 'The God-fearers', Appendix 2 in C.J. Hemer, *The Book of Acts in the Setting of Hellenistic History* (*WUNT* 49, Tübingen 1989) 443-447. M. **Goodman**, *Mission and Conversion: Proselytizing in the Religious History of the Roman Empire* (Oxford 1994) 117-119. A.T. **Kraabel**, 'The disappearance of the God-fearers', *Numen* 28 (1981) 113-126; reproduced in *Diaspora Jews and Judaism* (Atlanta 1992) 119-130; 'The diaspora synagogue', in D. Urman, P.V.M. Flesher (eds), *Ancient Synagogues* (Leiden 1995) 95-126. L.I. **Levine**, *The Ancient Synagogue* (New Haven 2000) 273 and passim. I. **Levinskaya**, 'God-fearers: epigraphic evidence', *The Book of Acts in its Diaspora Setting* (Grand Rapids 1996) 70-80. J.M. **Lieu**, 'The race of the God-fearers', *JTS* 46 (1995) 483-501. S. **McKnight**, *A Light among the Gentiles: Jewish Missionary Activity in the Second Temple Period* (Minneapolis 1991) 110-114. R.S. **MacLennan** and A.T. **Kraabel**, 'The God-fearers – a literary and theological invention', *BAR* 12.5 (1986) 46-53. C. **Marek**, 'Der höchste, beste, grösste, allmächtige Gott: Inschriften aus Nordkleinasien', *EA* 32 (2000) 129-146. S. **Mitchell**, 'Wer waren die Gottesfürchtigen?' *Chiron* 28 (1998) 55-64; 'The cult of Theos Hypsistos in Late Antiquity', in P. Athanassiadi and M. Frede (eds), *Pagan Monotheism in Late Antiquity* (Oxford 1999) 81-148. J. **Murphy-O'Connor**, 'Lots of God-fearers?: *theosebeis* in the Aphrodisias inscription', *RBi* 99 (1992) 418-424. G.J. **Mussies**, review of R. & T., *Mnemosyne* 44 (1991) 293-295; 'Jewish personal names in some non-literary sources', in J.W. van Henten and P.W. van der Horst (eds), *Studies in Early Jewish Epigraphy* (Leiden 1994) 242-276. L. **Robert**, '*Nouvelles inscriptions de Sardes* I (Paris 1964) 41-47. E. **Schürer**, *Geschichte des jüdischen Volkes im Zeitalter Jesu Christi* III (Leipzig 1909) 150-188, esp. 174; Eng. tr. and revision, G. Vermes et al. (eds), III (Edinburgh 1986) 15-176, esp. 169. G.N. **Stanton**, 'Godfearers: neglected evidence in Justin Martyr's *Dialogue with Trypho*', in T.W. Hillard et al. (eds), *Ancient History in a Modern University*, vol.2 (Grand Rapids and Cambridge 1998) 43-52. R.F. **Tannenbaum**, 'Jews and God-fearers in the holy city of Aphrodite', *BAR* 12.5 (1986) 54-57. P. **Trebilco**, *Jewish Communities in Asia Minor* (Cambridge 1991) 152-155. P.W. **van der Horst**, 'Jews & Christians in Aphrodisias in the light of their relations in other cities of Asia Minor', in *Essays on the Jewish World of Early Christianity* (Freiburg / Göttingen 1990) 166-181. P. **van Minnen**, 'Drei Bemerkungen zur Geschichte des Judentums in der griechisch-römischen Welt', *ZPE* 100 (1994) 253-258. M. **Wilcox**, 'The "God-fearers" in Acts: A reconsideration', *JSNT* 13 (1981) 102-122. M.H. **Williams**, 'The Jews and godfearers inscription from Aphrodisias: a case of patriarchal interference in early 3rd-century Caria?', *Historia* 41 (1992) 297-310.

E.A. Judge

§26 A Jewish Deed of Marriage

Antinoopolis   80 x 29.5 cm   AD 417

Ed. Pr. — Colette Sirat, Patrice Cauderlier, Michele Dukan & Mordechai Akiva Friedman, *Le Ketouba de Cologne. Un contrat de mariage juif à Antinoopolis* (Papyrologica Coloniensa, vol. XII. Westdeutscher Verlag: Opladen 1986; = P.Ketub.).

[הופאטיאס הונוריאו אוג]או[ס]ט[א]ו [טו]א הנדאקאטון

[קאי פלאויאו קונס]טא[נ]טי]או קומיטוס טוא מגאלוא

[פריפסטאטאו קאי] פאטריקיאו בשתה שתיח]ת[ה דשבועה

[. . . . .]ה בירח כסליו בעשרין בה בארבעה בשובתה

[בעיר] אַנטינו לפרוטאטי דתיבאיס אנה שמ]ואל ב]ר סמפטי

[מן]סוס ושרי באנטינו אמרת ובעית מן דעתי מן צביי[ני]

[נפשי] למסב לי יאת מיטרא ברת לעזר מן אלכסנדריא וש[ריה]

[באנט]ינו בתולתה לאתה כנימוס [כ]ל[בנת ישראל ואנה אמ]ר[ת]

[שמו]אל בר סמפטי חתנה דאנה [זן ומפרנס]

בתולת[ה]ה כ[לתה]

בקושט[ה והיא] ק[בל]ת למ[ה]ו[י] מֻק[ו]רה י[ות]ה

לשמואל {ברת} בר סמפטי בדכו ובנ]קדו[שה וב]טהרה כנימוס בנת

ישראל צניעתה והכדין אפרן ית]ה[[לעזר]] אסתר אמה [ ]ו[

לאוקון הולוסטימ[א] פלגו [די]נ[ר] ק]ו[ו]לא[בו]מאפורין אנזרבון [המישה

גרמסין תרתי סטכוון דכתן חמשה גרמסין זוגין תרתין

[פל]גו דינ]ר]   ירין   באלאנרין חד פלגו ד[ינר]

[פר]יזומא   [פלגו די]נר זוג ד[.]אלין פלגו דינר זוג דפסקיאה פלגו

דינר [ז]וג   ון דינר חד זוג זונארין פלגו גרמה סלק סכום

חושבן מ[ניא דע]מרא ודכתנה עם קדיטס דידה]ו[ן תשעה דינרין ופלג

ותרי ד[ינר]ין [דהב] יהבת לכלתה תעבד לה שאירין וחתנה שמואל בר סמפטי

יהב למיטרא כלתה לעסק הדנה א[ל]לי דדהב סלק סכום

ע[ם] קדיטס דמניא שתשר דינרין   חללין וחליין

כתובה למיטרא ברת לעזר ואחריין וערבין וכל [מה דהוא קני וכל מה]

דהוא עתיד למקני בין נכסין בין קרקעין ממ[שכנין]

ויהוון אחריין [ו]ע[ר]בין] למזונין ולתכסין ול]   ותרין שטרי]

פרניה אתכתוו]ן ביניהון] ואתיהב חד ל[שמואל בר סמפטי

ב[ע]לה דמיט[רא]   ואתיהב חד [ללע]זר

ביר

                ש

                שלום

אנה שמו]אל בר סמפטי קבלת עלי כל] מה דכתיב [ומפרש בהדן שטר מראש ועד סוף]

בישראל

ממרומך

[In the consulship of Honorius Aug]ustus for the eleventh time
[and Flavius Cons]tantius the most magnificent *comes*
[and] *patricius*, in the sixth year of the sabbatical cycle
[ ] in the month Kislev on the twentieth of it, on the fourth (day) of the week
5   [in the town of] Antinous, the most glorious (city) of the Thebaid, I S[amuel son of S]ampat[i]
[from ...]sos and resident in Antinous, declare and ask of my own free-will and of [the desire]
[of my own soul] to take for myself Metra, daughter of Leazar, from Alexandria and [resident]
[in Antino]us, virgin, as wife according to the law [of all the daughters] of Israel and [I declare, I]
[Samu]el son of Sampati, the bridegroom, that I [will nourish and maintain]
10 the virgin, the bride,
in truth. [And she agrees to honour] Samuel daughter (*sic*) son of
Sampati in purity and in [holi]ness and [cleanness? according to the law of the daughters] of Israel
(who are) chaste. And this is the dowry given by <Leazar> Esther [her] mother: [a mole-coloured]
[tunic] in sprang-work, half a denarius; a short-sleeved hooded long tunic in the Anazarba style, [five]
15 grams; two coloured tunics in linen, five grams; two pairs of [...],
[a half denarius]; [...]; one bathing set, half a denarius;
[a gi]rdle, [half a] denarius; a pair of [...], half a denarius; a pair of bands, half
a denarius; a pair of [...], one denarius; one pair of girdles, half a gram; the sum total
for the items of wool and linen together with their [con]tainer(?) comes to nine denarii and a half.
20 And two [denarii of gold she gave to the bride] that she make for herself bracelets. And the bridegroom
Samuel son of Sampati gave to Metra, the bride, as consideration bridal gifts [...] of gold, the sum
total with the [container?] of items comes to sixteen denarii, round and pure, *ketubbah* for
Metra daughter of Leazar, and they are pledged and vouched for. And all [that he possesses and all that]
he will in future possess, both herds (movable property?) and immovable property are [pledged]
25 and will be pledged and guarantees for the food and for the clothing and for [... Two documents]
of dowry have been written [between them] and one is given to [Samuel son of Sampati]
[the hus]band of Me[tra and one is given to Leazar.]
... son of (name of scribe?)
Shalom.
30 I, Samu[el son of Sampati, personally accept all] that has been written [and defined in this document
from beginning to end.] In Israel
??

The papyrus is a marriage contract (*ketubbah*) in Aramaic and Greek, written in Hebrew characters. It records the union between Samuel, son of Sampati, and Metra, daughter of Leazar and Esther. The document is dated in transliterated Greek according to the civil calendar by the consuls, and in Aramaic according to the Jewish calendar by the year of the sabbatical cycle — for the use of which the editors cite near contemporary epitaphs from Touba — as well as by month (Kislev), and the day of the month and of the week.

The *ketubbah* fills the gap between the second century AD Greek and Aramaic *ketubboth* from Wadi Muraba'at and Nahal Hever (Cotton; Yadin, et al.) and those of the late ninth to eleventh centuries from the Cairo Geniza studied by Friedman; for Egypt it falls between those from Elephantine in the 5th century BC (Porten and Yardeni) and the Geniza contracts.[1] It therefore makes a significant contribution to our understanding of Jewish marriage practice and its divergent forms. The contracts from the Judaean Desert (i.e. Wadi Muraba'at and Nahal Hever) have been the source of considerable debate regarding their divergences from the norms implied by the Mishnah and later rabbinic sources. In contrast, our document as well as the Geniza contracts show a higher degree of conformity. The above *ketubbah* clearly reflects rabbinic marital formulae as preserved in the Palestinian tradition;[2] this contrasts with later *ketubboth* from the Geniza where most follow the Babylonian tradition. Thus our document attests the presence of Palestinian rabbinic influence in Egypt before the late Gaonic period. Palestinian influence is further suggested by the Aramaic dialect used in the document which is said to be Galilean, e.g. the transcription Leazar for Eleazar.

Offering further insight into the Jewish community in Antinoopolis in this period[3] and into the resurgence of Hebrew/Biblical influence, are the names of the husband, Samuel, of his father, Sampati, a transliteration of the familiar Sambathion, of his wife, Metra, perhaps by metathesis Martha, of her parents, Leazar and Esther, and of a witness, Shalom. Leazar's origin is described as Alexandria. The editors surmise that he may well have been a fugitive of the anti-Jewish riots there of AD 415. If so, it is not at all

---

[1] Extensive comparison with rabbinic and other relevant sources is invaluable in providing a context for the interpretation of our *ketubbah* document, and is used by the editors to fill the lacunae.

[2] The following features showing evidence of Palestinian tradition are to be noted:

    (a) The use of Wednesday (fourth day of the week, *l*.4) rather than Thursday to celebrate the marriage of maidens. See ed. pr., 32.

    (b) The document's use of the *homologia* form and the declaration 'I ... declare of my own free-will to take' — אנה ... אמרת מן דעתי למסב are attested in the majority of marriage contracts in the Palestinian style found in the Geniza. See ed. pr., pp.36-37. The editors note: 'A clause where the parties to the contract affirm that they act voluntarily and freely is practically always included in extant Jewish juridical contracts. However, in the *ketubboth* this clause characterises the Palestinian tradition, and it is absent in the Babylonian tradition.'

    (c) Recording the mutual obligations of the spouses, especially of the bride, is a feature of Jewish marriage contracts in the Palestinian tradition. See ed. pr., 39-40.

    (d) The guarantee clause is also said to be close to that of the Palestinian tradition. See ed. pr., 57.

    (e) In so far as marriage contracts in the Palestinian tradition record the mutual obligations of the parties, it is logical that they might have been written in duplicate, as our document, and vested in each party. See ed. pr., 58-59.

The editors note other minor grammatical coincidences between our document and contracts written in the Palestinian tradition, e.g. the omission of the conjunction ו before the second מן (i.e. מן דעתי ומן) in *l*.6 (p.38); the word נימוס = νόμος in *l*.8 (p.38); and the use of the term פרנה with the meaning of marriage contract accords with usage in the Palestinian tradition (p.60).

[3] The document appears to be the first to mention Jews at Antinoopolis.

surprising that the family would seek refuge in a city where other Jews could be found. From the valuation and nature of the listed property it would appear that the families were of modest means.

Bibliography

H.M. **Cotton**, 'The Guardianship of Jesus Son of Babatha: Roman and Local Law in the Province of Arabia', *JRS* 83 (1993) 94-108; H.M. **Cotton** & E. **Qimron**, 'XHev/Se ar 13 of 134 or 135CE: A Wife's Renunciation of Claims', *JJS* 49 (1998) 108-118; H. **Cotton** & A. **Yardeni**, *Aramaic. Hebrew and Greek Documentary Texts from Nahal Hever and Other Sites* (DJD XXVII. Clarendon: Oxford 1997); M.A. **Friedman**, *Jewish Marriage in Palestine. A Cairo Geniza Study* (2 vols. Tel Aviv & New York 1980-81); N. **Lewis** (ed.), *The Documents from the Bar Kochba Period in the Cave of Letters: Greek Papyri* (Jerusalem 1989); B. **Porten** & A. **Yardeni**, *Textbook of Aramaic Documents from Ancient Egypt* vol.2 Contracts (Jerusalem 1988); A. **Wasserstein**, 'A Marriage Contract from the Province of Arabia Nova: Notes on Papyrus Yadin 18', *JQR* 80 (1989) 93-130; Y. **Yadin**, J. **Greenfield**, A. **Yardeni**, 'Babatha's *Ketubbba'*, *IEJ* 44 (1994) 75-101.

J.M. Lieu

§27 A Jewish Deed of Marriage: Some Further Observations

Description of Document

The papyrus is described as fine. Spacing between lines indicates that economy was not a consideration. The writing appears professional, the editors (p.19) suggesting that the scribe may have come from Alexandria or perhaps even Palestine. The first dating formula and the listing of the trousseau are in transliterated Greek.[1] From the careful transliteration — note that he can either transliterate the Greek genitive (קומיטוס *l*.2) or, if he uses the Aramaic genitive form, he leaves the Greek noun in the nominative (דתיבאיס *l*.5 and דפסקיאה *l*.17) — the editors also surmise that he knew both Greek and Aramaic. The text shows a number of interesting corrections from which it is concluded that the scribe realised his error immediately but writing under the constraint of dictation was unable to stop to make the correction. Note in particular: (a) ברת בר (daughter son) in *l*.12 where instead of correcting the word the scribe rewrites it; and (b) the correction of לעזר (Leazar) to אסתר (Esther) in *l*.13. An alternative interpretation might be considered. In view of the fact that both corrections involve a possible confusion of gender, one could postulate that the errors arose initially by the scribe's use of an exemplar in which a person of the opposite sex was mentioned on both occasions. It might be objected that this is an unlikely explanation in the first instance, i.e. in (a) where the bride acknowledges her obligations to the husband. However, it must be borne in mind that this clause itself is unusual, for the declaration of obligation was normally unilateral and made by the groom.

The document consists of the following elements:

(1)   Date and location formulae (*ll*.1-5)

(2)   The presentation of the parties (identified by origin and residence) and the unilateral proposal of marriage (*ll*.5-8)

(3)   Recording of mutual obligations (*ll*.8-13)

(4)   A description of the bride's dowry with valuation (*ll*.13-20)

(5)   The bridegroom's gift (*ketubbah*?) with valuation (*ll*.20-22)

(6)   Guarantee clause of the bridegroom (*ll*.23-25)

---

[1]   The editors reconstruct the Greek behind *ll*.1-3 as follows:
['Υπατείας 'Ονωρίου Αὐγούσ]του [τὸ] ἑνδέκατον
[καὶ Φλαουίου Κωνσ]ταντίου κόμητος τοῦ μεγαλο-
[πρεπεστάτου καὶ] πατρικίου ...
The editors note the scrupulous care of the scribe even transcribing the declinable parts of the Greek words. They reconstruct the Greek behind *l*.5 as follows: ἐν 'Αντινόου (πόλει) τῇ λαμπροτάτῃ Θηβαίδος. Note that the transliteration uses the Aramaic genitive ד before 'Thebaid' and accordingly renders the name in the nominative, Θηβαίς. The list of dowry items has been reconstructed by re-transcribing the transliterated Greek and by an extensive comparison with other sources. The editors reconstruct the Greek behind *ll*.13-18 as follows:
. . . [χιτῶνα σπα-]
λακὸν ὁλοστήμονα δηναρίου ἡμίσεος· κολαβομαφόριον 'Αναζαρβαῖον [πέντε]
γραμμάτων· στιχάρια δύο λινᾶ γραμμάτων πέντε· ζεύγη δύο [2-5 letters]
δηναρίου ἡμίσεος· [6-7 letters]ιον [4-6 letters]· βαλανάριον ἐν δηναρίου ἡμίσεος·
[περί]ζωμα δηναρίου ἡμίσεος· ζεῦγος [5-6 letters]ίων δηναρίου ἡμίσεος· ζεῦγος
φασκιῶν δηναρίου
ἡμίσεος· ζεῦγος [5-7 letters] δηναρίου ἑνός· ζεῦγος [ζ]ωναρίων γράμματος ἡμίσεος.
Note that the list is not properly transliterated Greek. For example, the valuations are in Aramaic, as also is λινᾶ (דכתן, *l*.15) and the use of the genitive form דפסקיאה (*l*.17).

(7) Specification of the exchange of documents with the signature (?) of the scribe (*ll*.26-28)

(8) Signatures (*ll*.29ff.) — note the change of hands from *l.* 29 where the parties sign the document.

It is interesting that in our document the scribe uses transliterated Greek for features with a specific reference (i.e. the dating of the document and the dowry's content), whereas in religious formulae he reverts to Aramaic. It was unusual for Greek to be transcribed into Hebrew characters.[2] Most other examples of the transliteration of Greek into Hebrew script are mediaeval, although the editors cite a Byzantine inscription from Beth-She'arim in Galilee.[3] Besides Talmudic citations from the LXX versions of Theodotion and Aquila there are quotations in the Rabbinic literature of Palestine:[4]

זיטא איפטה איטה אכטו — ζῆ τὰ ἑπτὰ [μᾶλλον] ἢ τὰ ὀκτώ (R. Abbahu, third century)[5]

קורי פלי בריכסון — κῦρι, πολὺ βρέξον (R. Menahem in the name of Resh Lakish, third century)

פרא בסיליוס אונומוס אוגרפוס — παρὰ βασιλέως ὁ νόμος ἄγραφος (R. Eleazar, third century)

כורוסתי בייה — χαρίζεσθαι βίᾳ (R. Hela, fourth century)

Lieberman is of the view that such usage indicates the pervasiveness of Greek language and culture not only amongst the rabbis of Palestine but also in the general populace. One is also reminded of the postulated solution to the riddle of the number of the beast at Rev. 13.18. The key to the puzzle, it is suggested, is that the number 666 represents an isopsephism/gematria. As the letters of both the Greek and Hebrew alphabets were also used as numbers, the numerical value of the letters of any word could be added to produce a unique sum. When the Greek spelling of the name Nero Caesar is transliterated into Hebrew characters, the sum of the letters is 666, i.e. Νέρων Καῖσαρ —> נרון קסר = 200+60+100+50+6+200+50 = 666.[6]

The Evolving Nature of Jewish Marital Custom

The differences between Greek and Jewish marriages in antiquity have already been treated in a previous volume in this series. See *New Docs* 6 (1992) 1-18. Suffice it to note here that whereas Greek marriage was based on a consideration which was the agreed sum of property brought into the marriage by the woman, in traditional Jewish marriage its consideration was the bride-price, i.e. the money given or promised to the bride or her family by the bridegroom or his family. In other words, the obligation of

---

2 Equally rare are examples of Hebrew script between the 2nd and 9th centuries, and thus this papyrus adds substantially to our knowledge of its development, as is exemplified in the ed. pr. by a detailed table of comparison also illustrating the formation of the letters.

3 M. Schwabe and B. Lifshitz, *Beth She'arim*, vol. 2 (Jerusalem 1974) 121-3, and N. Avigad, *Beth She'arim*, vol. 3 (Jerusalem 1976) 22-3, 235.

4 The examples are cited from S. Lieberman, *Greek in Jewish Palestine* (New York 1965) 15-67. Lieberman (144-60) also discusses Greek and Latin proverbs which though translated into Hebrew/Aramaic occasionally retain transliterated Greek terms.

5 Cf. also Philo, *De opif. mundi* 124-5.

6 Interestingly, when the Latin spelling is transliterated, the sum is 616, i.e. Nero Caesar —> קסר נרו = 200+60+100+6+200+50 = 616, a variant reading noted by Irenaeus (*Adv. haer.* 5.30.1). On the transliteration of Caesar as קסר rather than the more usual קיסר, see *DJD* II 18 recto (AD 55/56, plate XXIX), an acknowledgement of debt dated in the first line to the second year of Neron Caesar: שנ[ה]ב תרתין לנרון קסר. Unfortunately, the papyrus is damaged and the last two letters of קסר are incomplete. However, as D.R. Hillers, *Bulletin of the American Schools of Oriental Research* 170 (1963) 65, observes, 'enough is preserved to show that no vowel-letter was written between the ק and ס'.

providing the financial consideration in marriage is reversed between the two systems. The obligation on the bridegroom to provide a financial consideration to his bride tends to be a feature of marital custom where repudiation is the unilateral right of the husband, as is the case in Jewish law, and acts as a strong disincentive against frivolous divorce by assuring the wife of continued financial support.

Before commenting directly on the above deed of marriage it is important to understand a number of changes which occurred in the Jewish formalization of marriage. First, in the OT the father gave his daughter in betrothal (e.g. Gen.34.12; Ex.22.16-7; 1Sam.18.25; Tobit 7.12-14) and received in return the bride-price or *mohar* (מהר) from the bridegroom.[7] This custom changed. The *mohar* was replaced by the כתובה — *ketubbah* (also known as the פורנא = φερνή) or bill obliging the sum's payment (on divorce or death) to the wife and secured by a pledge over the husband's property (cf. P.Yadin 18 *ll*.16-19; 21 *ll*.11-12). Jewish law set a minimum amount. The pledge assured the payment of the agreed sum, also called *ketubbah,* the term denoting both the deed and the agreed sum. In our marriage document Samuel guarantees the *ketubbah* of his bride (*l*.23), but in the wording of the deed the pledge over his present and future property, both movable and immovable, guarantees his bride's maintenance rather than the payment of her *ketubbah* (*ll*.23-25). The value of the *ketubbah* is sixteen denarii (*l*.22) consisting of the valuation of the property brought into the marriage by the bride (9.5 + 2 = 11.5 denarii) and the value of the bridegroom's gift (הדנה = ἕδνα, presumably 4.5 denarii). The value of the gift appears to have been added to the bride's dowry to form the basis of reckoning the *ketubbah.* Properly speaking neither the dowry nor the gift ought to form the basis of reckoning for they or their value were to be returned on death or divorce in addition to the value of the *ketubbah.* See below. Are we then to assume that the bridegroom was liable for the return of the property as well as the sixteen denarii promised as the *ketubbah*? Be that as it may, the use of the dowry to reckon the value of the *ketubbah* is interesting. It may explain the very unusual feature of the listing and valuation of the property brought to the marriage by the bride in the first instance and the fact that the bridegroom's guarantee relates to his bride's maintenance rather than the payment of the *ketubbah.* These changes indicate an assimilation to Graeco-Roman marital practice in Egypt.[8]

Second, in the OT period, there had been a separation between the husband's and wife's property. This changed possibly under Greek influence. The bride now brought property into the marriage either as *ṣon barzel* (צאן ברזל) or *melog* (מלוג). The *ṣon barzel* property was valued (*m. Ket.* 6.3) and recorded either in the *ketubbah* itself or in addition to it and became the property of the husband. On divorce either the property itself or the amount of its valuation was returned to the wife. The *melog* property (usually immovable property), however, remained the property of the bride or her father

---

[7] The *mohar* is only mentioned three times in the OT. The first is the price and gift (מהר ומתן) offered by Shechem to Jacob for the marriage of his daughter (Gen. 34.12). In the second, Saul tells David the grisly bridal gift he requires if David were to marry his daughter (1Sam 18.25). Finally, by law a man who seduces a virgin is obliged to pay her bride price (Exod. 22.16). Cf. Deut. 22.38-9.

[8] The question arises as to the significance of the terms כתובה and פרנה found in the document at *ll*.23 and 26. The answer is, no doubt, that the couple actually saw their arrangement as a Jewish marriage. The language of the document and the basis of the wife's obligations (*ll*.8 and 12-3) indicate that this was the case. One might also note the avoidance of potentially offensive titles and epithets in the dating formula in the first three lines, e.g. δεσπότης and αἰώνιος. The editors (p.26) note that such reserve does not appear to be used in Jewish documents written in Greek.

and was not recorded in the *ketubbah*. The husband, however, had right of usufruct of this property but was neither responsible for any loss nor benefited from any increase in its value. Our document shows the bride bringing what appears to be *ṣon barzel* property into the marriage. It is valued and recorded in our deed of marriage. This feature may also be due to the influence of Graeco-Roman marital practice. In Graeco-Roman law the wife's dowry (i.e. the property she brought into the marriage) both formalised the conjugal bond and was fundamental to the husband's obligation to maintain his wife. See *New Docs* 6 (1992) 3-4. The prominent listing of Metra's dowry and the fact that Samuel actually pledges his property (rather than in accord with usual Jewish marital practice being personally responsible) for his wife's maintenance may not be purely coincidental, but vitally related facets of our document. It is possible that the couple saw the dowry as obliging the bridegroom to maintain his wife.

Third, in the OT the *mohar* was a transaction between the bride's father and the bridegroom. Interestingly, the *ketubbah* was addressed as a unilateral proposal by the groom to his bride (e.g. see *m.Qid.* 2.1, 3.2). Parties to a *ketubbah* expressed the marital obligation in the words 'according to the law of Moses and Israel', e.g. Tobit 7.13, *DJD* II 20 *l*.3, *CPJ* 128, *P.Yadin* 10 *l*.1 and 18 *l*.7, *m.Ket.* 7.6, *t.Ket.* 4.9, *y.Yeb.* 15.3.14d, and *y.Ket.* 4.8.28d. In other words, the law of Moses and Jewish custom formed the basis of obligation in Jewish marriage. In our deed of marriage the proposal is unilaterally addressed by the bridegroom but the bride appears always to be spoken of in the third person. Cf. *m.Qid.* 2.1 and 3.2 which uses the second person. The editors argue that the form of our document is that of the Greek *homologia* and that in the majority of Geniza contracts the bride is addressed in the third person. The obligations of the bride are said to be 'in accord with the law of the daughters of Israel' (*ll*.8 and 12-3?).

To summarise, the above *ketubbah* document diverges from Jewish marital custom at a number of interesting points. The cause of this may be ascribed to the influence of Graeco-Roman practice. The divergences include:

(a)   The trousseau brought by the wife with its valuation is listed immediately after the proposal of marriage (*ll*.5-11) and its acceptance (*ll*.11-13), and before documenting the *ketubbah* (*ll*.20-23). As in Jewish law it was the *ketubbah* which formed the legal basis for marriage and the wife's dowry was not an obligatory part, its location here is extraordinary. Elsewhere the dowry was written separately and did not form part of the *ketubbah* itself (ed. pr. pp.14-5). Here, however, it is listed first and forms part of the value of the *ketubbah*. But the location in this instance does conform with Greek deeds of marriage, as also does the valuation of the trousseau by competent persons.

(b)   The trousseau is given by the mother of the bride rather than her father. Leazar appears to be both alive (note the absence of eulogies reserved for the mention of the name of the deceased, *l*.7) and still married to Esther (note that a copy of the contract apparently was to be handed to him, *l*.27).[9] Here also one finds parallels in the Greek deeds of marriage where persons other than the family's κύριος could give the dowry. See Häge, 26-7, and Modrzejewski, 264-5.

(c)   The value of the *ketubbah* appears to be calculated as the sum of the value of the bride's dowry and the groom's gift (i.e. הדנה — ἕδνα, *l*.21). This is unlike the *ketubbah* in Jewish marriage which is a debt owed by the husband to his wife and paid on divorce or his death. Such gifts, though not legally obligatory, are found in Greek deeds of marriage. The use of the term הדנה is also interesting as it shows an underlying attempt to understand and define the Jewish *ketubbah* by a Greek concept. A similar phenomenon is to be found in the Greek

---

[9] So ed. pr., 42. But one notes that the first point (i.e. that Leazar was still alive) rests on the argument of silence, whilst the second on a reconstructed section of the text.

attempt to understand the alimentation capital of Egyptian marriage as a loan (δάνειον). See Häge, 108-125.

(d)   In our document the *ketubbah* is secured by all the movable and immovable property of Samuel which then guarantees the maintenance and clothing of Metra (*l.*25). Such a guarantee, the editors note, is not found in any other *ketubbah*. In the Talmud it is the husband personally, and not his property, who is responsible for the upkeep of his wife. The property merely guarantees the payment of the *ketubbah* on divorce or his decease. Interestingly we find in Greek deeds of marriage (e.g. from Alexandria in the time of Augustus) a similar understanding of the husband's guarantee where the dowry is fundamental to the husband's obligation to maintain his wife: τὸν Διονύσιον ἀπεσχηκότα τὴν προκειμένην φερνὴν τρέφειν καὶ ἱματίζειν τὴν Ἰσιδώραν ὡς γυναῖκα γαμετὴν κατὰ δύναμιν κτλ — 'Dionysius having received the aforementioned dowry will maintain and clothe Isidora as a married wife to the best of his ability etc.' (BGU IV 1050). See further Häge, 75-91, and Modrzejewski, 261-4.[10] It is further paralleled in the marriage agreements between Jewish couples recorded in Greek. See P. Yadin 18, 37 and DJD XXVII 69.

Earlier Jewish Marriage Documents

(a) Fifth Century BC Marriage Documents in Aramaic from Egypt

The influence of Assyrian, Persian and Egyptian practice on the papyri of Elephantine is readily admitted (Kraeling, p.52). The influence results from the fluid nature of legal custom which was affected by successive conquests and attraction to the practices of the dominant power. In these papyri are a number of marriage contracts. Marriages are often mixed. For example, in Cowley 15 (435 BC) an Egyptian Ashor b. Seho marries Mibtahiah, the daughter of Mahseiah. Her previous marriage also appears to have been to an Egyptian (Cowley 14, 440 BC). In Kraeling 2, Ananiah b. Haggai marries Tamut who by virtue of her name and status was probably Egyptian.

Before the bride reached marriageable age, she may be betrothed by contract with compensation payable in case of default (Cowley 48). The marriage itself is agreed between the groom and the bride's *paterfamilias* (par. OT custom).[11] The proposal of marriage is addressed by the groom (in the first person) to the *paterfamilias* (in the second person). A *mohar* is usually exchanged from the groom to the *paterfamilias* (par. OT custom). In Cowley 15 (435 BC) the *mohar* is paid to the bride's father. In Kraeling 2 (449 BC) no *mohar* is paid. Here Ananiah b. Azariah contracts to marry Tamut, the handmaiden of Meshullam b. Zakkur. She is still in her master's power, as Kraeling 5 (a contract releasing Tamut and her daughter from servitude but obliging them to *paramone*, dated 427 BC) shows, even after her marriage. It is unclear whether her still being a maidservant affected the payment of the *mohar* in this instance, but this may well be implied in the fact that a *mohar* is paid for her released daughter. In Kraeling 7 (420 BC) Ananiah b. Haggai contracts to marry Tamut's daughter. The *mohar* is paid to her 'brother', Zakkur b. Meshullam, the heir and son of her and her mother's former

---

[10] Two further features of the *ketubbah* document might also be noted:

    (i) The recording of mutual obligations of both spouses is a feature of Greek contracts from Egypt, but is also found in Palestinian tradition (ed. pr. p.39).

    (ii) The fact that our document appears to be one of two copies, one given to each of the contracting parties, may reflect Greek practice (ed. pr. p.59). The creation of duplicate copies might be due to the fact that the contract records the mutual obligations of the parties, another feature of our document which shows possible Greek influence.

[11] In Cowley 18 (c. 425 BC), which is the end of a marriage contract, it is unclear how extensive the role of the bride's mother was. At least she appears to have provided the bride with the property she brought into the marriage.

master, and to whom she was still bound by the *paramone* contract of 427 BC. The evidence is somewhat ambiguous as to whose daughter she really was. Cf. Kraeling 5 *ll*.5-8 with Kraeling 4 *l*.18 and Kraeling 7 *ll*.3-4, 41 where she is described as Zakkur b. Meshullam's sister.

In these documents the bride's personal possessions which she brings to her husband's house are recorded and valued. The *mohar* appears to have been included in the total valuation of this property, even though it is recorded as given to the bride's *paterfamilias*.[12] Is it then a fictive payment? Against this suggestion it must be noted that the *mohar* is recorded as given and received. Also there is no guarantee clause for repayment of the bride's property, as one might have expected if the payment was fictive. Both features suggest an actual payment. The value of the *mohar* may have been affected by whether the bride had previously been married or not.[13]

Divorce could be initiated by either party. In the case of divorce the wife received back her property (inclusive of the *mohar* regardless of who initiated it). The person, however, who initiated the divorce appears to have had to pay the 'divorce money' which was a fixed amount and probably covered the cost of divorce (Kraeling, p.202). If the husband expelled his wife, an act which was not legal divorce, he had to pay a penalty which was agreed in the contract. In the case of death, either the surviving spouse inherited control of the property between them (Kraeling 2) or all property belonging to the deceased (Cowley 15, Kraeling 7). Again it would be of interest to know whether the legal status of the wife (in Kraeling 2 the bride is a handmaiden) affected her right to inherit from her husband and whether this accounts for the difference in the clause. However, it should be noted that in Cowley 15 and Kraeling 7 the stipulation is added that the wife inherits where there is no heir. It is also unclear what is meant by 'the property between them', but I assume that it refers to the property recorded in the contract as well as that jointly acquired after the marriage. Gifts, if given, are from the bride's family. There does not appear to be a gift from the groom to the bride.

(b) Second Century AD Marriage Documents in Aramaic from Palestine

The Aramaic contracts appear to consist of the following elements:

(I) Orientation

(a) Date and place: See P. Yadin 10 *l*.1, P. Mur. 20 *l*.1, 21 *ll*.1 and 6, XHev/Se 11 *l*.1. The day and month are given according to the Jewish calendar, the year according to Roman provincial dating.

(b) Naming of parties: 'N. son of N. from N. says to N. daughter of N.'. It will be noted that the wording of this section is in the third person. It serves to orientate the contract which from this point on is rendered in direct speech as the address of the groom to the bride. See P. Mur. 20 *ll*.1-2, 21 *ll*.1-2 and 6-7.

(II) The words of the groom to the bride

(a) Proposal: 'You will be my wife according to the law of Moses and the Jews/Israel, and I will feed and clothe you and through your *ketubbah* I will bring you in'. Unlike the earlier

---

[12] See Kraeling, 146, 201-2, against the reading of Cowley 15. Note that the total sum at Cowley 15 *l*.14 appears to have included the value of the *mohar* paid by the groom. For an English translation of the corrected text see Porten & Yardeni, p.33.

[13] Like later custom in Roman times, the price paid for an unmarried bride may have been twice that for a woman who had previously been married. Cf. Cowley 15 *l*.5 with Kraeling 7 *l*.5, but note that the amount in Kraeling 7 is restored.

contracts from Elephantine the proposal is addressed by the groom (first person) to the bride (second person). Also it is expressly stated that the marriage is in accord with Jewish law and custom (DJD II, p.110). A promise is also added to maintain the wife. See P. Yadin 10 *ll.*4-5, P. Mur. 20 *ll.*2-4, 21 *ll.*6-7, XHev/Se 11 *l.*2.

(b)   Statement of *ketubbah* and other obligations owed by the groom: 'I owe you the sum of ... together with your food, clothes and sexual relation.' See P. Yadin 10 *ll.*6-10, P. Mur. 20 *ll.*4-6, 21 *ll.*9-10(?), XHev/Se 11 *l.*3(?).

(c)   Promise to redeem and take back the wife, if taken captive. See P. Yadin 10 *ll.*10-11, P. Mur. 20 *l.*6.[14]

(d)   Provisions in case of death:

(i)   For sons to inherit the money of the *ketubbah*, if the wife predeceases her husband. See P. Mur. 20 *ll.*7-8, 21 *ll.*12-14.

(ii)   Again, if the wife predeceases her husband, for daughters to be maintained from the estate of the groom until they themselves marry. See P. Yadin 10 *l.*14, P. Mur. 20 *ll.*8-9, 21 *ll.*10-12.

(iii) If the husband predeceases the wife, for the bride to be maintained from the estate of the groom. Maintenance can be limited by repayment of the *ketubbah*. See P. Yadin 10 *ll.*15-16, P. Mur. 20 *ll.*9-11, 21 *ll.*14-16.

(e)   Guarantee: The amount owed by the groom is guaranteed by a pledge over all his property, both present and what he will acquire in the future. See P. Mur. 20 *ll.*11-13, 21 *l.*16(?). See also the wording of the traditional Jewish *ketubbah*.[15] It does not appear ever to guarantee the maintenance of the bride, as in the above *ketubbah* from Egypt and the Greek-language contracts, P. Yadin 18, 37 and DJD XXVII 69 (see below).

(f)   Promise to renew the document. See P. Mur. 20 *ll.*13-4, 21 *ll.*19-20.

(g)   Acceptance of the conditions of the contract by the groom. See P. Yadin 10 *l.*18, P. Mur. 21 *ll.*17-18(?).

(III) The signatures

(h)   On verso the signatures of the parties and witnesses. See P. Mur. 20 *l.*18, 21 *ll.*21-27, and P. Yadin 10 (verso) *ll.*1-8.

Many of the above features are typical of the Palestinian *ketubbah*, as reconstructed from the clauses recorded in *m.Keth.* 4.7-12 and *Qidd.* 3.1.[16] However, due to the fragmentary nature of the Palestinian contracts, no one document in its extant text contains all the above features. The surviving text of P. Yadin 10 contains I a, and II a, b, c, d2 and d3, but in all probability the document originally included all clauses.

P. Mur. 20 (*c.* AD 117, the groom is a priest from the sacerdotal family of Eliasib) appears to contain all clauses with the exception of II g. Unfortunately, the papyrus has lost about half of the text along its left-hand side. This is particularly significant as it is in this portion of the contract that the dowry was probably mentioned. The editors, however, conjecture that there was no mention of the *mohar* (i.e. the bride-price paid by the groom to the bride or her family), but only a mention of the dowry or property that the wife brought into the marriage (DJD II, p.110). The suggestion is prompted by the Greek document P. Mur. 115, and the Aramaic text is reconstructed on the basis of the traditional *ketubbah*. There are two difficulties with this editorial procedure. The first

---

[14] The editors of P. Mur. 20 had originally understood the clause to refer to divorce. The text of P. Yadin 10 shows this not to be the case.

[15] An English translation is cited at the beginning of the Mishnah tractate *Ketubbah* in P. Blackman, *Mishnayoth*, vol. 3 (Gateshead 1983) 123

[16] See Yadin, Greenfield, Yardeni, 'Babatha's *Ketubbba*', p.92.

concerns the appropriateness of using a marriage document between a Jewish couple but written in Greek to understand and interpret a legal instrument in Aramaic. The language of a document may well be significant in determining the legal system applicable in it. One has only to recall the rule that came to apply in Ptolemaic Egypt that the language of the document was determinative of the court and thus legal system (*P. Tebt.* I 5 *ll.*207-220, Tebtynis, 118 BC). Second, in reconstructing the Aramaic text from the traditional *ketubbah* no allowance is made for recording the *mohar* or promissory *ketubbah*, but instead the text is reconstructed from the promise to maintain the wife which follows immediately on the proposal and the obligations listed after the statement of the *mohar/ketubbah*. The prompt to this reconstruction appears to be the conjectured reading ועַ]לי at the end of *l.*4; the word begins the list of obligations after the statement of the *mohar/ketubbah*. But the reading is cast in doubt by the subsequently published Aramaic marriage contract, P. Yadin 10. Here, after the proposal and the promise to maintain the wife is found a statement of the *ketubbah* owed ('I owe you the sum of four hundred zuzin' — קים לך עלי כסף זוזין ארבע מאה) followed by a list of obligations. It is not implausible that a similar expression stood in P. Mur. 20, e.g. ... עלי קים לך. Cf. קים in P. Mur. 20 *l.*6. The reconstructed understanding of the debt as a *ketubbah* owed by the groom to his bride is further confirmed by the following fragmentary marriage contract, P. Mur. 21, where the sum is called כסף כתבתיך — 'sum of your *ketubbah*', *ll.*10 and 16.

Of interest in these documents is the fact that the proposal of marriage is made between the spouses. The bride no longer is represented by her *paterfamilias*. The document records the various obligations of the groom to the bride. In that sense it is a unilateral document which protects the rights of the bride. This explains the summary acknowledgement of the groom recorded at the end of each text. It will also be noted that the *mohar* has become the *ketubbah*, i.e. an amount promised rather than actually paid for the bride.[17] Also new to this type of document is the guarantee clause. The introduction of the guarantee is attributed to Shimon b. Setah in the first century BC (*m. Keth.* 4.7, *b. Keth.* 51a, 82b — 'all property which is mine are pledged for your *ketubbah*' — כל נכסי דאית לי אחראין לכתבתיך). As such its addition to the contract enabled the bride-price to become a promissory rather than an actual payment. One may ask whether the introduction of the guarantee reflects Greek legal usage. Of further interest is the fact that no document appears to record the property brought into the marriage by the bride. This is in contradistinction to the earlier documents from Elephantine and the contemporary marriage documents in Greek (see below). As such this feature attests the essentially Jewish legal nature of these documents.

(c) Marriage between Jews documented in Greek

There are five extant documents in this group. They are P. Mur. 115 (AD 124), 116 (?), P. Yadin 18 (AD 128), 37 (= DJD XXVII 65, AD 131) and DJD XXVII 69 (AD 130).

The documents are in two forms depending on who the parties are. These can be the groom and either the bride or her parent, who gives the bride away. The dowry in each instance is conceived in the Greek manner as being a transfer of property from the bride to the groom.

---

[17] The editors of DJD XXVII (pp.267-8) doubt that 'the money of the *ketubbah*' of P. Mur. 21 and P. Yadin 10 is the *ketubbah* of rabbinic marital practice. I see no justification for their scepticism, especially given the Jewish nature of much of these documents.

Type I: Contracts between spouses

This type contains two forms. They will be indicated in the analysis below.

(a) Date and place: P. Mur. 115 *ll.*1-2, P. Yadin 37 *ll.*1-3. The date follows Roman convention by year, month and day.

(b) Acknowledgement of marriage: This element is in two forms. The contract from Wadi Murabba'at has two parts: (i) naming and details of the parties (P. Mur. 115 *ll.*2-3); and (ii) acknowledgement of marriage (P. Mur. 115 *ll.*2-5). This division appears to reflect that found in the Aramaic *ketubboth*. See above. The contract from Arabia (P. Yadin 37) avoids the repetition of this construction by combining the naming and details with the acknowledgement of marriage (P. Yadin 37 *ll.*3-6). The acknowledgement of marriage in both forms is phrased objectively, i.e. 'N.N. (groom) acknowledges (third person) to have taken N.N. (bride) for a wedded woman'. In this regard both are different from the proposal of the *ketubbah*, which is subjective and addressed in the first person by the groom to the bride.

(c) Receipt of dowry: See P. Mur. 115 *ll.*5-6 and P. Yadin 37 *ll.*6-9. The dowry is conceived as brought into the marriage by the bride. It is variously called: προίξ (P. Mur. 115 *ll.*5-6, P. Yadin 37 *l.*6) and φερνή (P. Mur. 116 *l.*6). It may be minimally described as consisting of gold, silver, clothing and other female things. In P. Mur. 115 the editors note (DJD II, p. 252) that the amount of the dowry is the same as the legal minimum prescribed by the Mishnah (*m.Keth.* 1.2) for a virgin. As this is a document of remarriage (between the same spouses) they postulate that it may have been the sum taken out by the wife on the dissolution of the first marriage.

From this point on the form diverges.

P. Yadin 37

(d) Statement of the groom's obligations: Receipt of the dowry obliged the husband to feed and clothe his wife and their children in accord with Greek law and custom. See P. Yadin 37 *ll.*9-10.

(e) Acceptance of obligations: The obligations are accepted by the groom against his personal good faith and the risk of all his property, both present and future. Exaction for failure to meet these obligations was at the discretion of the bride or her agent. See P. Yadin 37 *ll.*10-13.

These features (i.e. d and e) appear absent from the contracts from Wadi Murabba'at, but are paralleled in the documents of Type II from Arabia. See P. Yadin 18. In DJD XXVII 69 the obligation is for the upkeep of the wife only.

(f) Acknowledgement of conditions: The groom was asked in good faith and acknowledged all the conditions of the contract. See P. Yadin 37 *ll.*13-14.

(g) Agreement of bride's guardian. See P. Yadin 37 *l.*15. Lewis (p.133) considers this as a sign that the father of the bride was absent or deceased. For the editors of DJD XXVII (pp.235-6) the use of a guardian is a sign of romanization. As the bride was no longer a minor but an adult, under Jewish law she did not need a guardian; the fact that she used one is paralleled in Graeco-Roman legal practice, though the usual term used there is κύριος rather than ἐπίτροπος.

P. Mur. 115 and 116

(d) The groom's obligations:

(i) Maintenance of the children (male and female) from the property of the husband: P. Mur. 115 *ll.*8-10.

(ii) Arrangements in view of death

— predecease of husband: the right of wife to maintenance or to her dowry (P. Mur. 115 *ll.*10-12, P. Mur. 116 *ll.*8-12).
— predecease of wife: sons inherit her *ketubbah* and after the groom's death a portion of his estate (P. Mur. 115 *ll.*12-14, P. Mur. 116 *ll.*4-8).

(e)   Guarantee or execution clause (P. Mur. 115 *ll*.16-18). Execution can be exacted from him or his property (present and future).

(f)   Signatures of parties and witnesses: P. Mur. 115 verso. All appear to sign in Greek; cf. P. Yadin 18 and DJD XXVII 69 below.

It will be noted that the clauses under (d) in P. Mur. 115-6 accord with Jewish marital practice. See the above analysis of the *ketubbah*. It is therefore of great interest that P. Yadin 37, which contains quite different clauses, states openly that the husband's obligations are according to Greek law and custom. Lewis (p.130) was inclined to see P. Yadin 37 as Jewish in nature, documenting the conversion of an arrangement of betrothal to one of marriage. It was occasioned by the bride's coming of age. The editors of DJD XXVII (pp.227-9) convincingly refute this, arguing that it is better understood as documenting the conversion of an unwritten marriage to a written one. It was the receipt of the dowry which then occasioned it. The Greek nature of the document is evident.

Type II: Contracts between the groom and the bride's parent

(a)   Date and place: P. Yadin 18 *ll*.1-3, DJD XXVII 69 *ll*.1-3. The date follows Roman convention with respect to year, day and month.

(b)   Giving of the bride by her parent: In P. Yadin 18 the marriage contract is between the bride's father and the groom: ὁ δεῖνα (bride's father) ἐξέδοτο τὴν ἰδίαν θυγατέραν αὐτοῦ παρθένον τῷ δεῖνι (groom) ... εἶναι τὴν δεῖνα (bride) γυναῖκα γαμετὴν πρὸς γάμου κοινωνίαν κατὰ τοὺς νόμους (*ll*.3-7). In DJD XXVII 69 (*ll*.3-5) it is between the bride's mother, Sela, acting through her guardian and the groom. The fact that the bride was given away in both instances does not imply that she was, in accord with Jewish law, a minor; the practice rather appears to reflect what is found in the Graeco-Roman papyri of Egypt. The naming is styled objectively from the bride's parents' perspective.

(c)   Description of the dowry and its mutually agreed valuation: The descriptive element is minimal, only naming such generic groups as gold, silver, clothing etc. Interestingly the dowry is described as brought into the marriage by the bride. See P. Yadin 18 *ll*.7-10 and DJD XXVII 69 *ll*.6-7. It is termed προσφορά and/or προίξ.

(d)   Acknowledgement of receipt of dowry by groom: The acknowledgement is phrased objectively, i.e. 'The groom acknowledged that he has taken from N.N. (bride) in cash forthwith from her father and owes her etc'. The value of the dowry (προσφορά) might be supplemented by a gift from the groom to his bride. The value of the gift is added to the sum of the dowry and together they constitute the προίξ. See P. Yadin 18 *ll*.10-15 and DJD XXVII 69 *ll*.8-9.

(e)   The groom's obligations: Receipt of the dowry obliged the husband to feed and clothe his wife and their children. See P. Yadin 18 *ll*.15-20. This obligation was expressed to be in accord with Greek law. The obligation is accepted by the groom against his own good faith and the risk of all his property, both present and future. Cf. also DJD XXVII 69 *ll*.10-11 Exaction for failure to meet these obligations was at the discretion of the bride or her agent. It is interesting to note the divergence of DJD XXVII 69 *ll*.9-11 at this point. Though the text is fragmentary, there does not appear to be an obligation to maintain the children and the obligation is not stated to be in accord with Greek law/custom. What follows in *ll*.11ff., however, appears from the extant text to be a statement of the obligations found in *ketubbah* documents (i.e. P. Mur. 20, 21, P. Yadin 10) and P. Mur. 115 and 116, i.e. in the case of the bride's predecease, the dowry was to be inherited by the male children and any daughters were to be maintained from the estate of the husband (*ll*.11-13); in the case of the husband's predecease (*ll*.14-15), the wife was to be maintained or she might receive her dowry and leave (DJD XXVII, pp.263-4, 270-3). This same sequence of conditional clauses is found in P. Mur. 20, 21 and 116. The clauses represent some of the court stipulations required of Jewish marriage.

(f)   Rescinding the contract: The groom agrees to exchange without argument this contract for the monetary value of the dowry, including the value of the supplementary gift, whenever asked by his bride. This is an interesting feature, for if one assumes that a Jewish wife could not initiate divorce, she does however appear to have been able to initiate the return of her dowry. The dowry is thus conceived as a debt owed by the groom to the bride which she could then call up at any time. The effect of such an action is unstated, but it is reasonable to assume that it would prompt the ending of the marriage. See P. Yadin 18 *ll*.20-23.

(g)   Penalty and execution clause: A twofold penalty applies if the husband fails to repay, with the wife or her agent holding the discretionary right of exaction against his person or property. See P. Yadin 18 *ll*.23-27.

(h)   Acknowledgement of conditions: The groom was asked in good faith and acknowledged all the conditions of the contract. See P. Yadin 18 *ll*.27-28.

(i)   Summary in two parts: The summary is in Aramaic and styled subjectively in the first person. The bride's father states that he has given his daughter to the groom according to the conditions of the contract. The groom then states that he is in debt (בחובה) for the agreed sum of money which is his bride's dowry (פרן - φερνή) in accord with the conditions of the contract. See P. Yadin 18 *ll*.68-72.

(j)   Signature of scribe. See P. Yadin 18 *l*.73.

(k)   On the verso the signatures of the parties and witnesses. See P. Yadin 18 *ll*.74-80 (only one signs in Greek, the others in Aramaic), DJD XXVII 69 verso *ll*.1ff (all sign in Greek as in P. Mur. 115).

There has been some dispute as to the nature of the marriages contracted in these documents. Are they Jewish or Greek (Hellenistic) marriages? Lewis (pp.76-82) understood it to be largely Jewish. The fact that the father gave his daughter in marriage is explained by Jewish custom, if she was still a minor. The laws referred to in P. Yadin 18 *l*.7 are Jewish and the expression parallels the wording of the more traditional *ketubbah* which is contracted according to the law of Moses and the Jews/Israel. Wasserstein (pp.108-113) rejects the Jewish interpretation of the documents' underlying legal conception. In particular, he notes the reference to Hellenistic law (*l*.16), the absence of any reference to the law of Moses and the Jews/Israel, and the fact that the bride is given away (*l*. 3), though she was not a minor.[18] He entertains the possibility that a separate *ketubbah* document may have been drawn up, but that the Greek document was contracted as an added safeguard for the bride, enforcible in a non-Jewish court (p.121).

One notes with interest that the summary and signatures are Aramaic and that in the previous generation the bride's father had contracted his marriage in a Jewish *ketubbah* written in Aramaic (P. Yadin 10). The linguistic residual might be seen as an indication of Jewish cultural continuity with assimilation to Greek custom where convenient. As the editors of DJD XXVII (pp.254-5) state: 'The Babatha Archive has taught us that the use of Greek in legal documents does not reveal Hellenized Jews: their signatures and subscriptions in Aramaic prove the opposite'. Further evidence of an underlying Jewish conception is the prevalence of clauses differentiating provisions for male and female children in the case of the predecease of the wife. With reference to DJD XXVII 69 Cotton (pp.82-5) argues for a greater degree of assimilation. Of particular interest is the absence of any reference to 'the law of Moses and the Jews', and nature of the dowry. The payment is unlike the *mohar* and *ketubbah* which is paid or promised to be paid from the groom to the bride. The dowry is in this and other Jewish marriage contracts

---

[18] See also Cotton, *JRS* p.77, on DJD XXVII 69. There is no indication that the mother in giving the bride away in this document was following Jewish law.

written in Greek (i.e. P. Mur. 115, P. Yadin 18, 37) a valued amount brought into the marriage by the bride. Unlike Wasserstein, Cotton seems to accept a greater degree of assimilation. She does not mention any parallel *ketubbah* document but notes instead: 'These Jews felt free to use legal forms which went together with the use of Greek language. They did not seem to be conscious of the existence of a prescriptive form for the writing of their marriage contracts'. She sees this as an indication that Jewish contractual forms had not yet become normative. The motive to adopt Greek legal forms was to make the contract enforcible in a gentile court, the initiative for this coming, no doubt, from the fact that the payment was now from the bride to the groom. Greater protection was thus offered to the bride.

The possible reference to a gentile court prompts one to ask what court. It is improbable that the Greek court of a city could be meant as this presupposed that the initiating party was a citizen. The Babatha archive provides the clue in that the actions against her son's guardians are brought before the Roman governor. It was the Roman court of a provincial official who heard cases by *cognitio*. This type of court offered greater legal freedom. The judge's legal thinking was invariably Roman; however, he was not compelled to employ any one legal system in deciding the case, rather he respected the legal conventions of the subject peoples, only overturning them in the odd instances where a convention or custom appeared barbaric. It is this freedom from the use of any one legal system that might explain the rather mixed nature of customs and conditions met in these documents which draw expressly from Greek as well as from Jewish legal practice.

There is a difficulty in accepting the Greek legal basis of P. Yadin 18, 37 and DJD XXVII 69, and that is the fact that the property of the husband, both present and future, does not secure the dowry, but rather the maintenance of the wife and her children. It is interesting to note that also in the above *ketubbah* from Egypt the same guarantee of maintenance is met. In Greek contracts from Egypt, the guarantee secures the return of the dowry only, though here no word is spoken of future possession in the guarantee clause. The latter is a feature, however, of Jewish documents. But it is of little use to appeal to Jewish law to explain the wife's right to maintenance, as here also the guarantee functions to secure the future payment of the *ketubbah*, if required either in case of divorce or death, e.g. P. Mur. 20 *ll*.11-13.[19] A parallel, however, is to be found in Egyptian marital practice. Here an alimentation capital was paid to the groom for the maintenance of his wife. In consideration of this amount the husband made yearly payments in cash or kind to his wife, and his property (present and future) was pledged as a guarantee of this.[20] Interestingly the Greeks considered the arrangement a loan. One might compare here the use of ὀφείλειν in P. Yadin 18 *l*.12. The clause may, however, have resulted from a confluence of legal conceptions. When the financial consideration of the marriage changed from an obligation on the groom (i.e. the *mohar*) to an obligation on the bride (i.e. the dowry), it is to be expected that the responsibility of the husband should be defined expressly in any subsequent document.

In summary, one finds from the study of the above *ketubboth* that it is difficult to understand Jewish marital contracts under any one legal system. Practice is not normative, but evolving. Customs and conventions are adopted from the surrounding cultures and are reflected in the clauses and language of the documents.

---

[19] See DJD XXVII, 269-70.
[20] See *New Docs* 6 (1992) 6-9.

Bibliography

H.M. **Cotton**, 'The Guardianship of Jesus Son of Babatha: Roman and Local Law in the Province of Arabia', *JRS* 83 (1993) 94-108; H.M. **Cotton** & E. **Qimron**, 'XHev/Se ar 13 of 134 or 135CE: A Wife's Renunciation of Claims', *JJS* 49 (1998) 108-118; H. **Cotton** & A. **Yardeni**, *Aramaic. Hebrew and Greek Documentary Texts from Nahal Hever and Other Sites* (DJD XXVII. Clarendon: Oxford 1997); A.E. **Cowley**, *Aramaic papyri of the fifth century B.C.* (Oxford 1923); M.A. **Friedman**, *Jewish Marriage in Palestine. A Cairo Geniza Study* (2 vols. Tel Aviv & New York 1980-81); G. **Häge**, *Ehegüterrechtliche Verhältnisse in den griechischen Papyri Ägyptens bis Diokletian* (Köln-Graz 1968); E.G. **Kraeling**, *The Brooklyn Museum Aramaic papyri : new documents of the fifth century B.C. from the Jewish colony at Elephantine* (New York 1969); N. **Lewis** (ed.), *The Documents from the Bar Kochba Period in the Cave of Letters: Greek Papyri* (Jerusalem 1989); J. **Modrzejewski**, 'La structure juridique du mariage grec', *Scritti in onore di Orsolina Montevecchi* (Bologna 1981) 231-68; B. **Porten** & A. **Yardeni**, *Textbook of Aramaic Documents from Ancient Egypt*, vol.2 Contracts (Jerusalem 1988); A. **Wasserstein**, 'A Marriage Contract from the Province of Arabia Nova: Notes on Papyrus Yadin 18', *JQR* 80 (1989) 93-130; Y. **Yadin**, J. **Greenfield**, A. **Yardeni**, 'Babatha's *Ketubbba*', *IEJ* 44 (1994) 75-101.

S.R. Llewelyn

ECCLESIASTICA

§28 Fragment from the Unknown Gospel (Papyrus Egerton 2)

Unknown provenance   Papyrus leaf (5.5 x 3 cm)   mid-II

Ed. — M. Gronewald in *Kölner Papyri*, vol. 6, eds M. Gronewald, B. Kramer, K. Maresch, M. Parca and C. Römer (Opladen 1987) 136-145 (= P. Köln 255).

verso (↑)   recto (→)

```
19  [        ]τοισυπαυτου[      ]    42  [ ]π[                        ]
    [      ]οις· ειγαρεπι [     ]        δεαυτωοιη[                   ]
21  [      ]επιστευσατεα[      ]    44  τονεπιδειξον[                ]
    [  ]ρ[ ]εμουγαρεκεινο[     ]        και ανενεγ´κον[             ]
                  `ϋ´                              `προ[ ´ ]
23  [    ]ντοισπατ[  ] σιν⟦η⟧μω[   ]    46  [ ]αρισμουως⟦επ⟧ε[       ]
    [    ] ε[       ].[          ]        [ ]ηκετια[  ]ρτανε  [      ]
            - - -                    48  [           ]¯[           ]
```

There is sufficient text to distinguish similarities to gospel accounts. More particularly, the verso and recto can be seen to continue the narratives on the verso and recto of Fragment 1 of Papyrus Egerton 2, or the Unknown Gospel (= UG), originally published by Bell and Skeat (P. Lond. Christ. 1, 1935):

verso (↑)

```
        - - -

    ]ι [
[  ....  ..] τοῖς νομικο[ῖς
[  ....]ντα τὸν παραπράσσ[οντα
[  ....]μον καὶ μὴ ἐμέ· [ ]α ..
5   [ ....] οποιεῖ πῶς ποιε[ῖ·] πρὸς
    [δὲ τοὺς] ἄ[ρ]χοντας τοῦ λαοῦ [στ]ρα-
    [φεὶς εἶ]πεν τὸν λόγον τοῦτο[ν·] ἐραυ-
    [νᾶτε τ]ὰς γραφάς· ἐν αἷς ὑμεῖς δο-
    [κεῖτε] ζωὴν ἔχειν ἐκεῖναί εἰ[σ]ιν
10  [αἱ μαρτ]υροῦσαι περὶ ἐμοῦ· μὴ ν[ομί-]
    [ζετε ὅ]τι ἐγὼ ἦλθον κατηγο[ρ]ῆσαι
    [ὑμῶν] πρὸς τὸν π(ατέ)ρα μου· ἔστιν
    [ὁ κατη]γορῶν ὑμῶν Μω(ϋσῆς) εἰς ὃν
    [ὑμεῖς] ἠλπίκατε· α[ὐ]τῶν δὲ λε-
15  [γόντω]ν ὅ[τι] οἴδαμεν ὅτι Μω(ϋσεῖ) ἐλά-
    [λησεν] ὁ θ(εό)ς [·] σὲ δὲ οὐκ οἴδαμεν
    [πόθεν εἶ] · ἀποκριθεὶς ὁ Ἰη(σοῦς) εἶ-
    [πεν αὐτο]ῖς· νῦν κατηγορεῖται
    [ὑμῶν τὸ ἀ]πιστεῖ[ν] **τοῖς ὑπ' αὐτοῦ**
20  **[μεμαρτυρη]μένοις·** εἰ γὰρ ἐπι-
    [στεύσατε Μω(ϋσεῖ)] · **ἐπιστεύσατε ἄ[ν]**
    **[ἐμοί·** πε]ρ[ὶ] **ἐμοῦ γὰρ ἐκεῖνο[ς]**
    **[ἔγραψε]ν** τοῖς **πατ[ρά]σιν ὑμῶ[ν]**
    [          ]ε[ .... ... ].[      ]
              - - -
```

And turning to the rulers of the people
he spoke this word: Search
the Scriptures; in them you
think you have life. It is these
which bear witness to me. Do not
think that I have come to accuse
you before my Father. Moses it is
who accuses you – the one in whom
you hope. When they began
saying: We know that God spoke
to Moses but as for you, we do not know
whence you came, Jesus replied and said
to them: Now is condemned
your unbelief in his
testimony. For if you had believed
Moses, you would have believed
me; since he wrote about me
for your fathers ...

recto (→)

- - -

25	[. . . . . . .]. ω[. . . .]. [ ]	... [to the crowd] ...
	[. . . . .] λίθους ὁμοῦ . . [ ]	to [pick up] stones together [and stone]
	σι[ν αὐ]τόν· καὶ ἐπέβαλον [τὰς]	him. And the rulers sought to lay
	χεῖ[ρας] αὐτῶν ἐπ' αὐτὸν οἱ [ἄρχον-]	hands on him
	τες [ἵ]να πιάσωσιν καὶ παρ[	to seize him and [hand him over?]
30	. . [. .]. τῷ ὄχλῳ· καὶ οὐκ ἠ[δύναντο]	to the crowd. And they were not able
	αὐτὸν πιάσαι ὅτι οὔπω ἐ[ληλύθει]	to seize him for the hour of his handing
	αὐτοῦ ἡ ὥρα τῆς παραδό[σεως·]	over had not yet come.
	αὐτὸς δὲ ὁ κ(ύριο)ς ἐξελθὼν [ἐκ τῶν χει-]	And so the Lord himself passing out of their
	ρῶν ἀπένευσεν ἀπ' α[ὐτῶν·]	hands departed from them.
35	καὶ [ἰ]δοὺ λεπρὸς προσελθ[ὼν αὐτῷ]	And behold a leper came to him
	λέγει· διδάσκαλε Ἰη(σο)ῦ λε[προῖς συν-]	and said: Teacher Jesus, while
	ὁδεύων καὶ συνεσθίω[ν αὐτοῖς]	travelling and eating with lepers
	ἐν τῷ πανδοχείῳ ἐλ[επρίασα]	in the inn I have caught leprosy
	καὶ αὐτὸς ἐγώ· ἐὰν [ο]ὖν [σὺ θέλῃς]	myself. If therefore you will,
40	καθαρίζομαι· ὁ δὴ κ(ύριο)ς [ἔφη αὐτῷ·]	I shall be clean. And the Lord said to him:
	θέλ[ω] καθαρίσθητι· [καὶ εὐθέως]	I will, be cleansed. And immediately
	[ἀ]πέστη ἀπ' αὐτοῦ ἡ λέπ[ρα· λέγει]	the leprosy left him. **And Jesus said**
	δὲ αὐτῷ ὁ Ἰη(σοῦ)ς [·] πορε[υθεὶς σεαυ-]	**to him:** Go and
	τὸν ἐπίδειξον τοῖ[ς ἱερεῦσιν]	show yourself to the priests
45	καὶ ἀνένεγκον [περὶ τοῦ κα-]	and offer for your
	[θ]αρισμοῦ ὡς προ[σ]έ[τ]αξεν Μω(ϋσῆ)ς	cleansing as Moses commanded.
	καὶ]	And
	[μ]ηκέτι ἁ[μά]ρτανε [ ]	sin no longer . . .
	[ ]⁻.[ ]	

- - -

The surviving text of P. Köln 255 (identified by bold lettering above) enables some correction to the reconstruction proposed by Bell and Skeat, notably at *ll*.42-43 (= Bell and Skeat 39-40). It is noteworthy in *l*.43 that the abbreviation IH̅ for IH̅Σ is also to be found elsewhere in the UG (for example at Fragment 2, *l*.50).

Debate on the UG has largely centred on its relationship to the canonical gospels. Several clear views have been expressed:

(i)   In respect of the synoptic gospels, arguments have been put for the dependence of UG on the gospels (Wright, Jeremias) and their independence (Mayeda, Dodd, Pryor).

(ii)   In respect of John's Gospel, arguments have also been put for John's dependence on UG (Bell and Skeat, Koester); for independence of one from the other (Mayeda); and for dependence of UG on John, quoting it either from memory or, less likely, copying it (Bell [1937], Dodd, Jeremias, Pryor).

The present fragment displays the same tendencies as the larger fragments published in 1935. Lines 19-24, reflecting the conclusion to the Jesus-Pharisees debate in John 5, continue the UG pattern of using only Johannine vocabulary in a 'Johannine' narrative, and of being relatively true to the Johannine text. It is thus difficult to agree with Jeremias, that 'the Johannine material is shot through with Synoptic phrases and the Synoptic with Johannine usage ...'.

Lines 42-48 conclude an account which is a reflection of several synoptic *pericopae* (see Bell and Skeat 29). Of greatest interest is the reflection of John 5.14 (and 8.11): μηκέτι ἁμάρτανε at the conclusion of the incident. The incident, therefore, while entirely synoptic-like in context, style and vocabulary, commences and concludes with clear recollections of the Johannine text (λίθους ὁμοῦ λιθάσωσιν αὐτόν – John 10.31; cf. 8.59; μηκέτι ἁμάρτανε – John 5.14; cf. 8.11). This may strengthen the claim that the author of the UG knows and treasures the fourth gospel, quoting it with reasonable care and due deference. If he knows any of the synoptic gospels, which can be questioned, he does not feel nearly as committed to their faithful reproduction. More likely is it that the UG reflects a time in early Christianity when living oral tradition and written word continued to live side by side and to influence Christian writers.

J.W. Pryor

Bibliography

K. **Aland**, *Repertorium* I (1976) Ap 14. H.I. **Bell** and T.C. **Skeat**, *Fragments from an Unknown Gospel* (London 1935). H.I. **Bell**, *Recent Discoveries of Biblical Papyri* (Oxford 1937). C.H. **Dodd**, 'A new Gospel', in *New Testament Studies* (Manchester, 1953). U. **Gallizia**, 'Il P. Egerton 2', *Aegyptus* 36 (1956) 29-72, 178-234. J. **Jeremias** in W. Schneemelcher (ed.), *New Testament Apocrypha* (vol. 1; London 1991) 96-99. H. **Koester**, 'Apocryphal and canonical gospels', *HTR* 73 (1980) 119-126. G. **Mayeda**, *Das Leben-Jesu-Fragment Papyrus Egerton 2 und seine Stellung in der urchristlichen Literaturgeschichte* (Bern 1946). John W. **Pryor**, 'Papyrus Egerton 2 and the Fourth Gospel', *ABR* XXXVII (1989) 1-13. **van Haelst**, *Catalogue* (1976) 586. D.F. **Wright**, 'Apocryphal gospels: the "Unknown Gospel" (Pap. Egerton 2) and the Gospel of Peter', in D. Wenham (ed.), *Gospel Perspectives: the Jesus Tradition outside the Gospels* (Sheffield 1984).

§29 Awaiting the Trumpet of God

Claudiopolis   Limestone block   late II/III?

Ed. — F. Becker-Bertau, *Die Inschriften von Klaudiu Polis, IK* 31 (Bonn 1986) 126-27 (no. 177). S. Şahin, *Bithynische Studien, IK* 7 (Bonn 1978) 54 (no. 5).

A block of reddish limestone broken off below and measuring 0.32m (h) x 1.06m (b) x 0.4m (t). The inscription was found re-used in the stairs of a house at Kandamis.

	οὐ χρυσὸς οὐκ ἀργύ-	Neither gold nor silver
	[ρ]ιν ἀλ<λ>' ὀστέα κατακί-	but bones lie here
	μενα, περιμένοντα	awaiting
	φωνὴν σάλπινγος· μὴ	the trumpet call. Do not
5	λύσις ἔργον θεοῦ γενετῆρ-	disturb the work of God the begetter
	[ος]	[...]

From a tombstone in Bithynia, this inscription raises a number of interesting issues for early Christianity. The editor, S. Şahin, has dated it as 'early Christian' without further precision. However, his use of other terminology to date inscriptions in the same volume suggests that he means thereby the late second century or the third century. There is nothing in either the content or the palaeography (particularly sigma, epsilon, and omega) which would challenge such a broad determination.

The author of the inscription was a Christian, as indicated by the biblical allusions (see below), who wished to secure the tomb from interference by graverobbers. In antiquity, among many cultures around the Mediterranean world (and beyond) it had long been the custom either to adorn the cadaver with items of jewellery indicating the person's social standing and/or to include various items, possibly as useful goods to accompany the deceased on the journey into the next world. While the latter would have had no place in Christian thinking and practice, the frequent warnings against disturbance that continued on Christian inscriptions (see, for example, Tabbernee, *passim*), as well as findings from later periods, may indicate that Christians of rank continued to be buried with adornments and other insignia of their status.

The most noteworthy feature of this inscription is that it is constructed almost entirely of New Testament echoes, thus serving as an exception to the observation of Feissel: 'Whereas funerary epigraphy is almost always the most common in all places, biblical quotations are relatively rare within this category, only a few dozen out of thousands of epigraphs.' (Feissel, 292) The most obvious is περιμένοντα φωνὴν σάλπινγος. The notion of the dead in Christ awaiting the sound of the trumpet finds its closest echo in 1 Thess. 4.16 (cf. 1 Cor. 15.52). The collocation of σάλπινξ with φωνή in certain ancient MSS at Matt. 24.31 may be thought to suggest that our author knew of this textual tradition. It should be noted, however, that in Matthew the trumpet sound does not explicitly awaken the dead — it is Paul who adapts the tradition in the light of the death of believers before the return of the Son of Man (cf. also Rev. 1.10 and 4.1).

Perhaps the most intriguing New Testament echo is to be found in *ll.*4-5: μὴ λύσις ἔργον θεοῦ. In Rom. 14.20 St Paul exhorts the Roman church: μὴ ... κατάλυε τὸ ἔργον τοῦ θεοῦ. New Testament commentators are divided in their opinion as to what

Paul meant: was he referring to the church, the οἰκοδομή of God, or was he referring to the new creation effected in an individual who believes? The association between *ll.*4-5 of our inscription and Rom. 14.20 is unmistakeable, each of which has: (a) a negative command; (b) a common verb root; and (c) the use of the phrase (τὸ) ἔργον (τοῦ) θεοῦ. Elsewhere in the New Testament the phrase is found only in the fourth gospel and denotes the spiritual/moral activity which God requires of humans, namely faith in Jesus Christ (see John 6.29).

In the papyri and in other inscriptions the phrase ἔργον θεοῦ has apparently not been found. However, between the second and fourth centuries the phrase is used among Christian writers with increasing frequency, with the following senses:

1. Creation as the work of God

1a. Man as the special work of God, the summit of creation (sometimes with reference to Gen 1.26)

2. Faith in Christ as the work which God requires (John 6.29)

2a. Other spiritual/moral values which God expects of humans

2b. Moral/spiritual values which God effects in humans

3. Christ, or the Holy Spirit, as *not* being a work of God

4. All that happens as the work of the all-pervasive God

While the Christological application of the phrase (#3 above) does not emerge until the fourth century (Basil, Epiphanius, Eusebius, Gregory of Nyssa, Athanasius), all other senses may be found prior to that date. In respect of 1a, two features are noteworthy. Firstly, the identifying of man in particular as the ἔργον θεοῦ owes much to the reading of Gen. 1.26. Indeed, on more than one occasion either the quoting of Gen. 1.26 (Chrysostom: μόνος ὁ ἄνθρωπος ἐν κτίσμασιν ἀσύγκριτον καὶ ἐξαίρετον ἔργον τοῦ θεοῦ ἐξ ὧν καὶ περὶ αὐτοῦ μόνου γέγραπται· ποιήσωμεν ... 'man alone is the incomparable and singular work of God amongst creatures apart from which also it has been written concerning him alone: Let us make ...') or the use of εἰκών or μορφή in context (e.g. Clement: ἤδη δὲ καὶ πάντας ἀνθρώπους ἑνὸς ὄντας ἔργον θεοῦ καὶ μίαν εἰκόνα ... 'actually all men are the work of one God and are one image ...') indicates that God as creator and man as the supreme ἔργον θεοῦ are associated in the early Christian mind. Secondly, it is not unknown for a writer to specify that every aspect of man, body, soul and mind, is the work of God. Indeed, both Athenagoras in the second century (οὐ μὴν οὐδ' ἐκεῖνο φαίη τις ἂν ὡς ἀνάξιον ἔργον τοῦ θεοῦ τὸ διαλυθὲν ἀναστῆσαι σῶμα καὶ συναγαγεῖν ... 'Nor in truth would one even say this, that it is an unworthy work of God to raise up and reconstitute the dissolved body ...') and Chrysostom in the fourth century (τὸ μὲν οὖν ἀναστῆσαι τῆς τοῦ θεοῦ δυνάμεως ἔργον ἐστὶν, τῇ γῇ κελεύοντος ἀφεῖναι τὴν παρακαταθήκην ... 'It is the work of God's power to raise up, commanding the earth to release its charge ...') are explicit in their claims that it is the work of God to raise the body.

The evidence, then, from the second century onwards suggests that an understanding of man, the human body, as the summit of the creating work of God, was well established in early Christianity. What is not found elsewhere is any direct assertion that dead human bones are the ἔργον θεοῦ. One is left to ponder why their disturbance would interfere with the work of God. Perhaps what lies behind such an association is the conviction that at the sound of the trumpet the very bones themselves will obey the voice of God (reminiscent of Ezek. 37) and be raised. They therefore were, are, and will be an integral part of the work of God in the person of the deceased.

The ascription of the metaphor γενητήρ to God is noteworthy on several counts. The term is not found in the LXX and is found only rarely in Greek literature of the period (Lampe cites *Orac.Sib.* 3.278 and 3.296). However, the cognate γεvv-words are common from the first century on. From the late third century, I have not yet found any Christian writer who uses the term of God, as begetter or father-creator, except in the context of Christological discussion. The term had become so closely associated with the debates over the person of Christ, and from that time on references are many to God as ἀγέννητος, Christ as begotten (γεννητός), and God as begetter (γενήτωρ or γενητής/γενετής). Prior to that period, while the term is found in a general sense referring to human birth, only Philo writes of God as the begetter-creator of all: πρὸς θεὸν τὸν γεννητὴν τῶν ὅλων ... 'to God, the begetter of all' (*Decal.* 107/8). The closest he comes to associating God's begetting with human beings is in *Spec.* 2.198: τὸν γεννητὴν καὶ πατέρα καὶ σωτῆρα τοῦ τε κόσμου καὶ τῶν ἐν κόσμῳ θεόν ... 'the begetter, father and saviour of the world as well as God of those in it'.

Finally, it is quite possible that *l*.1 is an intended echo of Acts 3.6: ἀργύριον καὶ χρυσίον οὐχ ὑπάρχει μοι — after which follows the command to the lame man: ἔγειρε καὶ περιπάτει.

As already noted, such an accumulation of biblical echoes is quite unusual in Christian inscriptions, and the sophistication of their associations indicates an integrated theological outlook on the part of the author. The text is devoid of classical echoes or any reference to traditional virtues on the part of the deceased. This, along with the anonymity of the deceased, would suggest a devout Christian of no significant rank or social or ecclesiastical standing.

Graves in the ancient world might be disturbed for one of two reasons: either in order to use the site for a further burial, and/or, as already observed, in order to rob it of its inclusions; in either case the bones might be disturbed and/or scattered. Theoretically, burial sites had the double protection both of statute laws and of piety (Schulze, 14 n.3 contains primary and secondary references). As a guard against the first possibility, some Christian inscriptions made reference to a financial penalty to be imposed (Tabbernee, #17) or the judgement of God (Tabbernee, #20, 33, 35 ⁻ ἔσται ... πρὸς τὸν θεόν). As a guard against the second possibility, some form of divine judgement is frequently invoked (Tabbernee, #35, 60-62, 64-66, 76). It is therefore noteworthy, though not unique (see Feissel, 290, for examples of such appeals to conscience on possibly pagan inscriptions from Bithynia and Scythia Minor), that in this inscription no such explicit warning is given but simply an appeal. (It is unlikely that the incomplete *l*.6 carried an explicit threat.) It is possible, however, that the appeal/command not to destroy the handiwork of God carries an implied threat — at least in the author's mind, if his/her integrated theological outlook linked Paul's teaching on God's οἰκοδομή in Rom. 14.19-20 with what he says in 1 Cor. 3.9ff, culminating in the threat of 1 Cor. 3.17: if anyone destroys God's sanctuary (i.e. the church), God will destroy that person.

It is finally noteworthy that an inscription of this period contains such a strong expression of resurrection hope unaccompanied by any statement of the ongoing life of the deceased, either by reference to sleeping (e.g. ἐνθάδε καθεύδη in Tabbernee #87) or by having entered an eternal state (e.g. Tabbernee #17, 81). Does the allusion to 1

Thess. 4.16 suggest the deceased is looked upon as now 'asleep in Christ'? Perhaps, though, as already suggested, and in a way reminiscent of Ezek. 37, it is dead bones which await the sound of the trumpet.

J.W. Pryor

Bibliography:

C. **Andresen**, *Einführung in die christliche Archäologie* (Die Kirche in ihrer Geschichte; Göttingen 1971) 49-51. W. **Calder**, 'Early Christian epitaphs in Phrygia', *Anatolian Studies* 5 (1955) 25-38. G. **Delling**, 'Speranda futura', *ThLZ* 78 (1951) 521-26. D. **Feissel**, 'The Bible in Greek inscriptions', in P.M. Blowers (ed.), *The Bible in Greek Christian Antiquity* (Notre Dame Press 1997). W.M. **Ramsay**, *The Cities and Bishoprics of Phrygia* (Oxford 1895-97). L. **Robert**, *A travers l'Asie Mineure* (Athens 1980) 140 no. 41; *Bull. Ep.* (1979) 567. V. **Schulze**, Grundriss der christlichen Archäologie (Munich 1919) 14. A. **Stuiber**, *Refrigerium interim* (Bonn 1957). W. **Tabbernee**, *Montanist Inscriptions and Testimonia* (North American Patristic Society Monograph Series 16; Mercer University Press 1997).

§30 The Earliest Dated Reference to Sunday in the Papyri

Oxyrhynchus   24.5 x 55 cm   2 October 325

Ed.:— R.A. Coles, H. Maehler and P.J. Parsons, *The Oxyrhynchus Papyri*, vol. LIV (London 1987) 170-4 (= P. Oxy. 3759).

The text is complete apart from some damage along the right edge. The papyrus has been cut from a roll containing price declarations of various guilds made to the *logistes* (P. Oxy. LIV 3747-53, all dated 26 March 319) and the following record of proceedings before the *logistes* written (*transversa charta*) on the back of this. A label (line 42) is written on the price-declaration side in the margin between declarations 3747 and 3748.

Verso (↓)

(ἔτους) κ̅ καὶ τ καὶ β̅, Φαῶφι ε̅. ἐν τῷ Κορίῳ ἱερῷ. ἐπὶ παρό[ντων]	In year 20 and 10 and 2, Phaophi 5, in the temple of Kore. In the presence
Διονυσοδώρου ὑπηρέτου καὶ Φανίου παρέδρου, Ποιμένιος ῥ(ήτωρ) εἶ(πεν)· Χαι-]	of Dionysodorus, assistant, and Phanias, assessor, Poemenius, advocate, said: 'Chaeremon,
ρήμων ἀπὸ τῶν αὐτόθι ἐντυγχάνει. οὐ δικαστήριον ε . . . . θ . . . . [συγ]-	one of the locals, petitions. I did not come (wanting) to contrive
κροτεῖν ἦλθον, μὴ τοῦτο νομίσῃς. καὶ ἑξῆς λέγοντος Ἰσχυρίων ῥ(ήτωρ) εἶ(πεν)· παρα-	a hearing, don't think this.' And while he proceeded speaking, Ischyrion, advocate, said: 'I object.
5 γράφομαι· πρὸ[ς] τίνα λέγει εἰπάτω. Ποιμένιος ῥ(ήτωρ) εἶ(πεν)· ὁ κύριός μου διασημ(ότατος)	Let him say with respect to whom he speaks.' Poemenius, advocate, said: 'My lord, *vir perfectissimus*,
ἔπαρχος τῆς Αἰγύπτου Φλάουιος Μάγνος πρὸς τὰ αὐτοτελῶς γενόμενα	prefect of Egypt, Flavius Magnus with respect to the independently made
ὑπομνήματα παρὰ τῇ στρατηγίᾳ βοηθόν σε δέδωκεν. καὶ γὰρ ἐπι-	memoranda at the office of the *strategos* has appointed you as helper. For orders
στάλματα ἐγένετο παρὰ τοῦ πραι(ποσίτου) πρὸς τοὺς δημοσίους π[ερὶ τοῦ]	came from the *praepositus* to the public (officials) concerning
παραδοῦναι τὴν νομήν. ἧττον ἐφρόντισαν πρὸς τοῦτο κ[αὶ ἀνη]-	the handing over of possession. They ignored this and
10 νέγκαμεν ἐπὶ τὸν κύριόν μου ⟦ . ⟧ τὸν ἔπαρχον καὶ . . . [c. 4]	we referred (it) to my lord ⟦...⟧ the prefect and ...
τερόν σε βοηθὸν ἔσχαμεν καὶ ἀξιοῦμεν τὴν νομὴν . . [. . παραδο]-	we obtained you as helper and ask that possession ... be handed
θῆναι. / ὁ λογιστὴς εἶ(πεν)· τί προσέταξ[ε]ν ὁ δεσπότης μου [διασημότατος]	over.' The *logistes* said: 'What did my master, *vir perfectissimus*,
ἔπαρχος τῆς Αἰγύπτου Φλάουιος Μάγνος; ⟦Ποιμένιος ῥ(ήτωρ) εἶ(πεν) ἀνα-⟧	prefect of Egypt, Flavius Magnus order?' ⟦Poemenius, advocate, said⟧

[[γ.]] καὶ ἀνεγνώσθη οὕτως· ὁ λογιστὴς τὰ
κατὰ νόμους ὁρισθέντα

15 ἐπιτελῆ καταστήσει, ὥστε συνχώρησον
ἀναγνῶναι τὰ ὑπομνή-

ματα ἀφ' ὧν ἐντελέστερον . . [.] ει ὅτι
οὐδὲν ἕτερον ὑπ[ο-]

λείπεταί μοι ἢ εἰσαχθῆναι εἰς τὴν νομὴν
τῶν οἰκοπέ[δων].

κατὰ κυρίαν γὰρ ἀπελίφθησ[α]ν οἱ
ἀντίδικοι. οὐ παρεληλυ-

θότες εἰς τὸ δικαστήριον κατὰ κυρίαν,
ἀπόφασιν ἐδέξαν[το]

20 καὶ ἔξωροι γεγόνασι κατὰ τοὺς νόμους. /
ὁ λογιστὴς εἶ(πεν)·

πρὸς τίνα λέγει εἰπάτω. Ποιμένιος
ῥ(ήτωρ) εἶ(πεν)· κατὰ 'Αράχθου
ἀνήνεγκε

καὶ Εὐδαίμονα καὶ Φίβιος καὶ τῶν σὺν
αὐτοῖς. 'Ισχυρίων ῥ(ήτωρ) εἶ(πεν)·

μαρτύρομαι ὅτι κατά τινων ἀνήνεγκεν ἐπὶ
τὸν κύριόν μου τὸν

ἔπαρχον καὶ κατ' ἑτέρων εἰσάγει νῦν.
τοῦτο μαρτύριον ἔσται μοι

25 τῆς παραγραφῆς. / ὁ λογιστὴς εἶ(πεν)·
αὐτὸ τὸ ἐπίσταλμα

ὃ ἐπέστειλας τῷ ἀντιδικοῦντί σοι
ἀνάγνωθι. καὶ ἀνεγνώσθη·

μετὰ τὴν ἀνάγνωσιν 'Ισχυρίων ῥ(ήτωρ)
εἶ(πεν)· παραγραφὴν ἐπηγ-

γιλάμην· περὶ ἑτέρων προσώπων τὴν
δίκην νῦν εἰσάγει,

περί τινων ἀνενεγκὼν ἐπὶ τὸν κύριόν μου
τὸν ἔπαρχον.

30 τὴν οὖν παραγραφὴν ἐπηγγιλάμην
θαυμαστὴν

οὖσαν καὶ ἐννομωτάτην· ὡς οὐδαμῶς
δύναται

εἰσαγώγιμον ποιεῖν τὸ πρᾶγμα ὁ
ἀντίδικος. καὶ ἑξῆς

λέγοντος Ποιμένιος ῥ(ήτωρ) εἶ(πεν)·
μαρτύρομαι τὴν φωνὴν

[...] and it was read as follows: 'The *logistes*
will fulfil what has been defined by law.

Therefore agree to
read the memoranda

from which more completely ... that nothing
else is left

to me than to be installed in possession of the
real estate;

for on the appointed (day) my adversaries were
absent. Having not come

to the hearing on the appointed (day) they
received judgement

and have run out of time according to the law.'
The *logistes* said:

'Let him say to whom he speaks.'
Poemenius, advocate, said: 'He appealed
against Harachthes,

Eudaemon, Phibis and those with them.'
Ischyrion, advocate, said:

'I bear witness that he has appealed against
certain people before my lord the

prefect and against others he now proceeds.
This will be my basis

of objection.' The *logistes* said: 'Let the order
itself

which you sent to your adversary be read.'
And it was read.

After the reading Ischyrion, advocate, said: 'I
have stated my objection.

Concerning other persons he now introduces
this suit,

concerning certain (persons) he appealed before
my lord the prefect.

Thus I have stated my objection, which is
admirable

and most lawful. Thus in no way
can

my adversary make the matter maintainable.'
And whilst he proceeded

speaking, Poemenius, advocate, said: 'I attest
his utterance

	αὐτοῦ ὅτι μὴ δύναται εἰσαγώγιμον εἶναι τὴν δίκην	that it is not possible that the suit be maintainable
35	ὅπως ἀξιῶ ἤδη εἰς νομὴν πέμπεσθαι τῶν οἰκοπέδων.	so that I ask now to be installed in possession of the real estate.'
	/ ὁ λογ(ιστὴς) εἶ(πεν)· ἐπειδὴ ἑσπέρας ἐγένετο πρόκριμα οὐδὲν	The *logistes* said: 'Seeing that evening has fallen, there will be no prejudgement,
	ἔσται τῆς κυρίας μήπω ἐνστάσης. ἐπείπερ μέρος τι	since the appointed (day) is not yet at hand. Indeed, seeing that some part
	τῆς ἐπιούσης κυριακῆς ἱερᾶς ἐπέκυψεν, ὑπε[ρ-]	of the coming sacred Lord's day has supervened,
	τεθήσεται μετὰ τὴν κυριακὴν ἡ δίκη μέχρι [οὗ ἀμ]φότερα	the suit will be carried over after the Lord's day until both
40	τὰ μέρη παρέσεται πρὸς δικαιολογίαν. ἐὰν ⟦γὰρ⟧ δέ τις ἀπολ[ει-]	parties shall be present for judgement. But if anyone shall be absent,
	φθῇ εἴ τι παρίσταται τῇ ἐμῇ μετριότητι ἀποκριθήσομ[αι.]	I will give whatever judgement appeals to my sense of moderation.

Recto (→)

ὑπομν(ήματα) μη(νὸς) Φαῶφι κ̄ (ἔτους) τ (ἔτους) β̄ (ἔτους) ἐπὶ Λευκαδίου λογιστοῦ.

1 Κορείῳ 18 ἀπελείφθησαν 22 Εὐδαίμονος 24 καθ' 27-28, 30 ἐπηγγειλάμην 36 ἑσπέρα

P. Oxy. 3759 is a copy of proceedings before the *logistes/curator* concerning possession of unspecified real estate. The matter had previously been presented by the plaintiff to the *strategos* (*ll.*7, 18-20) and the prefect (*ll.*10, 21, 23, 29). The *strategos* had apparently made his decision in the defendants' absence, but his orders through the *praepositus pagi* to the public officials were not respected. The plaintiff then petitioned the prefect who in turn delegated the case to the *logistes/curator*. An order (ἐπίσταλμα) was issued to the defendants, no doubt informing them of the charge and the impending hearing before the *logistes*. Two advocates represent the parties, Poemonius the plaintiff, and Ischyrion the defendants. The basis of Ischyrion's objection is that different persons are named in the hearing before the *strategos* and in the present case. He therefore argues that the case cannot be maintained. At face value this may indeed be so; however, we are unaware of underlying circumstances. We do not know on what basis the plaintiff's claim to possession rested. Also we do not know whether effective possession had changed hands in the period between the two hearings. If the latter had occurred, a case might still lie against the present defendants.

Dialogue proceeds between advocates and the judge in a fashion typical of *cognitio*. Under the empire there was a steady growth in this legal process, i.e. the use of *extra ordinem* courts.[1] It was a more streamlined procedure and in Roman legal terms not subject to the inflexibility of the older formulary system. It also relieved to some degree a plaintiff's reliance on self-help in the areas of summons and execution, giving the judge an active involvement in these steps as well as a freer choice of penalty to be meted out.

---

[1] *Cognitio* made inroads into the Roman legal system but this was not marked until the Flavian period. See P. Garnsey, *Social Status and Legal Privilege in the Roman Empire* (Oxford 1970) 66.

Penalties became harsher and applied with an attendant loss of social distinction across the various classes of citizen. The procedure involved the use of administrative personnel to hear cases rather than resorting to judges or the standing court system. In Rome this meant that the urban prefect increasingly used his court to decide cases. In the empire the provincial governors as well as certain other Roman officials (usually by delegation) could convene an *extra ordinem* court to hear cases. The emperor's court itself was *extra ordinem* and used as a remedy to redress injustice. See further the entry on imperial rescripts in *New Docs* 8 (1998) 129-44. *Cognitio* arose from and was supported by the administrative (as distinct from the legislative) action of the state.

The protocol or official record of a *cognitio* hearing, it is alleged, became the basis for the genre of martyr literature of both civil (Alexandrian) and Christian provenance.[2] It was the dialogue between parties and judge which afforded a literary opportunity to portray the faithful witness of the accused. The nature of the Christian genre is well enough known.[3] The Alexandrian martyrs were tried and sentenced before Roman emperors. Unlike the Christian martyrs who died because of their faith and aversion to the rite of sacrifice demanded of them, the Alexandrian martyrs died as representatives of Alexandria and in defence of the rights of Alexandrian Greeks.[4] It is widely held that official records formed the historical core to many of the accounts, both Christian and Alexandrian.[5] But the literature goes beyond a mere repetition of the protocol. For example, it often included narrative accounts of the martyr's torture and execution — it did not confine itself to judicial dialogue. The literature also uses the protocol form as a literary vehicle for its purpose of either religious or political propaganda. Thus in the case of the Alexandrian martyrs, as part of the literary fiction each martyr is considered as an envoy of the city and thus as its representative. The hostility of the emperor to the envoy — in all extant examples the Alexandrians lose their case — is portrayed as typical of his sentiment against Alexandria. Another literary addition to the protocol is the ridicule directed in the course of the dialogue against the emperor;[6] for it is highly unlikely that an official scribe would record such insults in a public record. In the literature the emperor is portrayed as stupid and easily influenced by others, especially the Jews. This was a particularly offensive portrayal given the hatred between Jew and Greek in Alexandria.

Returning to P. Oxy. 3759, we find that the judge in this hearing is unable to give a decision. He is quite clear in stating his reasons for this: evening has fallen and part of the coming Lord's day has intervened.[7] This is the earliest dated reference to Sunday in

---

[2] See R.A. Coles, *Reports of Proceedings in Papyri* (Brussels 1966) on the form and development of the protocol, especially on the use of *oratio recta* in the Roman period.

[3] See H.A. Musurillo, *The Acts of the Christian Martyrs* (Oxford, 1972).

[4] The charge or charges they faced are uncertain from the surviving evidence. H.A. Musurillo, *The Acts of the Pagan Martyrs* (Oxford, 1954) 113-114, suggests that a legal charge may not have been formulated and that condemnation was by imperial *coercitio*.

[5] Musurillo, *The Acts of the Pagan Martyrs*, 275, and *The Acts of the Christian Martyrs*, l-lvii (especially with the very brief accounts given in the *Acta Cypriani* and the *Acts of the Scillitan Martyrs*).

[6] Christian accounts are different from those from Alexandria in this respect. The Christian martyrs do not tend to abuse their judges. As Musurillo, *The Acts of the Christian Martyrs*, lv, states concerning the Christian martyrs, 'It is a different sort of ἀρετή that is being held up before the eyes of posterity.'

[7] The judge observes that the appointed day (i.e. the day before which the hearing should occur) had not yet arrived so that the matter could be deferred till later. Legal procedure set defined periods within which parties were to present themselves. There was no set day or time for the hearing as such, at least

the papyri. Constantine had issued his edict (*Cod. Just.* 3.12.2(3)) requiring judges, the urban populace and businesses in all trades to rest on the *venerabili die solis* in 321.

> Let all judges, people of cities, and those employed in all trades, remain quiet on the Holy Day of Sunday. Persons residing in the country, however, can freely and lawfully proceed with the cultivation of the fields, as it frequently happens that the sowing of grain or the planting of vines cannot be deferred to a more suitable day, and by making concessions to Heaven the advantage of the time may be lost.[8]

P. Oxy. 3759 is dated 2 October 325, some four years later. It is therefore of interest to note the the judge in P. Oxy. 3759 deferred his hearing of the case when he became aware that it was now Sunday. However, he does not refer to the day by the name used in the edict, i.e. not *dies solis* or its Greek equivalent, ἡλίου ἡμέρα. The reason for this no doubt is that in Egypt, to judge from the papyri, the names of the days in the planetary week were not particularly in vogue; so apparently the official chose instead a name which was generally in use, this being the Christian name for Sunday. Usage of this expression to name Sunday goes back at least to the late first century (Rev. 1.10 and Didache 14.1). Its initial provenance may have been Asia Minor or Syria; however, usage soon spread elsewhere through Christian communities which met on that day.[9]

Constantine's edict, though prohibiting judicial and commercial business, did allow agricultural workers to undertake their seasonal work. Here another, though unfortunately not precisely dated, papyrus is of interest. P. Oxy. 3407 is the letter of a landlady to two of her employees requesting that they send a team of oxen to her farm in order to haul rocks. The matter is of some urgency as the work was to be done αὔριον (tomorrow) which is the Lord's day.

| Oxyrhynchus | 8.5 x 25 cm | Fourth century |

Ed.:— M. Chambers, W.E.H. Cockle, J.C. Shelton and E.G. Turner, The Oxyrhynchus Papyri (London 1981) 108-110 (= P. Oxy. 3407).

π(αρὰ) τῆς γεούχου Παπνουθίῳ	From the landlady to Papnouthios
προ(νοητῇ) καὶ ʽΑτρῇ φρ(οντιστῇ)	the caretaker and Hatres the foreman,
χ(αίρειν).	greetings.
σπουδάσαται τὸν ταυρε-	Hasten to send the bullock-driver
λάτην μετὰ τῶν μόσχων	with his steers
5 καὶ τοῦ ζυγοῦ καὶ σχοινίω(ν)	and yoke, and
αὐτῶν ἐξελάσε ἐν τῇ	their ropes
σήμερον εἰς τὸ ἡμέτερον	today to our
ἐποίκιον ʼΑκινδύνου πρὸς	settlement 'Risk-free' to
σύρσιν λίθου τῶν κυρί-	haul the stone of
10 ων μου ἀδελφῶν Νεπω-	my lord brothers, Nepotianus

---

until the final stage was reached, i.e. when a third deferral was reached. This explains the judge's reasoning in P. Oxy. 3759. A set period had been fixed within which the matter was to be heard. The parties had presented themselves before the end of this period so that the matter could be deferred. See R. Taubenschlag, *Opera minora* vol. 2 (Warsaw 1959) 179-80.

[8] Translation by S.P. Scott, *The Civil Code* vol.12 (Cincinnati repr. 1973).

[9] S.R. Llewelyn, 'The use of Sunday for meetings of believers in the New Testament', *Novum Testamentum* XLIII (2001) 1-19.

	τιανοῦ καὶ Διογένους· οἴδα-	and Diogenes. You
	τε καὶ ὑμῖς ὅτι οὔκ ἰσιν ξέ-	know that they are not
	νοι. ἀλλὰ πάντως ἐν	strangers. But at all events
	τῇ σήμερον, ἐπειδὴ συν-	today, since they
15	έθεντο βαστάξαι ἐν τῇ	have agreed to take it away on the
	κυριακῇ(ν) ἡμέρᾳ, τουτ-	Lord's day, that
	έστιν αὔριον ιαˉ.	is tomorrow, the 11th.
	μὴ οὖν, ἀδελφοί, δόξητε	Do not, brothers, decide
	ἀμελῆσε καὶ ἐνεδρευθῇ	to disregard (this) and (thus) let
20	τὸ ἔργον τῶν ἀνθρώ-	the work of the men be hindered,
	πων, ἐμέναν δὲ οὐκ ὀλί-	and bring me
	γην ὕβριν προσηνέγκα-	no small distress.
	τε. περὶ δὲ τοῦ τροχοῦ	Concerning the wheel
	ἀρκετοί ἐστε. ἐν τῇ	you are capable (of deciding).
	αὔριον	Tomorrow
25	ὁ ἀδελφὸς Λούκιος ἀπαντᾷ	our brother Lucius is coming
	πρὸς ὑμᾶς.	to you.

3 σπουδάσατε 6 ἐξελάσαι 12 ὑμεῖς, εἰσιν 19 ἀμελῆσαι 21 ἐμοί

Constantine's edict permitted agricultural workers to attend to the cultivation of the fields as the times of sowing and planting could not necessarily be deferred. This is in sharp contrast with Jewish practice where even agricultural work was prohibited on the sabbath, e.g. Exod. 34.21, *m.Shab.* 7.2, and the criticism of Jesus over his disciples plucking grain on the sabbath, Mark 2.23-8.[10]

Of interest in P. Oxy. 3759 is the fact that the hearing ends at sunset. In Roman law trials could not continue after sunset (*Lex XII tabularum* 1.9), the reason being that justice had to be seen to be done.[11] However, the *logistes'* reasoning in P. Oxy. 3759 (see especially *ll.*37-39) implies that it is out of respect for the Lord's day that proceedings are suspended. Constantine's edict of AD 321 (*Cod. Just.* 3.12.2(3)) had required judges, amongst others, to rest on the *venerabilis dies solis*. Rordorf[12] argues

---

[10] On the relation between the Jewish sabbath and the Lord's day see R. Goldenberg, 'The Jewish sabbath in the Roman world up to the time of Constantine', *ANRW* II, 19, 1 (1979) 442-5. Of interest also is his discussion (425-6) of the synoptic gospels and their presentation of Jesus' sabbath conflicts. He argues that they present the conflicts as inter-Jewish legal disputes as to what constitutes a permissible violation of the sabbath. A rabbinic principle is stated and applied to the issue at hand.

[11] One might contrast the Roman practice with the description of the trial of Jesus at night as recorded by Mark (14.53-72 and followed by Matthew). However, there are a number of irregularities in his account. For example, the trial, which occurs at night in Mark, in Luke is convened in the morning (Luke 22.66-71). According to Luke Jesus was led to the house of the chief priest in the night (22.54), but the Sanhedrin was not convened until the morning. Also a trial before the Jewish leaders in the house of the high priest is irregular. The Sanhedrin had its own building and did not have to meet in the high priest's house. Josephus and rabbinic literature record no meetings at the house of the high priest. Only Mark and Matthew have the Sanhedrin not meeting in its building (Mark 14.53 and Matt 26.57, cf. Luke 22.54, 66). In Luke the Sanhedrin is convened in its own building. Mark's second convening of the Sanhedrin (i.e. in the morning, Mark 15.1) is also odd. See p.53 above.

[12] W. Rordorf, *Sunday* (Eng. trans., London 1968) 156-69.

that Constantine was influenced in his legislation by both Christian and civil respect for the day, and that it preserves Roman ferial arrangements whereby on festival days courts did not sit nor was business transacted (e.g. Cato, *De agr.* 140, Cicero, *De leg.* 19, 29, Macrobius, *Sat.* 1.16.9), though urgent work was exempted (e.g. Macrobius, *Sat.* 1.16.10-12). By contrast before the time of Constantine there was a clear distinction made in the churches between the Jewish sabbath, which was a day of rest, and Sunday, the day of Christian meeting. The earliest Christians worked on Sunday and probably assembled in the evening. The time of meeting later moved to the morning, but work on the remainder of the day was not precluded. It appears that Constantine's edict is the earliest evidence for the association between Sunday and resting on that day. Once made this association allowed the churches to apply to Sunday the Old Testament injunctions prohibiting work on the sabbath and enjoining that the day be kept holy.

P. Oxy. 3759 also attests the use of a twenty-four hour day commencing at evening. The judge stops proceedings because it was evening, realising that the Lord's day had started. Usual Roman practice was to count the new day as beginning at midnight, just as we do today (Varro cited by Gellius, *Noc. Att.* 3.2.7, Pliny, *Hist. nat.* 2.188, Censorinus, *De die nat.* 23 and 24, and Plutarch, *Quaest. Rom.* 84).[13] P. Oxy. 3759 is not the only evidence pointing to this different method of reckoning the beginning of a calendar day. The chronographer[14] of AD 354 provides tables of a number of planetary days listed in two sets (night and day) of three columns (hour, planet, omen). Since he lists the night hours before the daylight hours, it would appear that also for him the twenty-four hour day began in the evening. The reason for this change is unclear, though one cannot rule out the possibility that it was facilitated by Christian usage, especially as mediated through the texts of the Old Testament.

The Jewish system of time counted the days as starting at sunset (*m.Hull.* 5.5). Thus a vow made for a day is said to be valid till dark (*m.Ned.* 8.1). This system of calculating a day is best observed in the regulations governing sabbaths and festivals as it is here that it is important to define the limits of the day. Darkness (חשך) defines the start of the sabbath (*m.Shab.* 1.3,10,11; 2.7; 15.3; 23.3,4; 24.1; cf. also *m.Shab.* 1.8 and

---

[13] In Plutarch the reason given for the choice of midnight relates to the difficulty in determining the exact beginning and end of the day by either sunrise or sunset. (See above for the difficulties faced by the use of sunset in Judaism.) According to Plutarch, it was better to choose either midday (μεσουρανοῦν) or midnight (ἀντιμεσουρανοῦν) as the measuring point (for a relict of the [Umbrian?] use of midday to calculate the calendar day in Roman calendars see G. Radke, *Fasti Romani* [Aschendorff: Münster 1990] 14-20), the former being preferable as it precedes the coming day:

ἐπεὶ τοίνυν ἐν ταῖς ἀνατολαῖς καὶ δύσεσι τοῦ ἡλίου δύσληπτός ἐστιν ἡ ἀρχὴ διὰ τὰς εἰρημένας ἀλογίας, ἀπολείπεται τὸ μεσουρανοῦν ἢ τὸ ἀντιμεσουρανοῦν αὐτοῦ λαμβάνειν ἀρχήν. βέλτιον δὲ τὸ δεύτερον· φέρεται γὰρ ἐκ μεσημβρίας ἐπὶ τὰς δύσεις ἀφ' ἡμῶν, ἐκ δὲ μεσονυκτίου πρὸς ἡμᾶς ἐπὶ τὰς ἀνατολάς.

A number of authors comment on the religious aspect of the Roman definition of the day, e.g. Varro cited by Gellius, *Noc. Att.* 3.2.8-10, and Censorinus, *De die nat.* 23. See also W. Sontheimer, 'Tageszeiten' in *RE* II 4, 2, 2012. The significance of the calendar in religious matters is not surprising. Indeed, it was the religious requirement to celebrate festivals at their appropriate times which gave impetus to the creation of the calendar in the first place. Disputes also arose from the use of different calendars. Cf. the dispute within Judaism between the temple priesthood who used a lunar calendar and the sectarians of Qumran using a solar one. See p.41 above.

[14] *Chronica minora: Monumenta Germaniae Historica, auctores antiquissimi* IX, section 4. See figures 8-12 in M.R. Salzman, *On Roman Time: The Codex-Calendar of 354 and the Rhythms of Urban Life in Late Antiquity* (Berkeley 1990).

Synesius, *Epist*. 4 = *PG* 66.1332). But naturally as one is not always able to tell when exactly night falls, there is need to err on the side of caution at twilight (לבין השמשות). The stringencies of both days apply to twilight (*b.Shab*. 34b). Thus, the eve of the sabbath (ערב שבת, i.e. Friday) was a time of preparation for the following day. If preparations had not yet been made and there was uncertainty as to whether it was now dark or not, what was left undone (e.g. lighting of lamps, purification of vessels, the tithing of food etc.) should not be undertaken (*m.Shab*. 2.7). Similarly, though it was usual to circumcise a male child on the eighth day, if the child was born at twilight, it was circumcised on the ninth (*m.Shab*. 19.5). The same calculation of the day from evening can be seen in the various festivals, e.g. Passover and Feast of Unleavened Bread (Exod. 12.6, 18).

According to Bickerman's rule of thumb, societies using a lunar calendar tend to count the day from sunset (so the Athenians, Gauls, Germans and Hebrews) whilst those operating a solar calendar count from sunrise (so Babylonians, Egyptians, Zoroastrians).[15] This is no doubt a logical consequence of the celestial body chosen by which to calculate time and the sphere of its perceived influence; the sun by day and the moon by night, so to speak. The cultural dimension in defining when the day began was well known in antiquity and commented on; see Varro cited by Gellius, *Noc. Att*. 3.2.4-6, and Pliny, *Hist. nat*. 2.188.

As already observed, the Athenians used a lunar calendar and calculated the day from sunset to sunset (Varro cited by Gellius, *Noc. Att*. 3.2.4, Pliny, *Hist. nat*. 2.188 and Censorinus, *De die nat*. 23.3).[16] Unfortunately the evidence from literary sources is ambiguous due to the overlapping reference in the term 'day' (see discussion of Sontheimer below). But one is on somewhat firmer ground when the evidence concerns civil and official business. Here it is clear that the Athenians used a lunar reckoning of days (Aristotle, *Ath. Pol*. 43.2), supposedly introduced by Solon (Diogenes Laertius 1.59). This in itself suggests a reckoning of the day as beginning at sunset. This is further confirmed by a law cited at Demosthenes 43.62 according to which the deceased was to be carried out the next day before sunrise (ἐκφέρειν δὲ τὸν ἀποθανόντα τῇ ὑστεραίᾳ ᾗ ἂν προθῶνται πρὶν ἥλιον ἐξέχειν). It was only with the introduction of the lunisolar and Julian calendars that the evening epoch among the Greeks gave way to the morning epoch for calculating the beginning of a calendar day.

The Seven-Day Week

P. Oxy. 3759 also raises the question of the introduction of the seven-day week into Graeco-Roman society. At first it must be noted that the seven-day cycle is a purely arbitrary convention having no basis in stellar, solar or lunar calculations of time. It is thus culturally determined. Thus the Greeks had 3 ten-day cycles in a month, the days being numbered rather than named.[17] The Etruscans and Romans used an eight-day cycle consisting of seven days of work and a market day on the eighth (*nundinae*), the

---

[15] E.J. Bickerman, *Chronology of the Ancient World* (London 1968, rev. 1980) 13-4, and Sontheimer, 'Tageszeiten' 2011ff.

[16] All three authors, Gellius, Pliny and Censorinus, appear to depend on Varro for much of their information at this point. However, only Gellius (cf. also Macrobius, *Sat*. 1.3) acknowledges his source.

[17] Bickerman, *Chronology* 27 and 100 n.28.

days being named by alphabetical enumeration (i.e. A through to H).[18]   However, a seven-day cycle gained great currency in the ancient world, possibly through the influence of Babylonian and Persian practice, though Josephus was not disinclined to claim credit for this and other customs for the Jewish nation (*Contra Apionem* 2.282).[19]   More recently Rordorf[20] has taken up a similar position.   However, the independence of the Graeco-Roman planetary week and the Jewish week is perhaps best indicated by the fact that each had a distinct starting day (Saturday and Sunday respectively), and by the order of the named days in the planetary week which rests on the notion of planetary power and control over hours and days.[21]   Dio Cassius 37.18, when discussing the reverence of the Jews for the sabbath, states his belief that the reference of the days to the seven stars/planets was of Egyptian origin and only in recent time had found general currency amongst all people.

The evidence of Dio Cassius raises the question of the naming of the days of the week. The earliest evidence seems to suggest that the days of the seven-day cycle were numbered rather than named. In the LXX, as well as in the Hebrew Bible and rabbinic tradition, the days of the week were numbered with the exception of the sabbath (σάββατον/σάββατα[22] — שׁבּת)[23]; cf. Exod. 16.22,23, titles to Psalms 23, 47, 91-93,

---

[18] Bickerman, *Chronology* 59, and F.H. Colson, *The Week* (Cambridge 1926) 3-4. For a range of examples see the *Fasti* in A. Degrassi, *Inscriptiones Italiae* XIII (Rome 1963).

[19] See the discussion of ἑβδομάς by W. Sontheimer, 'Zeitrechnung' in *RE* II 9a, 2, 2463. He notes that for the Greeks a seven-day cycle may have had a sacral origin. As well, the period agreed with the seven-day phases of the moon. Against a lunar basis for the seven-day cycle see Colson, *Week* 3, where it is argued that the cycle cannot be made to fit a lunar month of between 29 to 30 days. See also Rordorf, *Sunday* 19-24. The Babylonians had to intercalate to make their seven-day week keep pace with the moon. On the important differences between the Babylonian evidence and the Jewish week see Schürer, *ZNTW* 6 (1905) 13-5.

[20] Rordorf, *Sunday* 28-30. He argues that the establishment of Saturn's day was facilitated by knowledge of and familiarity with the Jewish sabbath. It was then only a short step to the adoption of a seven-day week. He finds support for this Jewish influence in the reckoning of the calendar day from evening. Unfortunately for Rordorf, evidence for this method of reckoning is late (fourth century) and well after the time when the planetary week was introduced. As such it may reflect a later development not an original feature of the planetary week. See discussion above on the chronographer of AD 354.

[21] H. Dumaine, 'Dimanche' in *DACL*, 870, Schürer, *ZNTW* 6 (1905) 16, and Colson, *Week* 24, 32. Colson argues for the validity of Dio Cassius' second explanation for the order of the planetary days, i.e. Saturn, Sun, Moon, Mars, Mercury, Jupiter, and Venus, when the usual order was by descending distance from the earth (Saturn, Jupiter, Mars, Sun, Venus, Mercury and Moon). What lies behind this ordering is the belief that the planets control the hours and days of the week, a belief inconsistent with the tenets of Judaism. See 42-47 and 60. Cf. also Tibullus 1.3.8 and Tacitus, *Hist.* 5.4, which both show a belief in the planetary control of human affairs (Saturn not only has the highest orbit but also a special power, *praecipua potentia*).   More generally, however, Colson (17, 26, 39-41, 51-2, 60 and 81) argues that, though in origin independent, the Jewish week assisted the introduction of the planetary week in the Graeco-Roman world through the felicitous coincidence that Saturn's day (sabbath) was a day unsuitable for work, i.e. a day of *otium*. In support of the association between Saturn's day and sabbath he cites Tacitus, *Hist.* 5.4 and Tertullian, *Apol.* 16.9-11 and *Ad nat.* 1.13. The difficulty with Colson's hypothesis is that though the Romans were well aware of the Jewish sabbath, on the whole their treatment of it was negative. How then could it have had a formative function in the adoption of the planetary week?

[22] Σάββατον and σάββατα in Greek could either refer to a sabbath day or to the whole week.

[23] In the Jewish tradition the sabbath is a holy day. The other days of the week were referred to as profane or common (חול). See *m.Pes.* 5.1,8; 6.2.

Judith 8.6, *m.Megilla* 1.2, 3.6, 4.1, *m.Taanith* 2.9, *m.Keth.* 1.1, *b.Pes.* 112b.[24] Cf. also *Didache* 8, Epiphanius, *Pan. haer.* 70.12.3, and Eusebius, *Quaest. evang. ad Marin.* (= *PG* 22, 941). Friday might be called either the sabbath-eve (προσάββατον — ערב שבת / ערובא) or numbered as the sixth day.[25] Josephus, as far as I can see, only names two days, the sabbath (σάββατον or ἡ ἑβδομάς) and sabbath-eve (προσάββατον or παρασκευή). In the former instance he only uses the term σάββατον after offering an explanation of it for his readers (*BJ* 1.146, 2.456, *AJ* 1.33, 3.143, *Contra Apion.* 2.20-1, 27; his *Vita* is an exception).[26] Thereafter both terms can be used. Of particular interest is the collection of Roman laws and rescripts which granted Jews the right to keep the sabbath; cf. *AJ* 14.10.12, 20-3, 25; 16.6.2, 4.[27] The terms πρὸ τοῦ σαββάτου (*AJ* 3.255) and παρασκευή (*AJ* 1.163; cf. Matt. 27.62, Mark 15.42, Synesius, *Epist.* 4 = *PG* 66.1332) are used of Friday or sabbath-eve. Zeitlin[28] argues that παρασκευή is the pagan term used to describe the day of sabbath preparation whereas Greek-speaking Jews preferred to translate the term ערב שבה by προσάββατον. Thus Josephus' only use of παρασκευή is to be found in his citing of Augustus' letter conceding privileges to the Jews, one of these being exemption from acknowledging sureties on the sabbath and its day of preparation after the ninth hour. A similar sensativity in name usage is found in Justin Martyr (see below).

The New Testament and patristic writers follow the Jewish practice, e.g. Matt. 28.1, Mark 15.42, 16.2,9, Luke 24.1, John 20.1,19, Acts 20.7 and 1Cor. 16.2. They adopt the title 'sabbath' for Saturday and παρασκευή for Friday. The one exception is the title for Sunday, ἡ κυριακὴ (ἡμέρα), which appears to find currency from the end of the first century.[29] The question naturally arises as to why the gentile churches assumed a seven-day week when it was not part of their cultural tradition. Schürer traces it back to Paul and his introduction of regular weekly assembly.[30]

Decisive for the adoption of the seven-day week and the naming of its days in the Graeco-Roman sphere is the belief in the controlling influence of the planets over the hours of the day. Schürer[31] holds that it was the belief in the power and control of the planets which led to the adoption of the seven-day week. In other words, belief preceded practice. Decisive for this discussion is Dio Cassius' second account for the order of the planetary names.[32] According to this belief the planets in their various

---

[24] One might note the difference in naming Sunday between Hebrew (אחד שבה) and Greek (μία τῶν σαββάτων).

[25] See Schürer, *ZNTW* 6 (1905) 3 and 7.

[26] Josephus in his dating information makes allowance for his Graeco-Roman readers in other ways as well. For example, in citing dates of the Jewish calendar he will give the name of the Greek month (*BJ* 5.99, 6.250, *AJ* 3.248); but note the exception at *AJ* 11.281 when the date occurs in a cited letter.

[27] See R. Goldenberg, *ANRW* II, 19, 1 (1979) 415-22. Goldenberg argues that the repetition of the decrees suggests a continued reluctance among the Greek cities to respect Roman recognition of Jewish practice. The Roman concessions were founded on the recognition of the Jews as a nation and their religion as the official cult of an allied kingdom.

[28] S. Zeitlin, *JBL* 51 (1932) 268-9. παρασκευή, used with reference to sabbath-eve, is found in neither the LXX nor the works of Philo. The term usually refers to preparations, provisions, resources or equipment of a military, eating, celebrating or similar context. Philo refers to the sabbath, with most uses stressing the aspect of rest, e.g. *De cher.* 87, *De fuga* 174, *De mut.* 260 and *De Abr.* 28.

[29] See Schürer, *ZNTW* 6 (1905) 8-13.

[30] Schürer, *ZNTW* 6 (1905) 42, 1 Cor. 16.2.

[31] Schürer, *ZNTW* 6 (1905) 18.

[32] Dio Cassius' second explanation (37.19) accounts for both the naming of the days of the week and the difference between the order of days in the planetary week (Saturn, Sun, Moon, Mars, Mercury,

combinations by day and hour controlled the fate and destiny of the newborn. Interestingly, this belief was known to rabbinic sages and debated, especially in the third century. See *b.Shab.* 156a-b. R. Joshua ben Levi held that the day on which one is born controls his personal qualities, e.g. whether he is kind, good, wise, bad-tempered, unchaste etc. The days are named according to Jewish custom, i.e. day one, two, three, four, five, sabbath-eve, sabbath. R. Hanina, on the other hand, held that it was not the constellation of the day but of the hour which controlled one's fate (מזל שעה גורם). He then names the seven planets and describes the control that they exert on the personality of the newborn. The planets are named in the order: Sun, Venus, Mercury, Moon, Saturn, Jupiter and Mars. It will be noted that the listing corresponds to the order based on the planets' assumed distances from the earth (i.e. Saturn, Jupiter, Mars, Sun, Venus, Mercury and Moon). It was this same order that Dio Cassius gives; however, the Talmud accommodates the order to its own ordering of the days of the week and thus begins with the Sun, the first day of the week being Sunday. It will also be noted that the Talmud gives the distance not the day order. This is consistent with the view of R. Hanina who held that the hour not the day controlled one's fate. The order thus betrays the same process of allocating planets to the hours of the day as is found in Dio Cassius' second account. It may seem somewhat strange to find this belief in planetary control in rabbinic literature. However, it should be noted that the belief is in part qualified. The way in which the day of birth affects one's fate accords with God's creative act on that day. Thus, if one is born on the fourth day (Wednesday), one is wise and has a retentive memory because on the fourth day of creation God made the lights in the sky to separate day from night. More importantly, one finds that Israel and her children are exempted from planetary control, and that acts of charity circumvent fate.

In the Graeco-Roman world the earliest clear evidence (i.e. non-astrological work) for the practice of naming the days is in the reign of Augustus; cf. Tibullus 1.3.18 where the poet gives one reason why a journey cannot be made: *Saturnive sacram me tenuisse diem* — 'the sacred day of Saturn detained me.'[33] In the West of the empire the days

---

Jupiter and Venus) and the usual astrological order of the planets used in antiquity (Saturn, Jupiter, Mars, Sun, Venus, Mercury and Moon):

> Beginning to count the hours of the day and night from the first (hour), and assigning that to Kronos (Saturnus), the next (hour) to Zeus (Jupiter), the third to Ares (Mars), the fourth to the Sun, the fifth to Aphrodite (Venus), the sixth to Hermes (Mercurius) and the seventh to the Moon, in accord with the arrangement of the cycles as the Egyptians consider it, and repeating this also, covering the entire twenty-four hours, you will find the first hour of the following day comes to the Sun. And doing this for the next twenty-four hours by the same calculation as for the former, you will dedicate the first hour of the third day to the Moon, and if you should so continue through the remaining (days), each day will take the god appropriate for itself.

The astrological order of the planets was determined by their perceived distance from the earth, from farthest to nearest, i.e. Saturn, Jupiter, Mars, Sun, Venus, Mercury and Moon. The planets were also thought to rule over each of the twenty-four hours of the day in succession: the first hour by Saturn, the second by Jupiter ... the seventh by Moon, the eighth by Saturn again etc. By this calculation the last hour of the day was ruled by Mars and the first hour of the next day by the Sun. Each day was named after and controlled by the planet which ruled its first hour. Thus each hour of the day was controlled by two planets, one controlling (διέπων) the hour and the other controlling (πολεύων) the day itself. If this calculation is performed through the seven days of the week, the order in the naming of the days results.

[33] Colson, *Week* 35-6. On evidence for the spread of the planetary week in the Graeco-Roman world generally see Schürer, *ZNTW* 6 (1905) 19-34, Colson, *Week* 18-38, 124-25, and S. Bacchiocchi, *From Sabbath to Sunday* (Rome 1977) 241-47. Evidence for the use of the planetary week predominates in the

were named after the planets (Saturn, Jupiter, Mars, Sun, Venus, Mercury and Moon). However, this custom of naming of the days may have originated in the East, possibly Alexandria.[34] Here they were named by their planetary equivalents, i.e. Κρόνος, Ζεύς, ῎Αρης, ῞Ηλιος, Ἀφροδίτη, Ἑρμῆς, Σελήνη (Dio Cassius 37.19; cf. also Philostratus, *Vita Apollon.* 3.41). The days are rarely named in evidence from Egypt, e.g. P. Oxy. XLIV 3174 (ἡμέρα Ἑρμοῦ, AD 243), E. Ziebarth, *Aus der antiken Schule,* 2nd edn (Bonn 1913) §17b (ἡμέρα ῾Ηλίου, AD 327; see also *BASP* 17 [1980] 17).[35]

Interestingly, Justin Martyr calls the Lord's day (Sunday) ἡ τοῦ ῾Ηλίου λεγομένη ἡμέρα (Just. Mart., *1 Apol.* 67.3,7). Also of interest is the fact that Saturday is not called the sabbath but Κρονική. The use of the Greek names for the days of the week is not surprising as the author addresses his apology to the emperor Antoninus. In other words, he adapts his language so as to be understandable to his intended audience. The choice of name for Sunday also affords the author the opportunity to play on the name. On the *dies solis* as the day of resurrection darkness was dispelled. However, when Justin addresses his Jewish interlocutor, Tryphon, he reverts to the more usual Christian usage. Sunday is called μία τῶν σαββάτων.[36]

The seven-day cycle raises the question as to which day was considered the beginning of the week. Evidence is ambiguous and Gundel[37] suggests either Wednesday (Mercury) or Saturday (Saturn). Schürer, Colson and Salzman[38] argue for Saturday. However, due to Christian influence and the edict of Constantine in 321 (*Cod. Just.* 3.12.2(3)) Sunday came by the fourth century to be considered the first day. This same edict for the first time also gave the seven-day week civic importance thereby lending

---

West and it appears to have been more readily adopted there. In the East a reluctance to use the planetary names for the days of the week may have been due to a widespread rejection of the notion of planetary control, a notion which ran counter to the theological and moral tenets of God's omnipotent control of the world and man's freedom and responsibility for his actions. On another topic, one might note that when Dio Cassius describes the capture of Jerusalem in 38 BC, he states that it occurred on the day already then called Saturn's day: ἐν τῇ τοῦ Κρόνου καὶ τότε ἡμέρᾳ ὠνομασμένῃ, 49.22. However, one cannot necessarily conclude that at that time the planetary week was in use. Indeed, this would contradict Dio's claim elsewhere that the introduction of the planetary week was relatively recent: οὐ πάλαι ποτὲ ὡς λόγῳ εἰπεῖν ἀρξάμενον, 37.18. Rather the statement at 49.22 arises from the confused identification of the sabbath as Saturn's day. Cf. Dio Cassius 37.16-17 with Josephus, *BJ* 1.146-47, *AJ* 63-64. Rordorf, *Sunday* 10 n.1, 26-27, is of the view that evidence for the introduction of the planetary week is not to be found until the second half of the first century. His assertion is based on the misconception that the existence of the planetary week cannot be proved until all seven days are named or counted. This will necessarily under-estimate the date of its introduction. Colson offers a better criterion: a named planetary day combined with a concept of planetary control over that day. This we have in the Tibullus reference.

[34] W. and H. Gundel, 'Planeten' in *RE* 20, 2, 2143.

[35] The Western church retained the planetary/heathen names of the days, but the orthodox church replaced them by numbered days. See Gundel, 'Planeten' 2145.

[36] When speaking to Tryphon, Justin Martyr, *Dialog. cum Tryph.* 41.4, refers to Sunday, the day of resurrection, as the first day of the week. He draws a parallel between the Eucharist which was celebrated on Sunday (the eighth day, Saturday being the seventh) and circumcision which was performed on the eighth day, and sees a symbolic significance between the two. For the significance of the symbolism of eight in Gnosticism and its relevance in naming Sunday the eighth day here see R.J. Bauckham, 'Sabbath and Sunday in the post-apostolic church' in D.A. Carson (ed.), *From Sabbath to Lord's Day* (Grand Rapids 1982) 273-4.

[37] Gundel, 'Planeten' 2145.

[38] Schürer, *ZNTW* 6 (1905) 19, Colson, *Week* 24, 32, Salzman, *On Roman Time,* 31.

impetus to the dislodgement of the eight-day week (*nundinae*).[39] The edict also for the first time associated Sunday with resting and refraining from work. It was this new association of Sunday and the day of rest which permitted, indeed necessitated, the application of the Old Testament sabbath injunction to Sunday itself. However, it needs to be noted that the idea of refraining from certain activities was not readily accepted in the empire. Thus later the emperor permits, sometimes even reluctantly, exceptions to his legislation. For example, by an edict issued some months later (*Codex Theodosianus* 2.8.1) an exception was made for certain legal activities. It was legal disputation which was not fitting on the venerable day. Acts of emancipation or manumission were different and legal formalties could continue to be completed on that day.[40] Again, in CIL 3, 4121 the same emperor is seen to permit for a full year the holding of markets on Sunday in the province of Upper Pannonia.[41]

This latter point raises an interesting question about how the week was marked. The Roman *nundinae* was marked by a market every eighth day. The Jewish week by the sabbath service. So also our week is marked by set workdays and weekends. The cycle is reinforced by recurrent patterns of behaviour or ritual. The question then is: if Dio Cassius' statement about the general acceptance of the planetary week by the early third century is to be believed, what cyclical habit reinforced it in society? How would the weeks be bounded in popular consciousness? Christian (Sunday) or Jewish (sabbath) practice does not offer an adequate explanation for its general acceptance at this date. Is Dio Cassius' claim then an exaggeration?

S.R. Llewelyn and A.M. Nobbs

---

[39] Sontheimer, 'Zeitrechnung' 2463, and Schürer, *ZNTW* 6 (1905) 40. Constantine's edict did not end the use of the eight-day week immediately; both ran concurrently for much of the fourth century as the evidence of the chronographer of AD 354 shows.

[40] The text of *Codex Theodosianus* 2.8.1 reads:
> Just as it appears to us most unseemly that the Day of the Sun (Sunday), which is celebrated on account of its veneration, should be occupied with legal altercations and with noxious controversies of the litigation of contending parties, so it is pleasant and fitting that those acts which are especially desired shall be accomplished on that day. Thereafter all men shall have the right to emancipate and to manumit on this festive day, and legal formalities thereof are not forbidden. (Trans. C. Pharr, The Theodosian Code [New York repr. 1969])

[41] The relevant portion of the inscription reads:
> Imperator Caesar Flavius Valerius Constantinus ... also by the foresight of his piety has decided to endure markets on Sunday for a whole year with Valerius Catullinus, vir perfectissimus, commander of the province of Upper Pannonia administering (them).
> Imp(erator) Caes(ar) Fl(avius) Val(erius) Constantinus ... provisione etiam pietatis su(a)e nundinas die Solis perpeti anno constituit curante Val(erio) Catullino v(iro) p(erfectissimo) p(rae)p(osito) p(rovinciae) P(annoniae) super(ioris).

§31 Two Hymns to Christ, One to Mary

Unknown provenance   11 x 9 cm   VI/VII

Eds:— B. Kramer and D. Hagedorn, *Griechische Texte der Heidelberger Papyrus-Sammlung* (Heidelberg 1986) 21-24 (= P. Heid. 292).

The recto and verso contain two related texts written in very similar if not identical hands. The fact that the left edge of the recto (= right edge of verso) is cut indicates that the piece does not derive from a roll. The similarity of hand and relationship of the two texts, the editors suggest, indicate that the fragment derives from a single publication.

Recto

```
    - - - - - - - - - - - -

1        ]...[
         ]πατεραν εισ[
         ] ευλογητο[
     ο   [το]υς παιδες εν κ[αμινω]         you refreshed the youths
5        καιομενι δροσισας               in the blazing furnace
     ο   σταυρον υπομεινας               you endured the cross
         και τα εθνη καλ[εσας]           and called the nations
     ο   σταυρον υπομειν[ας και]         you endured the cross [and]
         το ηδωρ κ[                      water . . .
10   ο   εν ατη .[                       you in Hades ...
         .ουσ[

    - - - - - - - - - - - -
```

2 πατέρα (?) **4** παῖδας **5** καιομένη **9** ὕδωρ **10** Ἅϊδη

Verso

```
    - - - - - - - - - - - -

         ].νεκυησ[
         ]κυνιυντ.[
         ] κ(υρι)ε οτι εκ ταφου α[        ] O Lord, because from the tomb [
     δοξ]α τη δυναμι σσου κ(υρι)ε :- [    glory to your power, O Lord [
5        ]. του θανατου τα δεσμ[α]        ] the chains of death
         ] δοξα τι δυναμει σσου κ(υρι)ε ::-   ] glory to your power, O Lord
         ].ιων του θανατου                ] of death
         ]ρεν σοι δοξα τη δυναμι σου       ] glory to your power
     [κ(υρι)ε        _ τον θ(εο)ν της      O Lord ... ] God of ...

    - - - - - - - - - - - -
```

4 δυνάμει σου **6** τῇ, σου **8** τῇ δυνάμει

Fragments of two hymns to Christ, one on the recto, the other on the verso, are found on this papyrus, which was either the leaf of a codex or a single sheet. While very similar hands are in evidence (for the type cf. R. Seider, *Paläographie der griechischen Papyri II*

[Stuttgart 1970] no. 69), the subject matter and form of the two hymns are quite different.

The first hymn is extant in parts of ten lines with at least four verses of 14 syllables each, though, the editor observes, there are irregularities in the metre. All four verses begin with the article, ὁ, anticipating the aorist active participle (which modern English converts to a verb). Hagedorn observes that this is a very common construction used in the *epikleses* of anaphora prayers. He provides numerous examples from the corpus of early Christian hymns. The first of the four extant invocations of this hymn recalls the divine refreshment (ὁ δροσίσας) of the three youths (οἱ παῖδες) in Nebuchadnezzar's furnace (see Pr Azar 27; 3 Macc 6.6), the second and third invoke Christ as the endurer of the cross (ὁ σταυρὸν ὑπομείνας), a theme first encountered in early Christian literature in Heb 12.2 (ὑπέμεινεν σταυρόν), while the fourth is too fragmentary to permit identification of subject matter.

Unlike the first hymn, the nine-line hymn extant on the verso does not appear to have been constructed on the basis of a regular metre. Hagedorn notes that the acclamation — δόξα τῇ δυνάμει σου κ(ύρι)ε[ ] — is repeated in the reconstructed text, suggesting, plausibly enough, that it functioned as an antiphonal refrain. The theme of this hymn is the resurrection of Christ, the editor conjecturing that the refrain was completed by the words ὅτι ἐκ τάφου ἀνέστης. Hagedorn suggests, quite reasonably given the subject matter, that the hymn was used in the liturgical celebration of Easter.

****

Unknown provenance   6 x 14 cm   V/VI

Eds:— B. Kramer and D. Hagedorn, *Griechische Texte der Heidelberger Papyrus-Sammlung* (Heidelberg 1986) 34-38 (= P. Heid. 294).

Recto

	+ Νυμφοτόκε παρ- θένε Ξενίζει πάντας ὁ τόκος σου. Ὅτι τὸν κτίστην τοῦ κόσμου	Mother of the Bridegroom, Virgin, your offspring astonishes all because you gave birth against all
5	Παραδόξως τεκοῦσα‹ν› σὲ μεγαλύνομεν.	expectation to the creator of the world. We magnify you.
	Ῥητῶς, ὦ γλῶσσα, προσυμνοῖς Σέ,	Declare, O tongue, praise to you
10	τὴν σεμνὴν παρθένον, καὶ ἔτεκεν Τῷ λέγειν οὐκ αὐταρκοῦντες Ὑμνολογοῦσιν ἀκ- ούσαντες σὲ μεγα- λύνομεν. +	the holy Virgin who gave birth. To speak is impossible, (yet) having heard (it) they sing hymns. We magnify you.

Verso

15	Φωταγομῆτορ	Mother of the Lightbearer,
	παρθένε Χρισ-	Virgin,
	τὸν ἡμῖν τεκ-	who bore
	οῦσα αἰώνιον.	the eternal Christ for us,
	ψαλμοῖς καὶ	with psalms and hymns
20	ὕμνοις ᾄδον-	we praise
	τες Ὣς μητέ-	as the Mother
	ρα δεσπότου	of the Lord.
	σὲ μεγαλύνομεν.	We magnify you.

1 νυμφωτωκαι   2 παρθενη   5 πασραδοξος   6 μεγαλυνωμεν   7 ρυτως γλωσσαι   8 συ
10 το λεγεν   11 αυταργουντες   12 αγουσαντες   14 μεγαλυνωμεν   15 φοταγωμητωρ
16 παρθενη   20 υμνης αδωντες   21 μυτερα   23 μεγαλυνωμεν

P. Heid. 294 is a codex-leaf written in the somewhat cursive, awkward style of a scribe more familiar with coptic (for the type cf. R. Seider, *Paläographie der griechischen Papyri II*, no. 64). It contains the second part of a hymn in praise of the Virgin Mary in three metrical strophes in the form of an acrostic. Each metrical verse begins with a letter of the alphabet (N to Ω, shown here, but not on the papyrus, as an underlined capital) and ends with a raised slash (*paragraphus*, not shown here). The text on the recto (but not the verso) begins and ends with a cross. Each strophe contains four verses and the same concluding refrain, typical of hymns to Mary, namely, σὲ μεγαλύνομεν (cf. Luke 1.46).

C. Römer notes that there is an intriguing parallel to hand in the Hymn to Mary published by D. S. Gassisi in *BZ* 18 (1909) 345–46, which also features short invocations and an acrostic pattern, each verse concluding with the same refrain σὲ μεγαλύνομεν. She also conjectures that this hymn may be among the earliest witnesses to the veneration of Mary in Egypt. Alanna Emmett's 1982 discussion (see *New Docs*, vol. 2, 141–46) of a fourth-century Egyptian (?) hymn in Latin, possibly to Mary, also an acrostic, concludes with a catalogue (with dates) of early papyrus Marian hymns to which the Heidelberg hymn, and several recently published hymns noted by Römer, should now be added. Emmett's observation that the earliest hymnic references to Mary are prompted by the Christological controversies, that is, such hymns refer to Mary's role in the incarnation and in the birth of Christ, while later hymns are actually addressed to Mary, is borne out by the invocatory tone and comprehensive scope of the Heidelberg hymn.

The term φωταγομήτωρ, 'mother of the Lightbearer', which appears at the beginning of the third strophe, is nowhere else attested, though references to Christ as 'lightbearer' (φωταγωγός) are common enough (s.v. Lampe).

Mark Harding

INDEXES

WORD INDEX